SAPELO

THE UNIVERSITY OF GEORGIA PRESS   ATHENS

SAPELO

PEOPLE AND PLACE ON A GEORGIA SEA ISLAND

Buddy Sullivan   PHOTOGRAPHS BY BENJAMIN GALLAND

Publication of this book was supported, in part,
by the Kenneth Coleman Series in Georgia History and Culture.

Unless otherwise noted, all photographs in the book
were taken by Benjamin Galland.

Library of Congress Cataloging-in-Publication Data

Names: Sullivan, Buddy, author. | Galland, Benjamin,
    photographer.
Title: Sapelo : people and place on a Georgia sea island /
    Buddy Sullivan ; photographs by Benjamin Galland.
Description: Athens : The University of Georgia Press, [2016] |
    Includes bibliographical references and index.
Identifiers: LCCN 2016023745 | ISBN 9780820350165 (hardcover :
    alk. paper)
Subjects: LCSH: Sapelo Island (Ga.)—History.
Classification: LCC F292.MI5 S855 2016 | DDC 975.8/737—dc23
    LC record available at https://lccn.loc.gov/2016023745

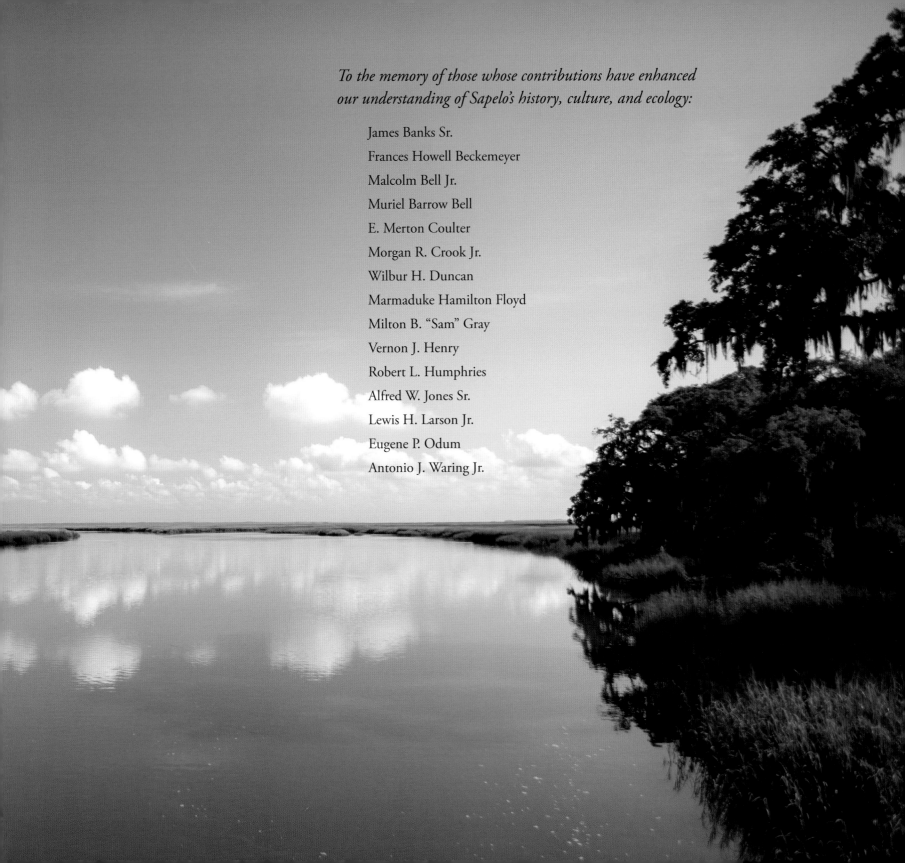

*To the memory of those whose contributions have enhanced
our understanding of Sapelo's history, culture, and ecology:*

James Banks Sr.

Frances Howell Beckemeyer

Malcolm Bell Jr.

Muriel Barrow Bell

E. Merton Coulter

Morgan R. Crook Jr.

Wilbur H. Duncan

Marmaduke Hamilton Floyd

Milton B. "Sam" Gray

Vernon J. Henry

Robert L. Humphries

Alfred W. Jones Sr.

Lewis H. Larson Jr.

Eugene P. Odum

Antonio J. Waring Jr.

Contents

Boxes

Preface

The sense of place has always been fundamental to an understanding of the native southern psyche. In no other region of the United States have the people attached themselves to their land—and their landscape—with quite the depth of passion, perception, and permanence, particularly in the generations preceding modern America. For native southerners it is the *land* that conjures and denotes the essentiality of *place*. For them, land is the clearest embodiment of permanence. Scholars have long argued over this notion, but when the concept is viewed from the perspective of three centuries, the sense of land, and land ownership, clearly devolves from centuries of peoples' association with the soil—and the local ecosystem in general—be they planter, sharecropper, slave, or freedman. Margaret Mitchell understood it best in *Gone With the Wind* when she rescued a hungry Scarlett O'Hara from the flames of Atlanta to return her home, to her familial land—"She sat down in the furrows and dug into the earth with hands that shook, filling her basket slowly . . . as God is my witness, I'm never going to be hungry again."

This is a book about Sapelo, a sea island off the coast of Georgia. Its recurring theme is that of place, and it examines how the people of Sapelo have for generations embraced the greater landscape and adapted to the land (and its soil), water, and marshes—the complete ecosystem. Sapelo's people have always been a tenacious and resourceful lot, be they Native American, Spanish missionary, cotton planter, slave, or free African American. All have been visionaries in their own way. People have come and gone, but Sapelo's land has always essentially been the same. It has only been used in different ways.

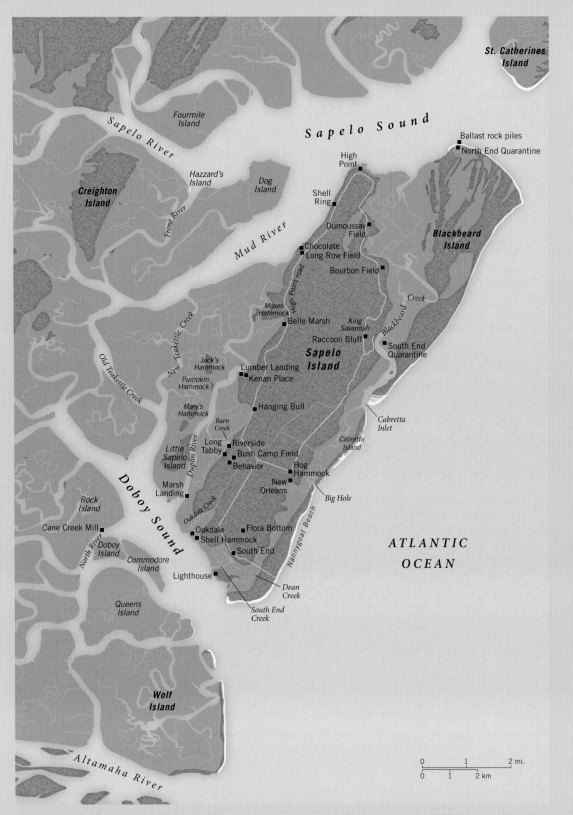

St. Catherines
Island

Sapelo River

Fourmile
Island

Sapelo Sound

Ballast rock piles
North End Quarantine

High
Point

Hazzard's
Island

Dog
Island

Shell
Ring

Creighton
Island

Front River

Mud River

Dumoussay
Field

Blackbeard
Island

Chocolate
Long Row Field

Bourbon Field

Creek

Moses
Hammock

High Point road

King
Savannah

Belle Marsh

Blackbeard

New Teakettle Creek

Raccoon Bluff

South End
Quarantine

Old Teakettle Creek

Sapelo
Island

Jack's
Hammock

Lumber Landing
Kenan Place

Pumpkin
Hammock

Mary's
Hammock

Hanging Bull

Cabretta
Inlet

Barn
Creek

Cabretta
Island

Duplin River

Little
Sapelo
Island

Long
Tabby

Riverside
Bush Camp Field

Behavior

Hog
Hammock

Marsh
Landing

New
Orleans

Big Hole

Rock
Island

Oakdale Creek

Nannygoat Beach

ATLANTIC
OCEAN

Cane Creek Mill

North River

Doboy
Island

Oakdale
Shell Hammock

Flora Bottom

South End

Commodore
Island

Doboy Sound

Lighthouse

Dean
Creek

Queens
Island

South End
Creek

Sapelo Island
in 1900

Wolf
Island

Altamaha River

0   1   2 mi.

0   1   2 km

To get to know Sapelo, it is important to understand the history of its land use and settlement patterns, particularly by viewing it through an environmental lens. Even as land use changes, however, my narrative will emphasize and reemphasize place and permanence within the island's natural environment, always the determining element of human existence on Sapelo.

Thomas Spalding, nineteenth-century planter of the island and slaveholder, perhaps best understood the significance of permanence and place here. After emancipation, many former slaves remained on the island of their birth and set about solidifying their foundation through community development. By getting to know Sapelo's people and subsequent generations on the island and understanding their concomitance to the land, one can begin to understand Sapelo itself. The relationship between people and land has not always been pleasant, and this story too will be told.

Although I have written extensively about the island over the past thirty years, *Sapelo: People and Place on a Georgia Sea Island* largely represents a fresh, objective approach. It incorporates new material, new insights, and a more focused story enhanced by the maturation of my own understanding.

Acknowledgments

No book is solely the product of its author. In researching Sapelo and writing this book, I have been fortunate to have the assistance of friends and colleagues on and off the island. I am indebted to those consummate professionals, including archaeologists David Hurst Thomas, Richard Jefferies, and the late Ray Crook, and scientists whose research on Sapelo has added to our understanding of the coastal ecosystem: Randal L. Walker, Alice M. Chalmers, and Merryl Alber, director of the University of Georgia Marine Institute at Sapelo. I am grateful for the help of historians Kenneth H. Thomas Jr., Martha L. Keber, Emory S. Campbell, Cornelia Walker Bailey, and June McCash. I thank my journalistic colleague Jingle Davis for suggesting this book and subsequently encouraging me from start to finish. I likewise thank my immensely helpful Sapelo colleague Aimee G. Gaddis, who prepared most of the historic images for the book; Lonice C. Barrett, commissioner of the Georgia Department of Natural Resources (retired), who brought me to Sapelo so many years ago; my astute editors at the University of Georgia Press, Patrick Allen and Jon Davies; and my friends and colleagues at the Georgia Historical Society (Savannah) and the Coastal Georgia Historical Society (St. Simons Island) for their research assistance over many years. Special thanks go to Alfred W. "Bill" Jones III for allowing the use of images from the collection of his ancestor Howard E. Coffin; to W. Noah Reynolds for use of images of his grandfather Richard J. Reynolds Jr.; and to Malcolm Bell III, who graciously provided several remarkable photographs of African Americans living on Sapelo in the 1930s, taken by his parents, Muriel and Malcolm Bell Jr. I also thank the anonymous reviewers who not only recommended publication of this book but also made helpful suggestions to improve the narrative.

SAPELO

CHAPTER I   Ecological Sapelo

The Natural Perspective

THE ISLAND is in a state of perpetual motion—endless, relentless, and completely subservient to the whims of nature. This constant movement is the one tangible aspect of Sapelo where the past is necessarily prologue, where the beginning will someday be the end.

The coastal islands drift, albeit imperceptibly, ever southward, perhaps at the rate of an inch per year. This movement is based on a natural phenomenon known as sand sharing, a process that reaches back to the genesis of what now constitutes the Georgia coast.

Sapelo and the other Georgia sea islands formed thousands of years ago as a collective transfer of upland soils and sediments; they continue to alter in an ongoing natural cycle perpetuated by winds, storms, tides, and ocean currents. The forces that created Sapelo began about two million years ago as the Pleistocene glaciers advanced to their southernmost point, establishing a temporary beachhead eighty miles east of the present shoreline. The ice sheet began melting eighteen thousand years ago, depositing water into the ocean and enabling the sea level to rise. Early sand-ridge and beach formations were alternately flooded by seawater and the eastward flow of melting glacier water, with its deposit of upland soil.

Sunrise on Nannygoat Beach

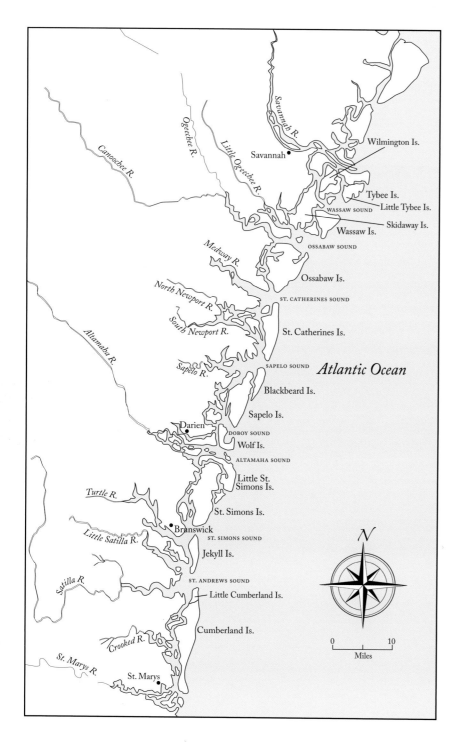

The age of the coastal islands is actually two-fold. Carbon 14 dating of submerged shell samples indicates that the main portion of Sapelo is twenty-five thousand to thirty-six thousand years old. Sapelo's uplands formed during several stages of the Pleistocene when the sea level was higher than at present. The seaward parts of Sapelo, including Blackbeard and Cabretta Islands, were formed four to five thousand years ago. They are Silver Bluff barrier island formations (late Pleistocene) and modern formations (Holocene).[1] The Georgia islands are situated in the most recent of a series of six Pleistocene shoreline complexes that increase in age and elevation the farther one moves from the present shoreline. Sapelo's shoreline is composed of fine quartz sands that cumulatively build to create beaches and dunes as an extension of the shallow, gently sloping sea bottom that extends seventy to seventy-five miles offshore as the Continental Shelf.[2]

The present stands of salt marsh around Sapelo are well developed and have been stable for the last five thousand years as Holocene formations. Earlier late-Pleistocene marshes, however, underwent frequent change—even disappearing at times in response to alterations in the sea level, creating unstable conditions. With adequate and relatively consistent sea-level heights in the Holocene, water-borne sediment deposits eventually built new marshes and beaches over the earlier Pleistocene deposits. Clays and fine sands make up the marsh deposits that form in the sheltered

The Georgia Coast

Deserted beach near high tide

Sapelo's beaches are constantly shifting with the effects of
offshore littoral currents off the Atlantic Gulf Stream.

areas away from the direct impact of the sea, accounting for the stable marsh belts along Sapelo's west side and South End, and between Sapelo and Blackbeard Islands. Another destabilizing cycle, however, may be in progress in light of evidence of pronounced sea-level rise along the south Atlantic shoreline.

The Georgia coast, about one hundred miles long, features a distinct island chain separated from the mainland by a four- to six-mile swath of salt marsh. From east to west, the islands feature sand beaches, dune lines, and a slightly elevated interior forest, often dissected by tidal sloughs and freshwater ponds. The marshes lie contiguous to the islands on their western sides. Penetrated by tidal creeks and rivers, the marshes extend westward to the coastal mainland. At its eastern edge the mainland is only slightly elevated but is buffered from the direct effects of tropical storms by the marshes and islands that lie seaward. Freshwater rivers—the Savannah, Ogeechee, Altamaha, Satilla, and St. Marys—empty into the Atlantic Ocean through sounds that separate the islands. A sequence of salt, brackish, and freshwater marshes follow the river channels upstream into areas of decreasing salinity.

An ocean current, the longshore littoral current, revolves counterclockwise off the Gulf Stream, flowing from the north along the Sapelo shoreline and constantly moving sand southward. The littoral current mixes with a strong outflow current moving from northwest to southeast on ebbing tides from Doboy Sound. The sandbars, beaches, and dunes of Cabretta Island and Nannygoat Beach are regularly altered by a combination of currents, tide flow, and wind conditions. Simultaneously, the accretion of sands washed southward from Blackbeard accumulate on the beaches on the southern end of Sapelo, with additional buildup of marsh west of the dunes and on the lighthouse tract. This natural sand-sharing process makes Sapelo Island one of the few remaining places on the East Coast where the phenomenon is evolving with minimal interference from human activity.[3]

The shoreline changes can be readily observed from a study of topographic maps and navigation charts of the area over the last two hundred years which show a progressive erosion of the north end of Blackbeard Island and a concomitant accretion of beach on Sapelo's South End. Much of the sediment from the sharply eroded, truncated dune ridges on the north end of Blackbeard has been deposited on the lower part of Sapelo, where the beaches are accreting and the dunes are increasing in size. Both islands have shifted southward about three-quarters of a mile during the present Holocene high stand of the sea. At the same time, the accumulation of sand

Nannygoat Beach's sand dunes accrete and erode due to seasonal changes in weather and full moon tides.

on Sapelo's South End has created natural obstacles to the Doboy Sound entrance. Continually shifting shoals and sandbars in the inlet, not all of which are exposed at low tide, account for numerous shipwrecks and ship groundings over the last two centuries by vessels approaching the inlet. Some of the sand from Nannygoat Beach is also washed southward by the prevailing winds and currents. The cycle of erosion and accretion is constant. Sand eroded from one area of beach is deposited in offshore sandbars; then that sand is washed back onto the beach, building up dunes.

The beach itself consists of fine quartz sands mixed with small amounts of crushed shell. On Nannygoat, the beach varies in width as it slopes gradually from dune base to water's edge, with its narrowest portion on the north across the inlet from Cabretta Island. Typical of the gently shelving southeastern shoreline, the water is very shallow for a considerable distance off Sapelo's shore, averaging only about eight feet a mile from the beach at mean low water.

The changing dynamics of Sapelo's beaches do not affect people as there is no development on the island near beach areas. These changes can, however, be detrimental to nesting areas for turtles and shorebirds such as the American oystercatcher, Wilson's plover, least tern, gull-billed tern, and black skimmer. These species rely on the stability of the beaches near the high-tide line to lay their eggs.[4]

Marine turtles regularly nest and lay their eggs on Sapelo's beach during the summer, the most prevalent species being the Atlantic loggerhead (*Caretta caretta*). From May to early September female loggerheads come to the beach at night, often during the flood stage of a spring tide, to lay from 120 to 130 eggs on dry ground close to the dune line. Most of the eggs fall victim to natural predators, but some hatchlings survive and return to the sea. Other large marine turtles may have nested on Sapelo in the past, including the Atlantic hawksbill, Atlantic green, and Atlantic leatherback.

Sapelo's sand dunes are quite fragile. New dunes nearest the beach are the most unstable and are under constant alteration by "blowout" from strong winds and

Sea oats help stabilize the sand dunes.

Native near-shore vegetation includes
Spanish bayonet, red cedar, and scrub oak.

"washover" from a combination of storm waves and northeasterly winds. Dune buildup near the beaches typically occurs in periods of calm weather with onshore winds. As seen from the air, the lower end of Nannygoat displays dune lines in large arcs curving around the southern tip of the beach, with sand accruing in the embayment washed by Doboy Sound's currents, lying just southeast of the lighthouse.

When constructed in the early nineteenth century, the lighthouse was on an island sand spit separated by a creek from the main island. Like Nannygoat Beach, the lighthouse spit is Holocene but is positioned well behind the beaches and dunes; it is also subject to accretion, but in a different way. Nineteenth- and early twentieth-century maps and photographs reveal a gradual buildup of marshes projecting south of the lighthouse. A 1932 photograph of the tower places it very near the waters of Doboy Sound, whereas marshes have since filled in a considerable area south of the tower, a clear illustration of the buildup of the South End through the sand-sharing system.

Sapelo Island has two distinct lines of sand dunes, with the inter-dune meadow in between. Closest to the beach are the active and back (primary) dunes that undergo frequent alteration through the effects of the littoral current, spring tides, and northeasters. East of Dean Creek, less than half a mile west of Nannygoat, is a high, wooded ridge of older dunes that are revealed as primary dunes in mid-1920s aerial photographs of the South End—further evidence of the natural accretive effects associated with barrier island sand sharing.

Salt-spray-tolerant vegetation prevalent along the beaches and dunes plays an important role in the ecosystem. Natural plants that proliferate in the active dunes and the back dunes near the beach serve as stabilizers. The most prevalent on Nannygoat Beach are sea oats (*Uniola paniculata*), which serve as a binder to hold the active dunes in place. Other dune plants serving the same purpose are beach elder, beach hogwort, beach pennywort, water pennywort, beach sand-spur, panic grass, morning glory, and Spanish bayonet (*Yucca*).

In the inter-dune meadow, away from the direct effects of salt, are other stabilizing shrubs and trees, including wax myrtle, red cedar, sand live oak, buckthorn, groundsel, yaupon holly, tamarisk, Muhlenbergia, and prickly pear—a plant that can play havoc with the feet and ankles of unwary strollers through the sand. In recent years the Chinese tallow tree, an invasive species, has appeared in the inter-dune meadow and other areas of Sapelo. The dunes and meadow provide feeding habitat and shelter for a variety of animals, especially ghost crabs, rattlesnakes, and shorebirds.[5]

The southern tip of Sapelo Island at the entrance to Doboy Sound has seen a natural accretion of sand deposits for hundreds of years.

Behind the two dune lines a swath of salt marsh separates the Holocene beach from the Pleistocene upland, and is penetrated by Dean Creek, a tidal stream emptying into Doboy Sound near the lighthouse. In this area just north of the beach road are salt pans fringed by small oak and cedar hammocks. The western side of Sapelo features broad marshes traversed by the Duplin River and numerous small creeks, the chief of which are Barn Creek and Post Office Creek. In this section are a number of marsh hammocks that are the Pleistocene remains of ancient beach ridges.

Tides have a pronounced effect on Sapelo's shoreline as well as the inshore salt marshes. Tidal amplitude around Sapelo ranges from about seven feet up to about eleven feet on spring tides. Not surprisingly, the hydraulics of the tides greatly affects the ecology of the marshes. Tidal rise and fall is a key factor in active processes that occur in the marshes, and it accounts for the diversity of habitats for a number of organisms in the intertidal area. Most tidal creeks lie within steep mud banks and natural levees that create a pattern for the movement of water preceding its eventual

dissipation in headwaters on the marsh surface. Tidal waters flow across the low marsh levees only on the highest spring tides. There are two tidal cycles daily, with about six hundred square miles of marsh and creeks in coastal Georgia being inundated, drained, and refilled.

In an ebb tide–dominated regime, tidal dynamics are most noticeably pronounced in the waters of the estuarine sounds that provide the breaks between the barrier islands along the coast. Off Sapelo's South End, Doboy Sound has a strong outflow on the ebb tide. This tidal outflow is northwest to southeast. When combined with the input from the nearby Altamaha River and the north-to-south emergence of water from Old Teakettle Creek, tidal fronts are often quite distinctive, sometimes marked by narrow lines of foam running crossways to the water flow.

Recreational boaters and even local shrimp boat operators note that Doboy Sound can be some of the roughest water on the Georgia coast, depending on the wind direction. For example, if there is a prevailing southeasterly wind from offshore going against the strong outflow of current from the sound toward the ocean, the waters of the sound can be quite turbulent. The same effect prevails if the wind is from the northwest on a flooding tide. Doboy has a slightly lower salinity than the offshore ocean waters due to freshwater inflow from the Altamaha delta just to the south. The Altamaha River system is one of the largest in the eastern United States when including the inland Ocmulgee, Oconee, and Ohoopee Rivers. Substantial amounts of freshwater flow to the sea, mixing with the salt water from the Atlantic in the Altamaha delta just south of Sapelo. This brackish mix, occurring up to twenty-five miles inland, affects the hydrology of Doboy Sound, being more pronounced during periods of unusually high flow of freshwater from the interior.[6]

The Duplin River, largest of the streams lying entirely within the marshes of Sapelo, transits the western side of the island, emptying on its southern end into Doboy Sound. Except for rainfall and groundwater discharge from the nearby uplands, the Duplin receives no freshwater and thus can more accurately be defined as a large tidal creek or embayment. Along its six and a half miles, the Duplin has three distinct sections, or tidal "prisms." The lower component ends near Pumpkin Hammock, the second extends northward to Moses Hammock, and the third comprises the tidal creek branches of the upper Duplin.

Doboy Sound, one of numerous inlets separating the Georgia barrier islands

The Duplin River is Sapelo's largest
tidal stream.

The strong tidal currents and the lack of freshwater input generally keep the hydrological dynamics of the upper Duplin excluded from those of the lower section of the
river nearer Doboy Sound. Occasionally, during especially high spring tides, water in
the upper Duplin may merge with that of Mud River a short distance to the north.
Conversely, the lower Duplin can sometimes have lower salinity levels than that of the
upper sections during times of heavy discharge from the Altamaha River into Doboy
Sound. The Duplin estuary covers thirty-three hundred acres, about 15 percent of
which remains submerged at mean low water, with a tidal excursion of about three
miles.[7]

A survey of the Duplin by University of Georgia Marine Institute scientists in the
1950s determined that the river's water surface was relatively narrow at low tide. When
the water rises to six feet above mean low tide, however, it begins to leave the banks
and flow in a sheet across the marsh. Small increases in tidal height impel increased
volumes of water into the estuary, and as a consequence the tidal flow is turbulent.
This promotes greater turbidity, though marsh flushing is incomplete, with very little
freshwater entering the system. Most water in the estuary merely oscillates back and
forth rather than draining away to be replaced.[8] The sediments in the bed of the
Duplin are low in mud content and contain accumulations of shell material, much of
which is deposited from the oyster banks along the river. At Little Sapelo Island and
Pumpkin Hammock the river is eroding sandy Pleistocene deposits.

The intertidal habitat of the Duplin and its largest tributary, Barn Creek, is teeming
with marine organisms that receive nutrients from the marshes and in turn provide
food sources for saltwater fish species. The Marine Institute has conducted much of
its research in these marshes, and over the last half century it has made important discoveries relative to the feeding habits of sub-tidal species. Microalgae are productive
in the river, and these and other organisms provide a food source for juvenile menhaden, a plankton feeder. Menhaden, in turn, are preyed upon by larger fish and birds.
Flounder, bluefish, and yellowtail are other finfish predators in the estuary. Mullet are
deposit feeders, and mummichog live in the shallower creeks and headwaters where
they are rarely threatened by larger fish. Shrimp utilize the creeks off the Duplin
throughout the year and are especially prevalent during the summer. Larger predators
forage in the smaller creeks and marsh edges, such as mink and otter, as well as dolphins that feed around Marsh Landing dock on the lower Duplin. Birds feed in the
tidal waters too—pelicans, gulls, and terns nearer the sound, and blue herons, ospreys,
and egrets further up the Duplin.

Little Sapelo Island

One of the Duplin River
hammocks north of Little Sapelo

Salt marsh on Sapelo's South End

The University of Georgia's Eugene Odum, widely regarded as the father of modern ecology, once described tidal creeks as a great circulatory system driven by the pumping heart of the tides. While some of Sapelo's creeks are offshoots of the Duplin River, others flow directly into Doboy Sound, and still others are on the northeast side of the island near High Point and Dumoussay Field. Two larger creeks separate Sapelo from Blackbeard and Cabretta Islands.

All of Sapelo's creeks provide new water input to the marshes on each high tide, while flushing out and removing many of the by-products of marsh growth and marsh decay—detritus—on the ebb tide. Some of the creeks are almost bare at low tide, leaving exposed mud banks that serve as habitat to a variety of consumers such as fiddler crabs, herons, egrets, and marsh hens. On a flooding tide snails become active, while periwinkles and insects graze on the stems of the marsh cordgrass. Plankton and juveniles of various species enter the creeks with incoming tides, as do shrimp and fish when the water becomes deep enough.

Sapelo's salt marshes are composed of many plant species, but the most prominent is smooth cordgrass—*Spartina alterniflora*—which comprises about 90 percent of the marsh system and receives the greatest amount of tidal inundation. Despite its low diversity, the marsh is considered to be one of the most productive natural areas on earth.[9] The basis for the marsh food chain is detritus originating from the dominant vascular plant, the cordgrass. There are differences between the *Spartina* along the creek banks and that of the high marsh nearer the transitional zone that is composed of a mix of short *Spartina* and *Salicornia*. Low-marsh *Spartina* is taller and more luxuriant than other marsh flora and prevails along the creek and river fringes. All marsh life requires freshwater to carry on metabolic processes, and the marshes have unique mechanisms that allow them to extract freshwater from the saline waters of the estuary.

Marsh soils are anaerobic except near the surface and around the roots. Soil bacteria that break down accumulated organic matter require an anaerobic environment, with the rate of breakdown and the rate at which plant nutrients become available for new marsh growth being related to water-flow characteristics and the dispersal of waste products.[10] Plant zonation is always subject to elevation and hydrology, but a water table maintains the marsh sediments in a near waterlogged state in all but the highest intertidal elevations.[11] Consequently, there are highly different plant, soil, and microbial attributes between the low and high *Spartina* zones.

Eugene P. Odum: Ecologist of Sapelo

Eugene Pleasants Odum (1913–2002) was a pioneer in the study of ecosystem ecology. As a young University of Georgia zoology professor in the late 1940s, Odum was among the first in his profession to attach academic rigor to environmental teaching and research. While serving on the University's biology faculty committee he successfully incorporated ecology, and by extension, environmentalism, as a separate field of study. Up to that time ecology had generally not been an academic discipline in the scientific community.

Odum was among the first to clearly define the then-vague term "ecosystem," and he elaborated on it by writing papers for scientific journals as well as important textbooks. His most enduring work is a classic in the field, *Fundamentals of Ecology*. First published in 1953, the book was revised and reissued several times, translated worldwide, and became the standard text in the discipline. The work firmly and permanently established Odum's credentials as a worldwide authority in the natural sciences.

Odum's goal to broaden the study of ecology beyond the Athens campus was largely responsible for the establishment of a marine biological laboratory on Sapelo Island (see chapter 9), a facility that evolved into the University of Georgia Marine Institute. He frequently conducted research at Sapelo, playing a leading role in the first serious investigation of the salt marsh ecosystem and its critical role in the estuarine food web.

His elemental description and articulation of the marsh systems of the Southeast Coast as a huge, natural circulatory system underlaid future studies at the Marine Institute over the next half-century, studies that often expanded on his concepts. The early years of the institute were energized by Odum's field research in tandem with some of the first scientists he helped bring to the Sapelo research faculty, including Robert A. Ragotzkie and Lawrence Pomeroy.

Eugene P. Odum, the "father of modern ecology." (Courtesy of Betty Jean Craige)

As his career developed and his contributions expanded, Odum came to be known as the "father of modern ecology" by his colleagues, students, and friends. The rationale for this appellation is founded upon the cogency of his scientific rigor. Odum's thesis, continually refined over the years, was that the entire earth was a system of interconnected ecosystems. As a modern ecologist, he also became an environmentalist but not in the conventional sense that was in vogue in the 1970s and 1980s. Instead Odum saw himself as an independent thinker. He formed his own concepts and conclusions rather than always adhering to the playbook of the times or the mantras of others in the environmental movement. In this sense, his environmentalist independence enabled him to eschew the more fashionable aspects of the growing movement. Arguably, his thinking outside the box may have resulted in some of his most important contributions to the environmental movement and the study of ecology.

"Gene Odum encouraged his students to see the social implications of ecosystem science," his biographer asserts. "Odum's focus on the whole brought interconnectivity—and hence social responsibility—to the fore." He was a "proselytizer of holism, and his message of interconnectivity insured a generation of ecologists." Odum's own words serve to define the basis of his beliefs. In *Fundamentals of Ecology* he wrote, "The landscape is not just a supply depot but is also the *oikos*—the home—in which we must live." From there his theories of the interconnectivity of the earth's ecosystems expanded and came to be embraced by a widening scientific and lay audience.

Odum's later works further explicated his reasoning and principles. *Ecology and Our Endangered Life-Support Systems* (Sinauer, 1989) incorporated a societal connection to ecology and environmentalism and provided his commentary on the dangers of overpopulation, the importance of recycling, and the "environmental utility of tax and zoning policies," among other socio-economic observations directly relevant to Earth ecology.

SOURCES: Betty Jean Craige, *Eugene Odum: Ecosystem Ecologist and Environmentalist* (Athens: University of Georgia Press, 2001); E. P. Odum, "Living Marsh," introduction to Robert Hanie, *Guale: The Golden Coast of Georgia* (San Francisco: Friends of the Earth, 1974), 19–28.

Salt marsh requires nitrogen and phosphorus as nutrients. Phosphorus is abundantly available in both the soil and tidal waters, but nitrogen availability is more complicated. The use of this common air element by *Spartina* requires its conversion to ammonia nitrate or nitrite through blue-green algae on the marsh surface and bacteria within the soil.[12] Thus, the adaptability of the marsh to natural processes in a saltwater environment makes it a unique plant species.

Twice-daily tidal cycles convey nutrients into the marshes, export detritus and nutrients back into the estuary, and provide a large surface area for phytoplankton production. Tidal flushing maintains a desirable vertical distribution of nutrients and detritus. The base of the detritus food chain is decayed *Spartina*, which is attacked by microorganisms.

Marine Institute research has determined that bacteria found in Sapelo's marsh mud are an important link in the food chain. In the late 1950s, John Teal found the important detritus-algae feeders of Sapelo to be fiddler crabs, periwinkle snails, and nematodes. Their utilization of marsh organic matter accounts for about 55 percent, leaving

Spartina alterniflora is the most prevalent plant of Sapelo's tidal marshes.

about 45 percent available for support of finfish, crabs, shrimp, oysters, and other estuarine fauna.[13] Further investigations found that marsh algae form a thin stratum "between a dark, nutrient-rich, anaerobic sediment, and an illuminated, aerobic, comparatively nutrient-poor water column." Thus, the algae habitat is subjected to rapid changes in light, temperature, pH, salinity, and nutrients that can have correspondingly rapid effects on the photosynthetic rate. Benthic productivity was found to represent about 12 percent of the net primary production of the macrophytes in the Sapelo marsh. About 75 percent of this production occurs during ebb tides, with the exposed creek banks being the most productive areas.[14]

In the higher intertidal zone between the *Spartina* and the upland, areas subjected to less frequent tidal inundation, other marsh-type plants are prevalent. Glasswort and salt grass appear mixed with the shorter cordgrass. Black needlerush (*Juncus roemerianus*) develops as patches amid the cordgrass, with its thin gray-brown stalks and sharp points. Other salt-tolerant plants mixed with the short *Spartina* in this zone are marsh bulrush and sea oxeye. Also featured in the higher zones are salt pans—barren sections of flat, packed soil that are free of vegetation because of excessively high salinity.

Clumps of vegetation lying amid *Spartina* marsh along the fringe abutting a tidal creek, or even a short distance apart from the uplands, are known as hammocks. These formations of high ground feature a mix of similar vegetation, including red cedar,

Marsh mudflats at low tide

sabal palm, wax myrtle, and yaupon holly. Hammocks range in size from less than an acre to several acres. Little Sapelo Island, on the lower Duplin, is considered a large hammock even though it comprises two hundred acres of upland, a hundred of which are subject to occasional tidal inundation. There are several other named hammocks along the Duplin north of Little Sapelo: Mary, Fishing, Pumpkin, and Jack. Like Little Sapelo they have Pleistocene bases surrounded by Holocene marshes.

A variety of marine organisms use the marshes as decomposing *Spartina* detritus gradually dissolves and is flushed by the tides to provide them with food. Numerous consumer species inhabit the marsh ecosystem, with the major groups comprising zooplankton, benthic invertebrates, insects, fish, reptiles, birds, and mammals. Benthic macro-invertebrates are the most conspicuous of the consumers, particularly the fiddler crab (*Uca* genus), marsh mussel (*Geukensia demissa*), and marsh periwinkle (*Littorino irrorata*). Noticeable along some creek banks are oyster reefs. Oysters (*Crassostrea virginica*) settle on solid surfaces along the banks and sub-tidal water; as filter feeders they

Black needlerush interspersed with *Spartina* cordgrass

use marsh nutrients as an important food source. Oyster beds can alter tidal flow in the creeks by creating pools and small breakwaters.

In the early decades of the twentieth century, Georgia salt marshes supported a sizeable oyster industry, but overexploitation and the failure to replace shells led to its near collapse by the 1960s. Another beneficiary of marsh nutrients directly related to human commercial use is the Atlantic blue crab (*Callinectus sapidus*), the majority of which are taken in the sounds and the smaller rivers and creeks. Crabs use the marshes and creeks as habitat during their juvenile and subadult stages.

Of even greater economic significance, the marsh is critical in supporting the coastal shrimp fishery, long a multimillion-dollar industry on the Georgia coast, with peak production in the middle decades of the twentieth century. While coastal shrimp (*Penaeus*) spawn in the open ocean, they migrate to the inshore waters as juveniles and depend on marsh-produced nutrients during their growth stages before returning to the sea.

At low tide, the ubiquitous fiddler crab, particularly the sand fiddler (*Uca pugilator*), is frequently observed scuttling along the mudflats foraging for food near its burrow. Fiddlers extract food from the substrate based on differing feeding stimulants

Live oak

in response to levels in the food resource.[15] Gradients in biotic and abiotic factors resulting from tidal flooding affect the distribution of marsh organisms, with the structural characteristics of *Spartina* providing refuge from predators for some species. The periwinkle prevalent in the marshes is a favorite of predators, particularly the blue crab.

Scientists on Sapelo have frequently studied the effects of predation by crabs on snails in the low marshes. For example, it has been demonstrated that the distance from the marsh edge, density of vegetation, and the duration of tidal inundation affects the ability of crabs to seek food in the marsh. The amount of time available to them to forage is key. The conclusion is that there is a decreasing rate of predation by the crabs on the snails with increasing tidal elevation.[16]

Sapelo Island's uplands are dominated by a mixed maritime forest characterized by stands of mature live oak (*Quercus virginiana*) and several varieties of pine (*Pinus*). There are distinct ecologies and forest zones on Sapelo: upland hardwood maritime forests, lowland hardwood forests, and old and new pine plantations, the latter being more prevalent on the North End. The upland forest comprises a mixed oak-hardwood community with less presence of pine. Here there are live oak, laurel oak, bay, holly, magnolia, slash pine, and cabbage palm (*Sabal palmetto*) with an understory dominated by wax myrtle, broomsedge, and panic grass. The oaks with their low, spreading limbs support various vines and epiphytes (air plants), the latter dominated by Spanish moss and resurrection fern. The latter epiphyte appears dead and dried out in its dormant phase but springs to life, lush and

Resurrection fern and live oak

green, during periods of rainfall. Wending their way around the gnarled, thick lower trunks and limbs of the oaks are grapevines and Virginia creeper. Spanish moss is a bromeliad and features tiny green flowers, hardly visible. Moss is a distinctive feature of the oaks but can also be observed on other tree species.

The lowland forests are typically found in Sapelo's wetter areas and comprise live oak, water oak, loblolly pine, black gum, sweet gum, and sweet bay, set amid thick understories of palmetto and wax myrtle. Much of the pine forest, particularly in the Reynolds Wildlife Management Area, was planted for commercial harvesting by Howard E. Coffin and R. J. Reynolds Jr. Recent management practices in the Sapelo pine forests by the state of Georgia have included the harvesting of pine timber to thin the more mature stands, with prescribed burning to control the understory. Scientific studies have demonstrated that these practices have impacted the marshes adjacent to Sapelo, mostly in the Duplin River watershed, due to runoff and groundwater seepage.

Timber management also provides open food habitat for deer and other animal species and facilitates the healthy growth of the maritime forest. Mixed stands of oak and pine are scattered all over the island, with a closed oak canopy beneath many of the pines. Selective cutting of pine by the state has resulted in the development of cleared habitat for deer herds and has hastened the regeneration of natural oak and other hardwoods in parts of the timbered areas. Large sections of the maritime forest are dominated by pine-palmetto vegetation, with the pine canopy rarely closed. Though pine is cut selectively, natural seeding remains effective in some areas. Saw palmettos form dense thickets four to five feet tall amid the pine forests and are often interspersed with other vegetation.[17]

In Sapelo's central highlands are several open grasslands, probably the result of human modifications for agriculture and pasturage in the nineteenth and early twentieth centuries. An example is King Savannah, which has thick stands of Bahia grass (*Poaceae notatum*) planted earlier as forage for cattle herds. Several areas are clear and open, evidence of antebellum agricultural fields. The open tract on the South End now serving as the island's grass airstrip was once the scene of cotton and sugar cane cultivation, as were similar fields at Flora Bottom, Kenan Field, Bourbon Field, and Chocolate.

Several grass ponds that remain wet throughout the year are found on Sapelo, most being quite small (two acres or less), and are composed of grasses, sedges, and other emergents. Two larger freshwater ponds are noteworthy. The human-made pond on

Mixed pine and oak growth in Sapelo's lowlands

Freshwater pond on Sapelo's South End

the South End near the Marine Institute was built in the mid-1920s by Coffin and is a brackish-freshwater home to a community of alligators that occasionally move between the freshwater and the nearby salt marsh during the summer, as well as populations of cottonmouths (water moccasins) and other water-based snakes.

Another human-made freshwater pond, the ninety-acre Reynolds Duck Pond, was built as waterfowl habitat by Coffin in 1927 on the North End immediately west of Dumoussay Field. Coffin built a tide gate at the north end of the pond to facilitate the outflow of excess freshwater into the marsh. The water control structure is a flashboard riser constructed of tabby, with a culvert leading under a dike to the marsh. There are rookeries at the pond for blue heron, ibis, egrets, gallinules, and several species of ducks.

Sapelo Island's soils are derived primarily from quartz sands and generally have high permeability, a condition that results in low water-holding capacity and rapid leaching. Soils range from deep, well-drained sands to poorly drained thick black loam surfaces and subsurface horizons of gray sands. Most of the soils, however, range from moderately well-drained to poorly drained.

The island's soils are generally highly acidic, whether they are well-drained or poorly drained (depending on the area of the island). According to the most recent soil survey of Sapelo (1961), the island's soil pH ranges from 4.1 to 7.4 among the twelve identified soil types inventoried.[18] Additionally, nineteenth- and early twentieth-century agriculture resulted in the clearing, ditching, and draining of many of the upland areas of Sapelo, considerably altering the island's natural hydrology.

Hydrological factors also come into play on Sapelo's beaches. High salt concentrations in dune sands inhibit the vertical percolation of rainwater through the dunes. This limited water supply reduces the amount of vegetation on Sapelo's seaward side. The close proximity of ocean salts directly affects beach and dune vegetation by excluding most species, often altering individual plants that are able to maintain growth in those areas. The salts also exert an influence on vegetation in the intertidal zone between the marshes and the upland, and they tend to limit species diversity. The abundant nutrients, however, enable the relatively few species in these areas to be highly productive. Conversely, west of Nannygoat Beach there are salt pans in the high marsh that are so concentrated in salts, usually two or more times that of seawater, that few vascular plants can grow there.[19]

The most cultivable soil on Sapelo is the Ona-Scranton fine sand series, which is moderately well-drained, with a sandy surface. The areas of the island's greatest agricultural productivity in the antebellum plantation period were on Ona-Scranton soils. These supported the cultivation of sea island cotton and provision crops at Long Row Field (Chocolate), High Point, Dumoussay Field (upper end), Bourbon, Kenan Field, Long Tabby, and the Duplin River hammocks. Palm Beach fine sand is dark and well-drained and found on level areas of sand ridges near tidal marsh. With proper fertilization, this soil was also used for cotton cultivation, particularly at Dumoussay Field, at Chocolate (north section), on Little Sapelo Island, and near the Sapelo mansion. Many of the Ona-Scranton and Palm Beach soils are now forested with pine (chiefly loblolly), with mixed stands of live oak, all indicative of earlier agricultural activities.

Rutledge fine sand is poorly drained and covered by water part of the year with black gum, cypress, and pine. With adequate drainage the soil is well suited for pine plantations. Although too wet for most crops, Rutledge sand supported small areas of rice cultivation at Raccoon Bluff and Hog Hammock in the late nineteenth and early

North End duck pond near
High Point

twentieth centuries. It was also useful for livestock pasturage in areas such as Raccoon
Bluff, Root Patch, and Flora Bottom. St. Johns fine sand is poorly drained and found
in damp areas, with vegetation of sabal palm, palmetto, huckleberry, gallberry, and
scattered pines.

Leon fine sand, similar to Ona-Scranton, is moderately well-drained and sandy and
usually found in sloped areas of the island. Leon sand supported the cultivation of
subsistence crops at Raccoon Bluff and King Savannah in the postbellum era and early
twentieth century. The natural vegetation includes saw palmetto, pond pine, gallberry,
and wire grass. Rutledge and St. Johns are the predominant soils on Sapelo, and they
comprise a sizeable portion of the interior uplands of the island, including Root Patch,
King Savannah, and large sections northwest and southwest of Raccoon Bluff and
north and west of Hog Hammock.

Sapelo's soils include high-phase tidal marsh, zones close to marsh that are non-
cultivable but are sufficiently above the frequent influence of salt water to allow vegetation of red cedar, live oak, and coarse grasses. These areas include parts of Little
Sapelo Island and the lighthouse tract, and the back-dune meadows west of Nannygoat
Beach and Cabretta. Sapelo's beaches are soils continually scoured by the sea and

wind, fronted by the barren white sands of the dunes on distinct ridges paralleling the beaches; high tidal marsh has vegetation of wax myrtle, marsh elder, saltwort, and sea oxeye, with low marsh comprised almost exclusively of smooth cordgrass and black needlerush.[20]

The foregoing indicates modification of large portions of Sapelo by human activity over the last two and a half centuries, primarily for agriculture, cattle raising, and timbering. Successive private owners of the island constructed irrigation and drainage ditches, drained low-lying areas, and built levees and embankments to facilitate agriculture and timbering. Since Sapelo has no freshwater streams, irrigation ditches were dug by slave labor in the nineteenth century to facilitate crop cultivation and watering of livestock. Some of these original ditches were improved and enlarged through dynamiting operations implemented by Coffin in the 1920s. Evidence of the ditches is conspicuous in many places on the south and central portions of Sapelo.

Wildlife abounds in Sapelo's uplands, marshes, and beach areas. Annual counts have identified almost two hundred species of birds on Sapelo at varying times of the year. In the marsh and on the waters of Doboy Sound, the Duplin River, and the tidal creeks are found brown pelicans, herring gulls, laughing gulls, ring-billed gulls, and double-crested cormorants. Present on the beaches are American oystercatchers, shearwaters, petrels, loons, clapper rails, plovers, gulls, terns, and skimmers, among others. Around the tidal sloughs and marshes are black sanderlings, clapper rails, several species of herons and egrets, wood storks, and white ibis. In the forested uplands, grassy savannas, and marsh fringes it is common to observe several species of hawks, ospreys, turkey vultures, kestrels, coots, woodpeckers, mockingbirds, and ducks, including teals, scaups, canvasbacks, and mergansers. The occasional bald eagle is observed, and in the spring and summer cattle egrets are present, as is the spectacular painted bunting, one of the most impressive of Sapelo's bird species.

Mammals common to the island are white-tailed deer, raccoons, opossums, squirrels, bats, otters, minks, armadillos, and feral hogs and cattle, the latter being descendants of the open-range dairy herd belonging to R. J. Reynolds. Eastern diamondback rattlesnakes populate the dunes and uplands, water moccasins are in the wetter areas, and numerous species of nonvenomous snakes are commonly encountered in the less-cleared areas.

It is likely that much, perhaps most, of the flora and fauna encountered today on Sapelo is not the same as those present during the Archaic period (10,000–3,000 BP).

During the Archaic, most of Sapelo was covered by a climax forest, which would have reduced the available food supply in the spring and summer. There would have been browsing areas available in the shrub-herb layers of the island ecology, but these would not have supported the large deer herds and other wildlife that prevail on the island today with open pastures and second- and third-generation forest growth.

As oak species matured in the Archaic, the fall and winter months would have produced sufficient acorn fall to support deer in greater numbers as time went along. Spanish moss and plants growing in the high marsh would have provided additional food. The remaining vestiges of the maritime climax forest from that period disappeared when large areas of the island were cleared for agriculture and oak timbering in the eighteenth and nineteenth centuries. If the early climax forest was not seriously depleted during the proto-historic and aboriginal agricultural eras, then it almost certainly was during the colonial period and after.

Sapelo Island's climate is classified as subtropical, consisting of brief, relatively mild winters, and warm, humid summers. Cold temperatures in some winters prevent tropical or subtropical vegetation from persisting, but the climate is sufficiently mild to allow some species characteristic of warmer areas to grow and reproduce naturally. The average date of the earliest frost at Sapelo is December 3, with the latest being March 2, allowing an average growing season of 276 days.[21] Intense summer showers account for much of Sapelo's annual precipitation, which averages 51.7 inches. The wettest months are usually June, July, and August with the driest being October and November. The least amount of annual rainfall on Sapelo was 32.9 inches in 1954. The highest was seventy-five inches in 1964, a hurricane year with Dora, a strong category-two storm in early September. Heavier rainfall in August and September is often associated with tropical systems.

Several hurricanes from 1989 to 2005 passed near the Georgia coast, but none caused serious damage. Most East Coast hurricanes tend to follow the warmer waters of the offshore Gulf Stream. Brunswick, Georgia, just south of Sapelo Island, is the westernmost point away from the Gulf Stream of any section of the south Atlantic coast. Only ten storms between 1886 and 2014 carried hurricane-force winds into the Georgia coast. The most damaging storms directly affecting Sapelo occurred in 1804, 1824, 1854, 1893, 1896, 1898, 1944, and 1964. The worst of these was the October 1898 cyclone that left much of Sapelo and the nearby islands under several feet of water due to an extremely high tidal surge.

CHAPTER II   Archaeological Sapelo

The Early Occupiers

ATIVE AMERICANS were using Sapelo Island as a food-gathering source by 4500 BP. The predominant group of gatherers was the Guale, a Muskhogean-speaking agrarian component of the Lower Creeks that may have had initial contact with Europeans as early as 1526. In the last fifty years there has been extensive study done on the Guale and their living patterns along the middle Georgia coast between the Altamaha and the Ogeechee Rivers, including the islands from St. Simons to Ossabaw.[1] The initial Guale contact with Europeans near Sapelo Island was possibly in 1526 during an unsuccessful Spanish attempt at establishing a colony some scholars think was in or near Sapelo Sound (see box, p. 48). Later there was sustained contact from about 1570 to 1684, a period during which the Spanish established a chain of missions in their provinces of Guale and Mocama along the southeastern coast.[2]

Permanent Guale settlements were on the mainland, as well as on the islands, including Sapelo and St. Catherines. Mainland Guale also used the islands seasonally during food-gathering periods. Based on archaeological evidence, Sapelo was occupied during the Late Archaic (ca. 2500–1000 BC), a period associated in the Southeast with the production of fiber-tempered ceramics. On Sapelo, the Guale used vegetal fiber—usually Spanish moss—mixed with the clay of their manufactured pottery to prevent cracking during the firing process. Scattered evidence of this pottery has been found on Sapelo on the high ground abutting the Duplin and Mud Rivers and Blackbeard Creek, including areas away from shell middens (refuse heaps).

The island was less populated in the Woodland phase (ca. 1000 BC–AD 1000), and only a few traces of artifact evidence have been documented. One Woodland phase occupation site has been identified at Moses Hammock, beneath a shell midden attributed to a later phase. Sapelo's Guale population increased during the two phases of the Late Prehistoric (Mississippian) period: the Savannah phase (ca. 800–1350), and the Irene (ca. 1350–1570). Sapelo's Mississippian sites are characterized by a number of large burial mounds at Kenan, Bourbon, and Dumoussay Fields, with additional evidence documented at Long Row Field, Moses Hammock, and High Point. The Guale mounds on Sapelo were encircled by shallow ditches, from which came the materials used in the mound construction. Mounds were typically repositories for large numbers of burials.

Guale towns were governed by a local *mico* (chief), who presided over a council, similar to most Muskhogean groups. The prevalence of the chiefdom as an organized political entity began to manifest itself in the Mississippian period from about 800. Spanish reports in the 1590s note that the Guale councils met in large, circular structures, some of which were capable of accommodating three hundred men. Beyond the archaeological clues little is known of Guale social organization, but Spanish documents do indicate a form of marriage was observed following Creek patterns, while the *mico* apparently had multiple wives.

The Guale were prolific users of tobacco. The pipe was apparently the constant companion of the Guale men, the soothing vapors of its tobacco providing a source of solace and pleasure. Even in death the Guale and his pipe were not separated—the pipe was buried with him in order that he might continue to smoke in the afterlife. The Guale commonly used a small pipe with a bowl made of clay and a long stem of reed. The ceremonial pipe, or calumet, was larger and of more intricate design. Pipe fragments are quite common in the mounds investigated by archaeologists over the years.

During the late Mississippian period the Guale, like other indigenous groups on the Southeast Coast, transitioned from a purely game-hunting society to one that also used agriculture. Coastal populations developed maize cultivation from about AD 1000, with increased development of agriculture to supplement their fishing, hunting, and foraging. The Guale eventually became primarily agrarian. Archaeological evidence

demonstrates their considerable expertise with cultivation of beans, squash, melons, pumpkins, and maize, the latter ground into flour for making flat, round cakes. With shell hoes, Guale women cultivated the land, growing the vegetables. They also cured and dressed the skins of deer and other animals killed by the male hunters and manufactured the clay pots used for cooking and storage. Archaeologists have found many fragments of these pots in burial mounds and middens.

Crops were grown based on the Guale's increased understanding of local soil and weather conditions. Guale planters adapted to the lack of adequate fertility found in the sandy coastal soils and developed proportionality to their farming techniques and the types of crops cultivated. Father Sedeno of the Santa Catalina mission on St. Catherines Island noted that "the Indians are scattered because they do not have that with which to clear trees for their fields, so they go where they find a small amount of land without forest in order to plant their maize; and the land is so miserable they move with their households from time to time to seek other lands that they can bring to productivity."[3]

Meat was plentiful. Herds of buffalo roamed the mainland forests, and deer proliferated in the woods and grassy savannas. The Guale hunted white-tailed deer on Sapelo as a year-round dietary staple, using the skins for clothing and for barter. Guale men bow-hunted using arrows made of reed, mulberry, or cedar, tipped with fishbone or chipped beads of flint. Other game included bear, turkey, raccoon, and rabbit. Live oak

acorns, gathered in the fall in great quantity beneath the tree canopy, were sweet and were eaten raw. Berries and persimmons were available in spring and summer, and wild grapes were abundant in the fall.

Shellfish was an important food for the Guale during the Archaic. Various species could easily be collected from creek banks without requiring watercraft. Mussels and periwinkles abounded in the salt marsh, and since intertidal oysters form beds along the creek banks it was relatively easy for the Guale to harvest these. In addition to shellfish, the Guale ate large quantities of finfish. Consumable fish species included sea trout, Atlantic croaker, yellowtail, drum, and shad.[4] Guale men traveled the tidal creeks in dugout canoes commonly made from cypress logs hollowed out by means of fire. The Guale used the dugouts to search the waterways for food and to visit their neighbors on the islands and mainland.

Artifact analysis based on a century of archaeological field investigation indicates considerable Guale activity on St. Simons, Sapelo, St. Catherines, and Ossabaw Islands during the Mississippian period. Guale settlement patterns on Sapelo were concentrated on the western and northeastern sections of the island in the higher elevations contiguous to the marsh and at points where tidal creeks offered access to the high ground.[5] The occupational sites have been identified as Kenan Field on the Duplin River, Long Row Field south of Chocolate, the strip on the northwestern portion of the island from the Shell Ring to High Point, and Dumoussay and Bourbon Fields in Sapelo's northeastern quadrant. Scattered shell mound evidence also points to Guale presence on the South End, several hundred yards east of the Marine Institute campus.

Archaeologist Morgan R. Crook Jr. conducted a systematic survey of Guale sites at Kenan and Bourbon Fields in the mid-1970s, concluding that settlements were present at both. Amplifying fieldwork at Bourbon conducted earlier by Clarence B. Moore, Crook determined that testing of ceramic and mortuary findings from two large mounds suggested the Savannah and Irene periods, while pottery analysis from the site further validated a Mississippian provenance.[6]

The several archaeological phases of the Mississippian period, about 800–1500 AD, were marked by changes in Guale pottery patterns such as tempering, stamping, and incising with increasingly decorative embellishment. These evolving techniques were clearly identifiable from the Savannah and subsequent Irene phases of the late Mississippian era, and they continued to be developed in the mission period in the early seventeenth century.

The Savannah archaeological phase in coastal Georgia began about 800 and represented maturing cultural development by the Guale and neighboring groups as they exploited the local estuarine waters and oak forests for sustenance. Both the Savannah and Irene phases, the latter continuing into the early historic period, were characterized by large nuclear settlements, dispersed smaller seasonal settlements (particularly on the islands), and extensive platform mounds and burial mounds.[7] Archaeological finds provide compelling evidence of seasonal mobility of the Guale between the islands and the mainland.

Field investigations relating to Native American life patterns on Sapelo Island have been conducted for over a century. It cannot be overstated, however, that this research has been made more difficult by the degree to which Sapelo's land has been used and altered by human activity from around 1750 to the modern era. Plantation agriculture, continued cultivation by Sapelo's freedmen in the postbellum era, and extensive timbering and road building in the first half of the twentieth century disturbed the evidentiary footprint of prehistoric and early contact period Native Americans on the island.

It must also be understood that early investigative archaeology was quite rudimentary. There was a general absence of definition in the academic aspects of the discipline and a concurrent lack of appreciation for this. A caption in the *Savannah Morning News* in November 1898 is typical: "No Treasure Ever Found in the Mounds and No Giants Either." This attitude was symptomatic of widespread misconceptions about the then-undocumented aboriginal societies of pre-Columbian coastal Georgia.

In 1872, William McKinley, a Milledgeville, Georgia, attorney, submitted a paper to the *Smithsonian Annual Report* based on his investigations of burial mounds on Sapelo. The document reflected his unscientific observations during a May 1871 visit to the island. He described a number of shell aggregations and detailed three burial mounds, noting that "great mound-circles were doubtless for councils or games." He included a reference to a mound named "Druid Grove" or "Spalding" near the old Spalding house on Sapelo's South End, placing it on a map accompanying his report. Regarding a mound complex situated in the center of the island, McKinley noted "These cemetery-mounds are very ancient. . . . Sapelo Island is famous for its wonderful moss-hung live oaks; but the largest-bodied tree on the island, one over four feet in diameter at the stump, and seven feet in height, to just below the first fork, grows on top of the biggest burial mound at the place marked Kenan."[8]

The first archaeologist to employ scholarly rigor in investigative field research on Sapelo was Clarence Bloomfield Moore, a Philadelphia academic who conducted studies on the Southeast and Gulf Coasts in the 1890s and early 1900s. His detailed field notes and drawings, when published in 1897 as *Certain Aboriginal Mounds of the Georgia Coast*, documented for the first time Native American social life in the region. This book included an assessment of his work at Sapelo in 1896.[9] While McKinley and Moore had different professional backgrounds, their common interests and observations, in tandem with the validity of their notes and didactic reports on Sapelo's mound complexes, provided later generations of researchers with critically important insights into aspects of pre-Columbian life on the island.

C. B. Moore's interest in southeastern coastal aboriginal societies was inspired by a series of articles published in the *American Naturalist* from 1892 to 1894 on the "Shell Heaps of the St. Johns River." Moore's meticulous attention to detail in the methodology of his field collection, and his subsequent documentation of aboriginal sites visited between 1894 and 1918, have enabled his findings to be used continuously through the years. He and his staff traveled the Gulf of Mexico and the southeastern Atlantic coast in addition to making trips along several interior rivers. The annual fieldwork was usually conducted from October through April, after which Moore returned to Philadelphia for the summer to collate and rewrite his field notes and make public his latest research.

Moore began his explorations by chartering two steam vessels, the *Osceola* and the *Alligator*. Soon thereafter, he realized the need for a customized research vessel. Thus, in 1895 the *Gopher* of Philadelphia was moved south and reconfigured to suit his requirements at a shipyard in Jacksonville, Florida.[10] The steamer was designed to navigate shallow coastal rivers to access remote areas, to serve as a field laboratory during the research season, and to be used as an onsite repository for his artifact collections. The *Gopher* was used in 1896–97 and 1898 during Moore's two visits to Sapelo Island.

Both McKinley and Moore investigated the Bourbon Field mound complex in the northeastern part of the island, then the property of New Englander Amos Sawyer. Each noted in his respective report that this area contained the largest of the burial sites observed on the island. A landing at Bourbon Field served as the anchorage for the *Gopher*, according to Moore's field notes.[11]

McKinley's 1872 Smithsonian report includes a description of a mound complex in a place he identifies as "Bobone field," a colloquialism used by the African Americans

Bourbon Field is the site of several burial mounds and has undergone extensive archaeological field research.

residing in that section of the island. In his 1897 report, *Certain Aboriginal Mounds*, Moore noted that "Boobone" was a small black settlement. He wrote, "Extending back from the landing is an extensive tract of rich land, undulating with shell deposits, long under cultivation, the property of Amos Sawyer, Esq., of Arlington, R.I. to whom we are indebted for cordial permission to make complete archaeological investigation."[12]

McKinley and Moore studied two mounds at Bourbon. In one mound "about one quarter of a mile S.E. by S. from the landing" Moore documented 192 points of human remains, including 115 skeletons.[13] His report indicated that the two mounds were 150 yards apart, the largest measuring seventy-two feet in diameter at the base and eight feet in height, the second being thirty-eight feet in diameter at the base and three feet, four inches in height. In the larger mound Moore recovered pottery vessels, clay tobacco pipe bowls, conch shell chisels, conch bowls, shell beads, and polished stone axes. When McKinley had measured the mound earlier, in 1871, he recorded the

largest as being seventy feet in diameter at the base and nine feet in height, and he recorded no measurements for the smaller mound, adding that the "entire surface of [the] field is dotted and white with hundreds of shell-mounds, from two to four feet high, and from fifteen to fifty feet base."[14]

It appears that both McKinley and Moore did fieldwork in the same area but made divergent observations. It is therefore problematic in determining whether the two simply saw things differently or whether during the twenty-five years of land use between their respective visits crop cultivation and climatic impacts had altered the site. Agricultural activity certainly occurred at Bourbon Field during much of the post-bellum period. When including more recent analyses, almost two hundred middens have been mapped at Bourbon, and the appearance of both aboriginal and European ceramics suggests extensive use of the site in the Mississippian and Spanish periods. With the archaeological excavation of considerable amounts of Spanish pottery, some researchers have concluded that Bourbon was the likely site of Mission San Joseph de Sapala.

Moore's 1896–97 investigations also included a mound at Dumoussay Field, a little over a mile north-northwest of Bourbon, a site known earlier as Mackays Old Fields. The north end of Dumoussay was accessed at high tide via McCoy's (Mackay's) Creek, a stream branching off Blackbeard Creek north of Bourbon and flowing due east of High Point. The mound here, about a quarter-mile from the landing amid a field then overgrown with pine, was a burial site with human remains documented at fifty-one points, including forty-two skeletons. The Dumoussay mound featured hundreds of low shell middens twenty to fifty feet in diameter. Materials recovered from the mound indicate a late Mississippian, Irene phase, setting for the Guale site. There likely were several sites of Guale settlement in different eras on the North End of pre-Columbian Sapelo. For example, the Yonge and DeBrahm survey map of 1760 delineated a small "Indian town" in the marsh east of High Point and another on the neck of land later known as Dumoussay Field.[15] McKinley noted that "[n]o other [burial mound sites] are known; but very much of the intervening central part of the island is impenetrable palmetto thicket, and it is possible other mounds exist in this thicket."[16]

Neither McKinley nor Moore excavated the extensive mound complex at Kenan Field, the latter being denied access to the site by the owner, Spalding Kenan. Subsequent investigation by Morgan R. Crook and others has determined that Kenan Field is the largest archaeological site on Sapelo Island, covering about sixty hectares (148 acres), with two burial mounds and 589 shell middens. There is evidence of two large structures at Kenan that may be Mississippian examples of council houses. The Guale likely had a "large, low platform" (according to Crook) constructed over one of the mounds, with several temple or platform mounds arranged around a plaza. Crook, who conducted his investigations at Kenan Field in 1976 and 1977, referred to the tract as "archaeologically complex," suggesting that much more research needed to be done at the site.[17]

Kenan's most prominent feature is the large mound (Mound A), near the center of the site, with a smaller mound at the southern edge of the field near the north bank of Barn Creek. There is a long, low earthen embankment that extends west to east across Kenan Field about five hundred feet south of Mound A. The remains of middens are quite numerous. These are recognized as low rises composed principally of oyster shell. These extensive refuse piles are scattered over the village and provide an important

Kenan Field, site of Sapelo's most extensive burial mounds

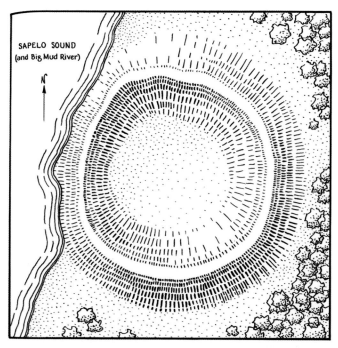

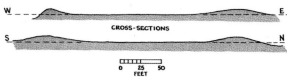

Plan of Sapelo Island Shell Ring No. 1, with elevations, based on a field drawing by Clarence B. Moore, 1897. (From *The Waring Papers: The Collected Works of Antonio J. Waring, Jr.*, edited by Stephen Williams [Athens: University of Georgia Press, 1968]; reprinted by permission of the University of Georgia Press)

source of information about the diet of the Guale. With its documented complexity, Kenan Field was clearly the site of a prominent Guale town on Sapelo, based on both the archaeological footprint and the Spanish manuscript record. The pottery types recovered at Kenan certify Guale occupation of the site during the Mississippian and early Spanish periods.

Probably the earliest of Sapelo's prehistoric sites is the Shell Ring complex in the northwestern section of the island, the most prominent feature of which was often referred to as the "Spanish Fort" in the eighteenth and nineteenth centuries. This aboriginal formation is regarded as one of the largest and most intact of the few remaining southeastern shell rings. McKinley's 1871 observations brought this unique formation to the attention of the anthropological community for the first time. He identified three rings south of High Point: the larger, most prominent one still much in evidence, and two smaller rings only three feet high "in an open field long cultivated." Of the larger ring, McKinley noted that it was

240 feet wide; 9 feet high; base, 30 feet; no gateway; built of earth and shells, densely overgrown with live oak, palmetto, myrtle, grape-vines, which perfectly mask it; western side built along the very edge of the table land; so as to front a salt marsh and the Mud River as a wall 20 feet high; on the north, skirting a fresh water flag and bulrush marsh or stream, 150 feet wide, separating it from circle No. 2, which is 210 feet wide, in an open field long cultivated; mound now rising 3 feet on 20 feet base, composed of shell and earth; area plain. Circle No. 3 is 150 feet wide, just like No. 2. These circles are surrounded by hundreds of shell mounds, about 3 feet high, on bases of 20 to 50 feet, which crowd, without visible order, a field of one hundred acres or more, bounded on the west by salt marsh and inland salt river, and on the east by fresh-water jungle. On all these shell-mounds and over all the plain are found fragments of Indian pottery, both plain and ornamented. No funeral-mounds are nearer than three miles. The shells are all of mollusks yet living in the neighboring waters, the oyster, clam, conch, scallop, & c., which fact, and the broken pottery, show plainly that these shell-mounds, indicated by dots on the map, in countless number, are ancient camps of the Indians or mound-builders, where they dwelt, while the three great mound circles were doubtless for councils or games.[18]

The Shell Ring today

McKinley's description indicates that the area was large and somewhat disturbed, probably because of the rings being used as a convenient source for oyster shells in the early nineteenth-century construction of tabby buildings on Sapelo Island. Moore referenced the Shell Ring in his 1897 publication as "Aboriginal Enclosure at Sapelo High Point," noting,

> Near the northwest end of Sapelo Island, overlooking Sapelo Sound and at periods of storm, washed by the water of Big Mud River which has laid bare a section of the walls, is an almost circular aboriginal fortification or ceremonial enclosure . . . having a diameter, including the walls, of somewhat over 300 feet. The walls have an average height of from 5 to 7 feet, and a thickness of about 50 feet at the base. They are flattened on top where at present they have an average width of from 10 to 15 feet. They are covered with forest trees, and are composed exclusively of shells, mainly those of the oyster, with the usual midden refuse intermingled, such as fragments of bone, bits of earthenware, and the like.[19]

An important dissimilarity emerged from the findings of the two archaeologists: Moore's report noted, "Earthenware in fragments, shattered bones of the deer and a fragment of a temporal bone from a human skull were met with." Because Moore was actually excavating at the Shell Ring site in 1896–97, and McKinley was only making visual observations a quarter-century earlier, it appears that their interpretations of the ring mounds are somewhat contradictory.

A more rigorous investigation of the site was conducted half a century after Moore by pathbreaking coastal archaeologists Antonio J. Waring Jr. (1915–64) and Lewis H. Larson Jr. (1927–2012). In 1949 and 1950 they documented the largest ring as having an interior diameter of two hundred feet, noting that it "seemed likely that the Shell Ring was the site of many small habitations. The occupants apparently piled the rapidly accumulating shell beside their small dwellings; later they moved, and new shell was then piled on the former habitation site." Waring and Larson concluded that the area inside the ring was intentionally "kept scrupulously clean" by the Guale since it was found to be devoid of shell.[20]

Like Moore, Waring and Larson noted that the composition is largely oyster shell, with a mix of clam, mussel, and whelk. Dating of fiber-tempered pottery remains indicate a Late Archaic or Early Woodland period provenance for the site. Radiocarbon dating of oyster shell remains places the starting date of building the ring at about 3,800 years before the present, plus or minus 350 years. The construction of the ring over several thousand years by the Guale was apparently quite purposeful, a planned

Archaeological
evidence indicates that
the Shell Ring was
both a pre-Columbian
Guale settlement and a
ceremonial site.

project spanning generations of Native Americans. Artifacts excavated in 1950 included animal bone, projectile points, fiber-tempered pottery, tools, and ornaments. The two nearby smaller rings observed by McKinley in 1871 have been validated by more recent investigation using advanced scientific techniques and analysis.

The research of archaeologist Victor Thompson starting in 2004 validated the findings of Waring and Larson regarding settlement patterns at the Shell Ring sites. Thompson posited that the largest formation was likely a permanent settlement during the Late Archaic period, ending around 1000 BC. The interpretation here is that there were actual structural elements—housing—inside the circumference of the ring, while the ring itself was a gradual accumulation of waste and shell deposits by the Guale. After the Archaic the Shell Ring ceased to be a settlement but continued to evolve as a ceremonial site. The Shell Ring settlement possibly transitioned a few miles south to Kenan Field, where a substantial Guale town was in evidence through several periods, including Late Archaic and Mississippian (Late Prehistoric).[21]

Mission San Joseph de Sapala

For most of the seventeenth century, Spanish authorities at St. Augustine occupied the coast of Guale (later Georgia) and maintained a system of Franciscan missions ministering to the Native American people of the coast and asserting Spanish hegemony in the region. The mission initiative began with Christianizing the Timucuans of northeastern Florida, followed by expansion into Mocama and neighboring Guale immediately north of Mocama. In 1587, the Spanish established their provincial capital at Guale, an Indian pueblo (village) and mission on St. Catherines Island, designated Mission Santa Catalina after the 1597 Guale uprising. Santa Catalina became one of the key outposts in the territory of La Florida.

The mainland Guale town and mission of Tolomato was another important seat of power, probably exceeding even that of Guale (Santa Catalina) in prominence prior to 1597. Recent scholarship has argued for a location of Tolomato either at Sutherland's Bluff or Harris Neck in present-day McIntosh County since records indicate that it was near the Guale town on St. Catherines Island.[22] The Guale uprising (Juanillo's Revolt) began at Tolomato in late September 1597. It was a spontaneous rebellion precipitated more by internal friction and competition among the Guale chiefdoms than resentment of Spanish authority over their local affairs.[23] Five Franciscan priests were murdered at the Guale missions, the first being Fr. Pedro de Corpa at Tolomato, quickly followed by the slaying of Fr. Aunon and Bro. Badajoz at St. Catherines, Fr. Rodriguez at Tupiqui, and Fr. Berascola at Talaje/Asajo.

The response of Spanish authorities was swift: the new governor of St. Augustine, Mendez de Canzo, after hearing reports of the murders, dispatched forces into Guale seeking retribution. On November 2, 1597, Spanish attackers destroyed a Guale town on Sapelo Island, followed several days later by the destruction of Tolomato and St. Catherines.[24] Peace was restored following the eventual capture and execution of the leaders of the revolt, and from 1604 until 1610 Franciscan missions were established or reestablished in Guale, including Santa Catalina, Talaje/Asajo, and San Joseph de Sapala.

By 1660 there were five principal missions in Guale: San Joseph on Sapelo Island, San Diego de Satuache on the mainland near the mouth of the Ogeechee River (later moved to St. Catherines Island), San Phelipe de Alava on the North Newport River, Santa Clara de Tupiqui on the Sapelo River near present-day Pine Harbor (moved to

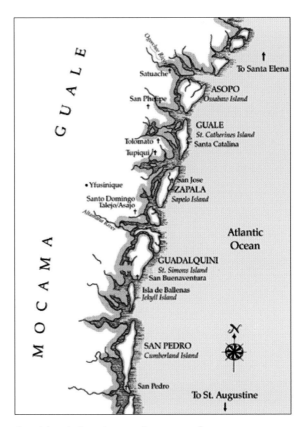

Spanish mission sites on the coasts of Mocama and Guale. (Author's collection)

Sapelo Island about 1674), and San Domingo de Talaje/Asajo, just east of present Darien at the later Fort King George site (moved in 1661 to Cannon's Point on St. Simons Island as Asajo).

The discovery of the Santa Catalina mission in 1981, after several years of systematic searching by teams led by David Hurst Thomas of the American Museum of Natural History's Department of Anthropology, opened an era of renewed interest in southeastern Spanish missions.[25] Thomas's published findings over the next three decades fueled vigorous archaeological and manuscript research by scholars to gain a clearer understanding of more than a century of Spanish activity in Guale. The discoveries at St. Catherines through the archaeological investigations of Thomas and his colleagues (still ongoing in 2016) have had significant contextual implications for research related to the Sapelo mission, San Joseph de Sapala (Zapala).

While San Joseph has been the focus of scholarship and field research since the mid-1970s, only in recent years has quantitative tangible evidence been yielded relating to the mission and its interaction with the Guale. Investigations by archaeologists Richard Jefferies, Christopher Moore, and Victor Thompson from 2003 to 2013, in tandem with manuscript research by John Worth, Amy Bushnell, and others, have resulted in important new interpretations of Sapelo's mission history that had been overlooked or misinterpreted by earlier historians.[26] Modern archaeological analytical techniques and forensic research skills have enabled increased historical synthesis from disparate fragmentary evidence.

Although the exact year is uncertain, San Joseph de Sapala was established between 1604 and 1610 during the period following the 1597 revolt when the Spanish were reestablishing their mission presence and encouraging more Guale to settle on the coastal islands.[27] In its early years the Sapelo mission was small, being listed as a *visita*, a subsidiary mission supervised by resident friars of the mainland Talaje/Asajo mission. The importance of San Joseph de Sapala apparently increased as the mission was recorded as a *doctrina*, or regular mission, in 1655. Additionally, Yamasee Indians had established a small settlement on the lower part of

Vásquez de Ayllón in Sapelo Sound?

Manuscript research in the 1980s provided compelling evidence that the environs of Sapelo Island may have been the site of the first European attempt to place a permanent colony in the continental United States. In 1526, only thirty-four years after the landfall of Christopher Columbus in the Western Hemisphere, a Spanish colony was established on the Southeast Coast by a Toledo-born lawyer and planter, Lucas Vásquez de Ayllón. This preceded by thirty-nine years the 1565 Spanish settlement of St. Augustine, regarded as the first permanent U.S. municipality. Ayllón's colony, San Miguel de Gualdape, was short-lived. It lasted only two and half months before hunger, disease, internal strife, and a Guale uprising forced its abandonment. Based on Spanish archival research, historian Paul Hoffman calculated that San Miguel was located in or near Sapelo Sound. Sapelo and St. Catherines Islands and the McIntosh County mainland at Harris Neck, Sutherland's Bluff, and Creighton Island were site possibilities. Earlier theories placed San Miguel in South Carolina at Winyah Bay or near the Savannah River.

Ayllón (ca. 1480–1526) was a wealthy Spanish sugar planter and *oidor* (judge) on the island of Hispaniola. In 1521 he financed an exploratory expedition to the Atlantic coast of North America, with two navigators, Gordillo and Quejo, establishing a base in the Santee River–Winyah Bay area. Ayllón secured rights of colonization from Charles V of Spain in 1523. The expedition was formed to place a colony in what was thought to be a fertile region envisioned by Ayllón as a new Andalucía.

Departing San Domingo (Haiti) in July 1526 with six ships and about six hundred colonists, including soldiers, sailors, African slaves, Dominican priests, women, and children, the expedition arrived at Winyah Bay on August 8. Ayllón determined that conditions there were not what he wanted, and a setback occurred when the *capitana* (flagship) carrying many of the expedition's supplies ran aground in a storm and sank at the mouth of the Santee.

Information from Spanish navigational records reveals that Ayllón's reconnaissance of the coast to the south led his expedition to the vicinity of Sapelo Sound (which he called Bahia de Zapala). There Ayllón found suitable soil conditions, a freshwater source, friendly Guale Indians, and the spacious anchorage afforded by the sound. The observations of contemporary Spanish historians Oviedo, Chaves, and Herrera support the notion that San Miguel de Gualdape was founded on lands rimming Sapelo Sound. Was it on the upper end of Harris Neck? On the north end of Creighton

Detail from Diogo de Ribeiro Mappamondo (map of the world), 1529, delineating southeastern North America including "Tierra De Ayllon." (Land of Ayllon)

Island? The high commanding land at Sutherland's Bluff? Or on one of the larger islands—Sapelo or St. Catherines? Oviedo's account described the colony's site as being flat, with expanses of adjoining salt marshes and vegetation comprising oak, cedar, and palmetto. He noted the use of local fish and shellfish by the colonists since the original supplies of maize and olive oil had been depleted by the Feast of St. Michael in September, the time of San Miguel's founding.

Disease—typhoid and possibly smallpox—took a toll on the Spanish colonists, as did unusually cold weather that fall. The settlers also succumbed to the ravages of hunger because of declining food sources, partly due to troubles with the local Guale. Ayllón himself became sick and died on October 18. An improvised cemetery began to fill. This burial ground, containing the graves of Ayllón and close to four hundred of his fellow colonists, will almost certainly be the primary archaeological signature if the site of the doomed colony is ever found.

By mid-November the remaining colonists abandoned San Miguel, boarding their ships and returning to San Domingo. Out of the 600 that started with the expedition four months earlier, only about 150 returned, and Ayllón's young widow, Ana Bezerra, was left to pay the exorbitant debts incurred from the venture.

Searches for Ayllón's colony began in the Sapelo Sound area in the 1990s. Previous investigations had uncovered Spanish artifacts in the region—at Thomas Landing on the north end of Harris Neck, at the Lebanon plantation on the South Newport River, on a large hammock (Wahoo Island) east of Harris Neck, on the north end of Creighton Island, at Pine Harbor at the western extremity of Sapelo Sound, and on Sapelo and St. Catherines Islands. But none of the artifacts are dated earlier than 1550. Noted one report, "The negative evidence does not

Sixteenth-century Spanish olive jar used as an all-purpose storage container, the equivalent of a modern-day cardboard box. (Author's collection)

necessarily refute Hoffman's hypothesis; however, San Miguel, in its exposed location, may have been buried in sand dunes," or it may have been in an area now submerged by the ocean tides. To date, no trace of San Miguel has been found—"not a bone, a potsherd, or a nail. But they are there somewhere, among the fish camps and condominiums, and palmetto woods. The Spanish dead of long ago still sleep in the once cruel land of Ayllón."

SOURCE: Paul Hoffmann, *A New Andalucia and a Way to the Orient: The American Southeast during the Sixteenth Century* (Baton Rouge: Louisiana State University Press, 1990).

A typical Spanish mission as it would have appeared at San Joseph de Sapala and nearby Santa Catalina. (Courtesy of artist Joe Durrett)

Sapelo by the mid-1660s, as well as on neighboring St. Simons, interacting with the Guale at both places.

In the spring of 1661, a rival group, the Chichimeco (also known as the Westo), staged attacks from the mainland on the Guale and Mocama mission provinces, "sacking the churches and convents and killing the Christian Indians."[28] The Chichimeco made an unsuccessful attack on Sapelo by boats from Talaje. With difficulty, most of these attacks were repelled, and for a time optimism again prevailed on the Guale coast. Fr. Jacinto de Barreda, the priest then assigned to San Joseph de Sapala, wrote in April 1663 that the Chichimeco threat had been so reduced that "it is not suitable that there be infantry in this province, because in having them it would follow much damage and destruction . . . to the few people which there are in each town . . . and they [Guale] are so annihilate[ed] and perishing."[29]

Nonetheless, the attacks signified the beginning of the end for the Guale missions. In response to the raids by the Chichimeco and their English allies from the new South Carolina colony, the mainland missions were relocated to the island missions in the 1660s and early 1670s. Small military garrisons were stationed at St. Catherines and Sapala for protection. A 1675 report from the resident priest at San Joseph,

Fr. Juan Bauptistas Campana, to the presidio at St. Augustine noted that "between men, women, children and pagan, fifty persons" were then in residence at the Sapala mission.[30]

In the spring of 1680, the English and Chichimeco attacked Santa Catalina and burned the town, which compelled the abandonment of the mission by the surviving Spaniards. The combined missions of Santa Catalina and Satuache were relocated across Sapelo Sound to the combined mission of Tupiqui and San Joseph. Spanish counterattacks from the south compelled the Yamasee in Guale to retreat north and ally themselves with the English.

Due to the overcrowded conditions at San Joseph created by elements of what had once been four separate missions, the settlement on the west side of the island near the Shell Ring was enlarged, and a small Spanish garrison shored up its defenses. This site, while convenient to the inland passage, nonetheless lay exposed to attack by English marauders and potential resurgence of the Chichimeco. Artifact and manuscript evidence indicates that the Spaniards were active in the Shell Ring section of Sapelo before 1680.

There clearly was agricultural activity in that part of the island. En route to the Altamaha River to build Fort King George in 1721, Col. John Barnwell of South Carolina reported "putting ashoar [sic] at Sapola for Spanish Garlick & to look for figs; they got garlick but the figs were green."[31] In their 1760 survey of Sapelo, William DeBrahm and Henry Yonge cited the presence of an "oranges and limes garden" on the northeastern corner of the island near High Point. While the 1760 reference to citrus could possibly be the result of cultivation known to have occurred on Sapelo after 1733, the observation by Barnwell indicates the probability of Spanish activity around High Point in the mission period.

The consolidation of missions at San Joseph in 1680 is reflective of the concerns felt by the St. Augustine authorities as to the continued sustainability of their Guale outposts. Crowded conditions now prevailed at Sapelo Island. In a census of Guale and Mocama conducted by Capt. Francisco de Fuentes in June 1681, the *situado* at San Joseph included 186 Guale from the combined missions of San Joseph (34), Tupiqui (48), Satuache (47), and Santa Catalina (57), including men, women, and caciques (chiefs). In early 1681, Fr. Simon Martinez de Sala was appointed *doctrinero* (parish priest) of the four combined villages at Sapelo, having recently succeeded the controversial Fr. Juan de Uzeda, whose relationship with the Guale at San Joseph had

declined almost to the point of precipitating a revolt. Sala appears to have served at San Joseph until the mission's abandonment in late 1684.[32]

The increased vulnerability of the Spanish to the English and their Indian allies precipitated the decision in 1683 to abandon Guale and Mocama and relocate the missions south to Santa Maria on Amelia Island. During the remainder of 1683 and into 1684 the relocation was achieved, including the removal of the survivors of Santa Catalina and Satuache from San Joseph. Under increasing tensions fueled by frequent rumors of imminent pirate attacks, San Joseph was gradually deactivated. In late September 1684, Lieutenant Saturnino, commander of the military garrison, ordered the priest and the remaining Guale inhabitants to retreat to the mainland with the mission furnishings.

In early October, a pirate sloop of eight guns and eighty men anchored off Sapala, and on or about October 3, Saturnino and his small force withdrew and abandoned the mission. Two days later, the marauders landed and sacked the mission.[33] Soon after the raid, Yamasee occupied what was left of San Joseph until they were driven off by attacking Spanish forces in 1686. The Spanish burned the priest's "brick" house (likely burned clay wattle and daub) and the rest of the mission structures.

While a precise footprint for Mission San Joseph has not been established, archaeological evidence makes location somewhere on the North End of Sapelo a certainty. A North End site would have facilitated convenient communication by water, and perhaps smoke signals, between Sapala and Santa Catalina. John Worth notes that descriptions of San Joseph in relation to the mission of Asajo on St. Simons to the south "confirm the location of Sapala . . . at Bourbon Field." Worth points out that "using the more securely identified location of Asajo at Cannon's Point on the northern end of St. Simons, San Joseph de Sapala is consistently placed at a distance of some 6 or 7 leagues to the north in mission lists dating between 1675 and 1683 . . . Furthermore, the two lists predating the 1680 abandonment of Santa Catalina place Sapala only 2 leagues south of Santa Catalina."[34]

Bourbon Field was thus the favored site for the mission in the scholarly research of the 1990s. But while archaeological fieldwork has disclosed Spanish hardware and ceramic fragments at both Bourbon and Kenan Fields, there is increasing argument for the mission being in an area just north of the Shell Ring complex. All three areas were the scenes of great Guale activity on Sapelo Island before and during the Spanish period. Recent research, however, has created a strong possibility that the Shell Ring area was the mission site: "The low frequency and diversity of Spanish artifacts suggest that Bourbon Field is no longer a strong candidate for the mission site," note University of Kentucky archaeologists Richard Jefferies and Christopher Moore, adding that the area just north of Shell Ring II has yielded a higher concentration of Spanish materials.[35]

Archaeological fieldwork included searches for two primary types of Spanish pottery—majolica and olive jars, the latter being used for storage and shipping of grain, wine, and olive oil. Most majolica was colorful, tin-enamel-glazed tableware and utensils produced in Spain and Mexico. As for buildings, no evidence of structural remains such as those discovered on St. Catherines has been found on Sapelo. Mission buildings would include the *iglesia* (church), and the *convento*, a monastery or cloister, to house the Franciscan priests. Wherever on Sapelo it was located, the mission would have entailed a consolidated *doctrina*, being the main mission, and a community of the Guale who had been converted to Christianity.

Period Spanish manuscripts, including reports from priests and visitors associated with San Joseph, point to at least one, possibly two, Guale settlements on Sapelo. One of the town names reported is *Espogue*, a place mentioned in the Spanish records as early as 1578, when officials from St. Augustine en route to Santa Elena "were received as friends by the Indians in the village of Espogue on Sapelo Island. But when they accepted the hospitality, they and all their nineteen men were slain."[36]

Espogue may have been at Kenan, Bourbon, or Dumoussay Fields, or perhaps in the Shell Ring environs. Of equal interest is the town of Chucalate, which some archaeologists theorize was sited at Long Row Field (Draw Bark), a strip of land along Mud River immediately south of Chocolate plantation on Sapelo's northwest side. Archaeological investigations have suggested considerable Guale presence at Long Row Field, with numerous shell deposits documented there. C. B. Moore conducted a partial excavation of a small mound at Long Row during his April 1898 fieldwork, describing the area as having been plowed, with a mound thirty-four feet in diameter yielding the skeletal remains of eleven Native Americans.

It is likely that the name "Chocolate" was derived from Chucalate, perhaps as early as the 1750s. Antebellum maps indicate that much of the northwestern side of Sapelo along a narrow strip from the Shell Ring to Long Row Field, almost to Moses Hammock, was under cultivation in cotton and provision crops, and this land included Chocolate. Continuous agricultural activities resulted in the plowing and dispersal of hundreds of shell middens. The only ones remaining relatively intact are just north of the Shell Ring beyond a tidal slough. Relevant to this discussion is the fact that the 1760 Yonge and DeBrahm survey notes an "Indian Town" at High Point, and Kenan and Dumoussay Fields, but no such delineation at Bourbon. Dumoussay and Bourbon are tracts nearly contiguous to each other. Alternatively, "Indian Town" may indicate mounds or midden deposits observed by the surveyors in 1760 rather than conclusive evidence of actual "settled" areas. The same survey identified the Shell Ring as "Spanish Fort."

North End field investigations from 2003 to 2013 by Jefferies and Moore led to important new conclusions about prehistoric and mission-era Guale and Spanish activity in the Shell Ring area. Their findings substantiated the strong possibility that a mission, a Guale town, and a defensive emplacement were sited in that section of Sapelo. Near Shell Ring II, immediately north of Shell Ring I (the largest ring), European items were found indicating the presence of resident priests, Spanish soldiers, and

Guale Indians. Among the artifacts recovered were majolica, olive jar sherds, nails, glass, white clay pipe stems, spikes, lead shot, a matchlock trigger mechanism, and a cast iron ball, probably from a six-pounder cannon, along with considerable amounts of Guale-manufactured pottery.

No structural remains have been found at Bourbon or the Shell Ring of a mission church or housing for Sapala's Guale and garrison. Based on their observations, however, Jefferies and Moore concluded that "the artifact assemblage from north of the Sapelo shell rings support the argument for an occupation of the site by not only Guale Indians, but also the Spanish . . . making the area north of Shell Ring II a strong candidate for the location of the Spanish mission."[37]

A footnote to the intriguing story of the Spanish on Sapelo occurred in 1687. William Dunlop, an English mariner on a scouting expedition to report on Spanish attacks against the Yamasee along the coast south of Port Royal, made a reconnaissance of Sapelo Island, where he observed "very large plantations where we see the ruins of houses burned by the Spaniards themselves. We see the vestiges of a fort; many great Orange trees cut down by the Spaniards in September last. There was great plenty of figs, peaches, Artechocks, onions, etc. growing in the priests garden. His house had been of Brick & his small chappell, but all had been burned to ashes last harvest by themselves."[38]

Sapelo in the English Colonial Period

The influence of half-Creek interpreter Mary Musgrove during the years that Georgia was a proprietary colony had important ramifications for Sapelo Island. Her negotiations with the British government in the early 1750s led to the use of Sapelo for farming twenty years before the American Revolution. Sapelo had several private owners during the period, the first of whom surveyed the island for the first time. The surveyor's map and field notes provide important clues to Sapelo's somewhat murky mid-eighteenth-century history.

There was a period of almost fifty years from the time the Spanish abandoned their mission in 1684 until the founding of the Georgia colony in 1733, during which nothing of consequence seems to have occurred on Sapelo. With the English permanently established in South Carolina and the Spanish dominant in Florida, the relatively unoccupied Guale coast entered a period of uneasy calm. Writing of this period, Herbert Bolton called the future Georgia coast the "debatable land." Spain, while acknowledging England's settlements in Carolina to the Savannah River, claimed the territory south of that river, even though the English and their Indian allies had compelled the Spanish to abandon Guale during the attrition of 1675–84.[39]

When South Carolina rangers built Fort King George on the Altamaha River in 1721, a diplomatic firestorm erupted between England and Spain. The Spanish resented any English incursion into Guale, particularly one of a military nature. From the English perspective the Altamaha outpost was to provide early warning about any Spanish movements against the Carolinas, particularly considering the increasing importance of Charles Town as a trading entrepôt. These developments fueled an increasingly contentious commercial rivalry between England and Spain in the Caribbean basin.

In 1732, King George II approved a charter for the Georgia Trustees to establish a proprietary colony in the former Spanish province of Guale, with James Edward Oglethorpe leading the first colonists to Yamacraw Bluff to found Savannah a year later. In early 1736, Oglethorpe brought Scottish Highlanders to the Altamaha to establish the town of New Inverness, later Darien. At the same time he began an ambitious project to build a town and fortification, Frederica, on the west side of St. Simons Island. He placed additional military garrisons on Jekyll and Cumberland Islands, actions that contributed to the subsequent outbreak of the War of Jenkins Ear

Colonial Georgia and South Carolina in 1747, showing "Sapella I." The inset depicts English settlement on St. Simons Island. (Map by Matthaeus Seutter; courtesy of the David Rumsey Historical Map Collection)

(1739–48). The war's favorable outcome for England solidified its hold on Georgia from the Savannah River to the St. Marys, and it ended further Spanish claim to the region.

Based on an agreement between the Crown and the Creeks, and more specifically with Mary Musgrove, England had no legal claim to Sapelo Island being part of the Georgia colony. Musgrove (1700–1764), daughter of a Creek woman and an English trader, played an important role as an interpreter during Oglethorpe's negotiations with the Yamacraw in the formative years of the colony. Musgrove married Thomas Bosomworth, an Anglican minister, in 1744. They subsequently lived at Mary's trading post on the Altamaha River, where they engaged in the Indian trade while Mary continued to serve the Crown as an interpreter with the Creeks.

In 1747, Malatchee, a Creek chieftain and cousin of Mary, deeded to the Bosomworths the islands of St. Catherines, Sapelo and Ossabaw, lands that had been reserved for use by the Indians in a 1739 treaty with the English. This initiated a series of claims and counterclaims between the Bosomworths and English authorities, with Malatchee and the Creeks in the middle of the dispute, and all parties being manipulated by Mary. To placate the English, Malatchee and other Creek chieftains denied having deeded the islands to the Bosomworths.[40] At the end of the Trustee period, as Georgia was becoming a royal colony, the Bosomworths traveled to England, where in 1754 they pressed their claim to the three islands. The couple appeared before the British Board of Trade several times without a successful resolution.

While the Bosomworths were in England, London merchant Isaac Levy provided support, feeling their claims were legitimate. In October 1754, the Bosomworths agreed to give Levy half title to the three islands for £300 and additional monies accruing from any profits made by Levy from agricultural ventures he chose to pursue on any of the islands. Levy migrated to America with the intent to "settle & cultivate the said Lands." Levy's claim was on shaky legal ground, however, as the British government had not recognized the Bosomworths' claim.

Georgia colonial authorities subsequently concluded a new treaty with the Creeks in 1757 that ceded Sapelo, St. Catherines, and Ossabaw to Great Britain. Finally, in July 1759, official word of the disallowance of the Bosomworth claims was rendered. Soon after, Governor Henry Ellis and the colonial council determined that Mary Bosomworth should be compensated for her services as an interpreter with £2,100 from the proceeds of the sale of Sapelo and Ossabaw. The third island, St. Catherines, where the Bosomworths then resided, was awarded to them with clear title.

The public auction of Sapelo and Ossabaw in Savannah was advertised in December 1759. Meanwhile, Levy, having been left out of these arrangements while they were transpiring, was in high dudgeon and had issued in the *South Carolina Gazette* his own claim to the islands based on his moiety agreement with the Bosomworths five years earlier.[41] Despite his arguments, the British government refused to recognize Levy's claim, and the legal wrangling delayed the auction of Sapelo and Ossabaw until May 1760.[42] The conveyance of title for the two islands was finalized April 19, 1760, thus enabling the public auction to proceed. Sapelo and Ossabaw were sold for £2,050, which was paid to the Bosomworths. The matter finally ended on June 13, 1760, with a grant signed by Governor Ellis awarding St. Catherines to the Bosomworths. There Mary died in 1764, her gravesite marked by a small shell mound on the north end of the island.[43]

There had been some activity at Sapelo Island during the imbroglio between the Bosomworths and the colonial authorities. In August 1753, a party including Jonathan Bryan, a prominent South Carolina landowner, and William Gerard DeBrahm, cartographer and military engineer, surveyed the Georgia coast. A passage in Bryan's journal relating to Sapelo provides a useful mid-eighteenth-century glimpse of the uninhabited island:

> This afternoon we had a very agreeable View of the Island of Sapelo, the rising banks covered with Green Grass [marsh] with the evergreen Trees along the Banks . . . afforded a very Pleasant Prospect. On the Island about a Mile from the North End is the remains of an old Spanish Fort, in a pleasant green Field. Here is also a very pleasant Mount, with a fine running Stream of water at its foot. This Island is a most agreeable Spot, with fine land for Corn or Indigo, and would admit . . . eight or ten good Settlements. We turned into a creek called Tea-Kettle Creek which leads to Doboy Inlet, and lay by all night in a small Creek about a Mile or two from the Inlet; observed the South End of Sapelo to be much broken with Creeks and entirely divided into two separate islands, which are distinguished by great Sapelo and little Sapelo. These islands are about fourteen miles long and are very good for Stock. . . . We entered Doboy Sound, which is a very poor Inlet, with reefs of Sands running clear across, and a small Island to the South of the Inlet called Wolf Island. Dob[o]y Island is a little Hammock of about ten Acres.[44]

Bryan's 1753 mention of Doboy is interesting for it provides an early English reference to the inlet and island of the unusual name. Doboy Sound, which washes the southern end of Sapelo, and the small island called Doboy across the sound from Sapelo, are named for Jehan Duboys, or Dubois, a French ship captain who accompanied the explorer Jean Ribault on his second voyage to Florida in 1565. The reports of Duboys/Dubois attest to his investigations of the inlet that bears his name during a reconnaissance of the coast just before Spain began establishing its missions.[45]

At the public sale of the island in the spring of 1760, Grey Elliott acquired Sapelo for £725. Elliott was a colonial surveyor and auditor who later served on the royal governor's council and was speaker of the colonial assembly. The formal issuance of Elliott's grant signified his being awarded "9,520 acres being all those islands called Sapelo and being on the sea coast and bounded on the east and southeast by the Ocean, southwest by a north branch of the Altamaha River, and west by a creek called Tea Kettle and the marshes thereof."[46] At the behest of Elliott, a speculator, Sapelo was surveyed by Henry Yonge and William G. DeBrahm, certification of their "Plan of the Islands of Sappola" being filed on September 30, 1760. This represented the first systematic mapping of Sapelo Island. The survey, while detailing structural and topographic features, also divided the island into contiguous five-hundred-acre parcels, presumably based on Elliot's intent to sell all or parts of Sapelo for profit.[47]

Despite the lack of success in his litigious exertions against the British colonial authorities, Isaac Levy left an important imprint upon the mid-eighteenth-century history of Sapelo, which stemmed from his business arrangements with Thomas and Mary Musgrove Bosomworth. There is documentation of Levy engaging in agricultural activities on Sapelo, probably the cultivation of indigo and provision crops, during the period of legal maneuvering prior to the island being auctioned in 1760. Yonge and DeBrahm's topographic survey that year provides useful clues about Levy's farming initiatives from 1756 to 1760.

Others may also have had agricultural interests on the island at the time of Elliott's acquisition. Yonge and DeBrahm delineated fields under cultivation and several structures at the sites of later agricultural activity on Sapelo, most notably at Chocolate, High Point, Raccoon Bluff, and Kenan Field. Symbols of buildings are shown at all four locations. Some historians have incorrectly attributed these structures to remains of buildings from the Spanish period. However, it is unlikely that the survey's placement of the structures can be attributed to the Spanish era since the Spanish and English both reported the destruction of mission buildings during the time San Joseph was abandoned and shortly thereafter.

Based on Levy's own statements regarding crop cultivation at Sapelo and Ossabaw for several years prior to the auction of the islands, it is likely that at least some of the

structures on the 1760 Sapelo map represent his efforts to achieve farming profits on the island. Yonge and DeBrahm identified four buildings at Chocolate and two each at High Point, Raccoon Bluff, Kenan, and Barn Creek. Some of these are shown as very small, perhaps signifying outbuildings or sheds. There is a single structure just south of the three buildings at Chocolate, in the area later known as Long Row Field. A larger rectangular feature at Chocolate is shown that may represent a garden plot or livestock pen, with a small adjacent structure, probably a shed. The evidence points to Levy centering his farming at Chocolate, and there is a good possibility that it was Levy who first applied the name "Chocolate" to the site. This section was also under cultivation in the antebellum era and beyond.[48]

The survey laid out tracts in five-hundred-acre increments and identified sections of Sapelo as being forested by oak, pine, and cypress stands. Clues to the Spanish presence a century earlier were noted with "Oranges & Limes Garden" at High Point and "Spanish Fort" at the Shell Ring. Broken down, Yonge and DeBrahm denoted 7,700 acres of upland for the "Main Island of Sapolla," 1,600 acres for "Part of Sappola called Black Beard Island," and 220 acres of highland for the "six small Islands of little Sapolla." Parenthetically, the survey makes the earliest known official reference to Blackbeard Island as such, named for the English pirate Edward Teach (ca. 1680–1718), who is alleged to have frequented Sapelo Sound and other coastal Georgia sounds during three years of freebooting that eventually led to his death after the Royal Navy finally caught him.

The surveyors' notes appended to their map revealed that Sapelo and Blackbeard "abound with live Oak timber for ship building, Water Oak & red Bay, & on some part of it are good sawing pines. The land is intermixed with such as is proper for Corn, Indigo &c. with many conveniencys for Water & large Savannas capable of being improved for rice plantations, & upon every side of the Islands are large quantities of feeding Marsh for pasturage." South End features identified were "Tea Kettle Creek," two houses overlooking Barn Creek, a tract identified as "Jons Hamec [Hammock] Island, pond of fresh water" on the later site of the lighthouse and dunes at "Nanny Goat," and "Cabretta Island."[49]

Two years after Elliott bought Sapelo at auction he sold the island to Patrick Mackay (ca. 1700–1777), a figure of some importance in colonial Georgia. Mackay was Oglethorpe's agent to the Creeks, an endeavor in which he had little success due to his lack of experience in diplomatic and Indian affairs. He was prominent in colonial politics in the 1750s and 1760s and was a prosperous Savannah shipper, with his vessels

"Plan of the Islands of Sappola," surveyed by Henry Yonge and William DeBrahm in 1760, delineating farm buildings on the North End at Chocolate and sites of former Guale settlements. (Courtesy of Hargrett Rare Book and Manuscript Library, University of Georgia Libraries)

transporting goods to London, Lisbon, and Dublin. Mackay owned the entire island from 1762 until his death in 1777. He was one of a few planters in Georgia to experiment with cotton prior to the Revolution. Some accounts identify Mackay's Sapelo cotton as being of the black seed variety that later became an important staple in the coastal agricultural economy after the war.[50]

Mackay raised cattle and grew cotton, corn, and possibly indigo on the North End around High Point and on the tract that came to be known as Mackays Old Fields, later Dumoussay Field. The latter is a neck of high ground southeast of High Point, bordered on its west by marsh and a savanna (present Reynolds Duck Pond) and on its east by the Blackbeard Creek marshes.

Mackay built a house on the North End, but its precise location is unclear. Mackay probably built this dwelling at High Point. If so, this would have been the house later used by the French partners who owned Sapelo in the 1790s. There is some evidence, based on later French correspondence, suggesting that Mackay had a dwelling or a farm structure at the Old Fields tract, which would have been convenient to High Point. Mackay also had housing for his small slave contingent, likely at Old Fields, close to the farming operations. The North End was a good location for agriculture because of deepwater access to Sapelo Sound. Mackay had a wharf at High Point, both to ship his cotton to Savannah and to receive goods for his plantation. A landing at High Point remained an important communications link for Sapelo from the late eighteenth century through the nineteenth.

Mackay may have been a Loyalist during the Revolution based on his complaint to the royal authorities in Savannah that on the night of October 31, 1775, his schooner, *Earl of Chatham*, while anchored off High Point, was boarded in the night "in a hostile manner" by nine men and cut from her moorings. The vessel was taken to sea with one of Mackay's slaves and apparently was never recovered despite Mackay offering a reward of fifty pounds sterling for the capture of the perpetrators.[51] Mackay died on Sapelo in 1777. The affairs of his estate were managed by his widow, Isabella Mackay, and his planting operations continued for several years under the supervision of brothers William and Lachlan McIntosh.

It was publicly noted in 1784 that Sapelo Island, "the estate of Patrick Mackay, deceased, [was] now seized and to be sold by virtue of an execution, along with the stock of horses, cattle, hogs, sheep, etc." Sapelo and Blackbeard Islands were sold the same year at a Liberty County sheriff's sale to John McQueen, a transaction that may also have included some or all of Mackay's slaves.[52]

McQueen (1751–1807), a South Carolinian who moved to Georgia after the Revolution, was a land speculator with coastal properties at Cumberland and Jekyll Islands, at Thunderbolt near Savannah, and on the Savannah River. With the intention of taking advantage of the high prices being offered by northern shipbuilders for quality live oak, McQueen first bought half of St. Catherines Island for £4,500, following which he purchased Sapelo, Cabretta, and Blackbeard. McQueen did not live at Sapelo or St. Catherines, instead supervising his timber-cutting operations on the islands from his residence, the Cottage, at Thunderbolt.[53]

McQueen's heavy debt compelled him to sell Sapelo and Blackbeard to François Dumoussay de La Vauve in 1789, a transaction that led to the formation of the French Sapelo Company (Société de Sapelo) in 1789. In 1791, to escape his creditors, McQueen fled to St. Augustine in Spanish-held East Florida where he swore allegiance to the king of Spain, became a Catholic, and continued to indulge in acquiring large tracts of land at cheap prices. He received a grant for Fort George Island at the mouth of the St. Johns River, where he built a residence and sawmill to process his timber. McQueen died of a sudden illness in October 1807, just as he was initiating a scheme to smuggle African slaves into the United States in violation of the federal act that prohibited slave importation after January 1808.

CHAPTER III

French Interlude

Anatomy of a Failure

ERHAPS the most interesting period in Sapelo's history is a five-year interval at the end of the eighteenth century during which a group of French nobles seeking enterprise, profits, and new lives invested their fortunes in the island. It was an undertaking that began with promise but, through mismanagement, incompatibility, and increasing discord, ended in failure. The initiative was original and bold, yet it ultimately collapsed because it was founded on speculation. In short, the peculiar tale of the French Sapelo Company was a destructive concoction of legerdemain, intrigue, deception, and, at its worst, even murder, making for one of the most unusual episodes of coastal Georgia history.

Only one of the French investors emerged from the disintegration of the Sapelo Company to achieve success resulting from his migration to Georgia. Christophe Poulain DuBignon (1739–1825), the son of a poor Breton aristocrat, used his involvement in the Sapelo venture as the catalyst for becoming one of the leading cotton planters in the region. A mariner by profession, DuBignon had gone to sea at the age of twelve, then served nearly four decades as a sailor and captain in the French India Company and Royal Navy. The bourgeois noble was enjoying a comfortable retirement at the age of fifty in Brittany when the French Revolution erupted. As the disarray in France worsened, DuBignon looked to America as a place to which his family could escape.[1]

DuBignon's decision to migrate to Georgia began with a transaction involving Sapelo Island, a sanctuary far removed from the precarious uncertainties of life in troubled Brittany. The story of the French venture begins in February 1789, when François Marie Loys Dumoussay de La Vauve (1754–94) finalized an agreement by which he purchased the island from John McQueen for £5,000 sterling. The acquisition included the adjoining smaller islands of Blackbeard, Cabretta, and Little Sapelo. Legal complications attending Dumoussay's purchase arose from the start. McQueen placed a writ of attachment against Dumoussay for default of payment when the loss of a vessel valued at £1,000, used as partial payment for Sapelo, was wrecked near Savannah. To further confound matters, McQueen, encumbered by debt at the time of the sale, was compelled to flee to Spanish East Florida to circumvent the imminent prospect of bankruptcy. McQueen's creditors subsequently filed a legal claim to Sapelo to satisfy the obligations. Consequently, Dumoussay had no clear title to the island initially, requiring him to enter into a convoluted series of legal maneuvers before the matter was resolved in 1791.[2]

With characteristic enthusiasm and the zeal of a real estate promoter, Dumoussay set out to recruit investment partners in his Sapelo project. In the spring of 1790, Julien Joseph Hyacinthe Chappedelaine (1757–94), a young noble and protégé of Dumoussay, became the first to join the venture. The two had become friends several years earlier during their travels along the eastern coast of the United States, from Pennsylvania to Georgia. Chappedelaine was also acquainted with DuBignon, a fellow Breton.

Chappedelaine reported the Sapelo possibilities to other prospective investors in France. "There is an enormous quantity of wild game," he effused to his uncle, Picot de Boisfeillet, in July 1790. "Sapelo has a great deal of live oak and pine, immense meadows of one league and a half, and where the cattle feed always. The orange trees, lemon trees, and olive trees grow there. . . . There is, my dear uncle, the *Eden*." Chappedelaine appended to this exuberant piece the real crux of the matter: "If you have any funds, they cannot be better employed."[3] Chappedelaine wrote with similar enthusiasm to DuBignon, noting the apparently limitless potential afforded by investing in the Georgia island. Settling his affairs in Paris in the summer of 1790, Dumoussay continued to champion the Sapelo project. Meanwhile, in Brittany Chappedelaine met with DuBignon, Boisfeillet, and other potential investors.

Motivated by the increasing peasant violence against the landed class in Brittany, and concerned for the safety of his family, DuBignon made a decision. On July 20 he communicated to Chappedelaine that he would commit financially to the Sapelo proposal, and in the process he began a new, probably irreversible chapter in his life. He formally joined the newly formed Sapelo Company (Société de Sapelo) on October 5, 1790. In addition to DuBignon, Chappedelaine, and Dumoussay, the consortium included Pierre Cesar Picot de Boisfeillet (1744–1800), Pierre-Jacques Grandclos Mesle (1728–1806), and François Magon de La Villehuchet (1727–94), the latter as a joint holder of his friend Grandclos Mesle's fifth share of Sapelo. For Dumoussay, obtaining Grandclos as a partner was significant from a pecuniary standpoint. A wealthy and influential shipowner from Saint-Malo, Grandclos gave the company financial stability and leverage, at least initially. Grandclos did not intend to accompany the group to Georgia, preferring to remain in France to attend to his shipping business, but his financial commitment clearly enhanced the prospects for the company's success. However, events would gradually begin to overtake Grandclos. Because of his nobility, the future for his business (and his life) became increasingly tenuous as revolutionary fervor increased.

Largely due to the investment of Grandclos, the company was able to expand its acquisitions. Two houses were purchased in Savannah, and in February 1791 Dumoussay bought Jekyll Island from Richard Leake. Later that year he acquired for the company the southern half of St. Catherines Island.

With preliminary arrangements complete and the company formalized, DuBignon, Dumoussay, and Chappedelaine, with several of their servants and workmen, sailed for Savannah in November 1790. DuBignon was accompanied by his five-year-old son, Joseph. (His wife, Marguerite, and other son, Henri, followed in June 1792.) Also on the vessel was the Lefils family, en route to Georgia to begin a business in Savannah. DuBignon, Dumoussay, and Chappedelaine befriended the family and would associate with them throughout the short life of the Sapelo Company. The three investors arrived at Savannah in January 1791. Though not a partner, there was another player who had involvement with the company. Thomas Dechenaux (1767–1814), a Savannah commission merchant and fellow French émigré, came to represent the company as a factor for marketing its agricultural commodities and would assist the group in its growing legal entanglements.

It will be instructive at this point to place in context a component of the organizational process that was to have adverse consequences for the prospects of the company's success. Correspondence between the investors attests to the complexity of the ambitious yet often vaguely defined goals set forth in the initial stages of the joint venture. In particular, Dumoussay's lack of transparency became increasingly frustrating to DuBignon. There developed a growing conviction that there seemed to be little conceptualization of the gambit, either from Dumoussay or his associate, Chappedelaine.

Specifics were often in short supply. There was a plenitude of ideas on Dumoussay's part but painfully little transactional commitment to the proposals. Dumoussay compounded his deceptive tendencies by withholding key information in his frequent communications, most egregiously to Chappedelaine, his supposed friend and confidant.[4] The early enthusiasm of the two should have been tempered by a corresponding reality: more deliberation and research would have demonstrated that the venture entailed potential financial perils. Caution, nonetheless, was often thrown to the winds.

The seductive prospect of profitability was no doubt amplified by the youth or free-spirited nature of several members of the syndicate. Dumoussay was thirty-six,

High Point, an area of much of the French Sapelo Company's activity from 1790 to 1794

while Chappedelaine, at thirty-three, was the youngest. Others of the group were older, which made the transition to a new country, particularly the environment of Sapelo Island (which was not as hospitable as they had imagined it), more challenging. Boisfeillet was forty-nine, DuBignon was now fifty-one, Grandclos Mesle, who never went to Georgia, was sixty-two, and Villehuchet, who was at Sapelo only a short time, was sixty-three.

The financial duplicity of Dumoussay, which often left the other investors ignorant of what was transpiring, eventually led to animosity. The investors initially placed full faith in Dumoussay, who always presented an air of unconstrained assurance and competence and seemingly could be relied upon to act in the best interests of the group. Behind the veil of outward confidence, however, Dumoussay was prone to provide misleading information to his colleagues to enhance the prospects for profitability. One early example of this manipulation was an augury of future deceit. Dumoussay implied that the French navy would be the principal customer for Sapelo's live oak, with great profit to the investors. But in fact the French revolutionary government declined to accept the company's timber contract, refusing to incur the costs of shipping the oak from Georgia to France, information that Dumoussay neglected to report to the others.

Another matter was a harbinger of worse to come: in early 1791 Dumoussay fell delinquent on paying property taxes to Liberty County for the company's Sapelo holdings, and to Glynn County for Jekyll, resulting in both islands being placed on public auction that spring. An imminent collapse of the venture was only averted by the action of Villehuchet who bought Sapelo at the tax sale with his own resources. This gave the investors the opportunity—theoretically, if not in fact—to each obtain separate title deeds to Sapelo by virtue of the island's resale by Villehuchet to his colleagues.[5]

Dechenaux, who arrived in Georgia in 1792, acted as the company's factor for the shipment of commodities from Savannah as the partners sporadically raised cattle and cultivated sea island cotton, rice, corn, and sweet potatoes on Sapelo and Jekyll. Initially they owned the Sapelo land in common. A similar arrangement pertained to slaves, furniture, buildings, and a boat. Dumoussay purchased slaves in 1791, and by the time of the division of community property in September 1793 the partners jointly held fifteen slaves. Some in the group purchased slaves individually—Dumoussay eventually had fifty-one in his name to work his Sapelo and Blackbeard farming operations.

The shareholders occupied a communal house at High Point on the northern tip of Sapelo overlooking Sapelo Sound. While the dwelling may have been constructed by the French in 1791, it more likely was a house built about 1765 by island owner Patrick Mackay, and was perhaps modified by the French. Sharing the house as a common residence was poorly conceived, as events would prove. The arrangement proved unsuitable due to the age differences of the investors, the ebb and flow of their temperaments, and their disagreements—usually precipitated by increased displeasure over the paucity of expected financial windfalls.

Accordingly, two of the partners built, or started to build, their own houses on other parts of Sapelo. Dumoussay's dwelling was south of High Point near Spanish Fort (Shell Ring). DuBignon began construction of "Bel Air" overlooking the ocean on the South End, a dwelling that was planned to be roomy and comfortable and was begun with two brick chimneys. DuBignon probably began construction on or near the same plot of land in the oak grove upon which Thomas Spalding would later built his South End House in 1810. DuBignon's efforts went unrewarded, as he encountered financial trouble early in the project, and the house was never completed.

DuBignon's one-fifth Sapelo share was the southern portion of the island, on which he intended to cut and sell live oak timber. He also wanted to raise cattle at nearby Little Sapelo Island, a hammock across the Duplin River from Sapelo contiguous to his other South End properties, which he collectively called the Hermitage.[6] Also on the South End was Thomas Sterling, an overseer and mariner for John McQueen earlier and now possibly employed in a similar capacity by the company. Sterling lived in a house near Marsh Landing apparently built before the French arrived. This dwelling was later used by Thomas Spalding and his family until the completion of South End House in 1810.

Because of his maritime experience, DuBignon was the partner most interested in the possibilities afforded by live oak. Geographically, the island was ideally situated to supply timber to shipbuilding markets in the U.S. Northeast, the Caribbean, and Europe. One of the goals outlined in the company's October 1790 agreement emphasized the investors' timber plans, with a priority placed on cutting oak. Initially agriculture and cattle raising were to be subsidiary to timbering. Despite the energies of DuBignon and Dumoussay toward achieving these aspirations, things did not go well. Contractual difficulties with the French government and other potential buyers prevented the ambitions from being realized. Although some oak was sold, the effort was only marginally profitable.

Farming efforts, while modest in the aggregate, were somewhat more successful. The partners understood that to satisfy their financial encumbrances they must cultivate profitable staple crops, chiefly cotton and rice. Boisfeillet was particularly interested in the agricultural possibilities. In January 1793, he and his family arrived at Sapelo, and soon thereafter he assiduously began planting cotton and provision crops on a tract on the island's northeast side that later came to be called Bourbon Field. It was probably unrealistic to expect these initiatives to produce appreciable results. Boisfeillet lacked financial discipline, and his monetary commitments to the company fell in arrears. His initial interest in farming thus quickly diminished when profits were slow to materialize.

It is possible that insufficient understanding of the important linkage between agriculture and the prevailing ecological conditions amid the semitropical coastal

environment proved detrimental to the French, resulting in their flawed crop management practices. For instance, at Raccoon Bluff, a tract south of Bourbon, the company attempted to grow rice using rainfall and swamp water for irrigation, but the effort was only minimally profitable. Lack of success in cultivating cotton and rice in 1791 was attributable to extended drought and tidal flooding. The following year an overabundance of rain so delayed the timely sprouting of the cotton plants that the harvests were diminished.[7]

The livestock efforts also saw mixed results. The company raised hogs on the South End to take advantage of the abundant live oak groves where the hogs foraged for acorns. But the problem of nocturnal poachers from the mainland surreptitiously coming to the island to slaughter the stock was a recurring one. It was common knowledge locally that the French owners usually restricted themselves to their operations on the opposite end of the island, giving the poachers free rein on the South End.

With progress uneven and erratic, the enterprising Chappedelaine assumed the management of the day-to-day activities on the island while Dumoussay, frequently in Savannah, oversaw the company's tenuous financial affairs. Some useful work was nonetheless accomplished. A new chimney was added to the High Point house, a salting house was built, and an east–west fence was constructed across the island.

Letters from Chappedelaine to DuBignon while the latter was visiting in France testify to continuing optimism tempered by recurring frustrations: "Our crop has been extremely poor on Sapelo due to the bad weather," Chappedelaine reported in December 1791. "It is unbelievable how much fish of all kinds are in our creeks. Once we have built what is necessary we too shall take up fishing, but we must have at least 50 good negroes, [and] 4 good carpenters, to fell and bark our live oaks or green oaks for which there is a big market now."

In May 1792, Chappedelaine reported:

Dumoussay arrived and has seen for himself the hell we live in—*nothing like experience for a teacher*. After months of patience nothing is accomplished. Grousse [Villehuchet], the old man, wants to go to Jekyl [*sic*], I to Blackbeard, you to Bel Air and I think Dumoussay will choose the Point or the Spanish fort. I sent

High Point. The French investors had a communal dwelling in the grove of trees at left.

Le Cou and Cabaret to Blackbeard to put up some hay. . . . We have rearranged all your elegant kitchenware. . . . Boiled beef and roast are what our cooking consists of—though we still do some grilling. The pans serve us as cups of which we drink plenty of beer. The small vine with little leaves of which there is a quantity around the house at the Point and which we mistook for a small creeper has many grapes, big ones in bunches of 8 or 10, well filled out. Dumoussay seems inclined to settle at the Spanish fort and to dig a small canal there for our boats. There are possibilities to make something pretty there by having about 10 negroes work there for 2 or 3 years. We will probably end by having our houses built at Savannah and have them brought here to use already made. . . . The marsh near the old field of Mackay's is very good for hay. The grass which we burnt there is so thick and splendid we cannot walk there. Madame Belle's negro has finished cutting and thrashing the rice on Raccoon Bluff. We are going to Merritt's house on Blackbeard.

In the above correspondence, "Madame Belle" possibly refers to Boisfeillet's wife. Le Cou and Cabaret were workers brought from France by the investors. The latter was much given to rum and "was an ugly drunk, quarrelsome and violent, who tried to beat up the old man Villehuchet on one occasion."[8] Merritt's identity is uncertain, but he was probably an overseer in the employ of the French.

Living arrangements occasionally bordered on the volatile. Boisfeillet continually delayed in building a house at Bourbon because of money differences and title disputes with Dumoussay, a situation that caused increasing resentment on the part of the former. The relationship between Boisfeillet and Dumoussay had been acrimonious from the start and was eventually to have serious consequences for the company's stability. Upon their arrival at Sapelo in early 1793, Boisfeillet and his family had moved into the company's common house at High Point, a dwelling already occupied by Chappedelaine and Dumoussay. Because of ongoing friction with Boisfeillet, Dumoussay quickly tired of this situation and began building another house at Spanish Fort a mile and a half south of High Point. An increasingly vituperative relationship with his uncle compelled Chappedelaine to also leave the High Point residence several months later and move in with Dumoussay. Dumoussay may have built or used another house at Mackays Old Fields (later Dumoussay Field), a four-hundred-acre tract southeast of High Point that he acquired in the later division of property. It is more probable that a structure already existed at Old Fields, built by Patrick Mackay sometime after his 1762 acquisition of Sapelo. This dwelling may have been used by the company for housing the French workers brought to Sapelo.

By mid-1793 it was clear that the novelty of the Sapelo venture was beginning to wear extremely thin. It had been embarked upon without reasoned assessment or understanding, and Sapelo's day-to-day life had become an enervating combination of intrigue, hatred, jealousy, and, at the base of this, unrelenting mismanagement. Social interaction among the partners decreased and life together devolved as finances dwindled. A growing combustibility began to manifest itself in the spring of 1793. DuBignon, ill-tempered and demanding explanations, confronted Dumoussay over not having received title deeds to his Sapelo land. Unable to convert Chappedelaine or the pusillanimous Boisfeillet as allies to neutralize Dumoussay's continuing mendacity, DuBignon was out of patience. In May he renounced any future financial responsibility for the company's debts.[9]

Dumoussay's lack of transparency in managing the group's affairs gave ample cause for DuBignon's frustration, making his intent to withdraw from the partnership easily understandable. DuBignon now coveted Jekyll, and he proceeded to negotiate a property exchange that eventually enabled him to swap his share of Sapelo for the Jekyll shares held by Dumoussay and Chappedelaine. By the end of 1793, DuBignon and his family had relocated to Jekyll, where he began planting cotton to alleviate his financial burdens. It was a fortuitous decision, and his possession of sixteen bondsmen made him one of the leading land and slave owners in Glynn County in 1794 (behind James Spalding of St. Simons Island).[10]

Villehuchet had also become exasperated with the company's management. Embroiled in a contentious relationship with the temperamental Chappedelaine, he returned to France in May 1792. He had briefly entertained hopes of a happier separation from Sapelo. After spending time on Jekyll earlier that year, Villehuchet, like DuBignon, wished to possess the island for himself—"[B]oth Villehuchet and DuBignon may have had a heightened appreciation of Jekyll because of the therapeutic distance it afforded them from Chappedelaine and Dumoussay," DuBignon biographer Martha Keber notes perceptively.[11] A 1793 memorandum by the French consul at Charleston further validates the escalating discontent:

> I have given orders to receive the statement of Captain Dusolier, Commander, and of the crew of the little vessel from St. Domingue purchased by a French company that put in at Sapello [sic] Island. One of those who calls himself Comte de Chapeldelaine [sic] was obliged to trample the flag of this vessel under foot. His associates are named Poulain de Bignon, Marquis de Trois Feuilles [sic] and Duc

Tabby foundation remains of the house at High Point

Moussay [*sic*]. The rest of the partners live in France. Grand Clos-Mele [*sic*] of St. Malo is one. *They are all at daggers drawn and this establishment cannot maintain itself.* [12] [italics added]

DuBignon's intention to abjure the company in May 1793 precipitated a sequence of developments that marked the beginning of the end for the company. Both Villehuchet and Grandclos Mesle also withdrew their financial investment and called for a division of property. This was a serious blow since Grandclos, with considerable funds at his disposal, had theretofore provided much of the support in keeping the company afloat.

In the summer of 1793, at Dechenaux's request, the Liberty County Superior Court appointed arbiters to facilitate a Sapelo property settlement. Concurrent with the land division, the fifteen commonly owned slaves, livestock, equipment, and furnishings were to be distributed equitably among the investors once the company's common debt had been settled. In September the investors approved the terms for the dissolution of the partnership. A formal agreement was then signed at Sapelo Island on November 18 outlining the distribution of land, cattle, and other property, with plans set for the following May to finalize the division of assets. A witness to the agreement was Thomas Spalding, this apparently being the first official connection the young barrister had with the island that would be the setting for his plantation empire a few years later.[13]

The final disposition of assets in the spring of 1794 produced another installment in the ongoing feud between Dumoussay and the pertinacious Boisfeillet. The public sale of the company's livestock was held at Sapelo on May 20. Furious over being left out of the auction arrangements, Boisfeillet precipitated a public brouhaha with Dumoussay, charging him with deliberately failing to notify him about the sale. Several opprobrious exchanges of notices in the *Georgia Gazette* ensued in which Dumoussay called Boisfeillet a "liar," while insisting that the other partners had agreed to the auction. It is difficult to sympathize with Boisfeillet—he lived on Sapelo with the others and could not have been unaware of the plan to sell the cattle. The underlying issue was that Boisfeillet had no money—he simply made Dumoussay the target of his frustration. "Boisfeillet was at his petulant best. Cantankerous, short tempered, and unencumbered by regard for the truth, Boisfeillet sulked because his life on Sapelo was in disarray," notes Keber, succinctly characterizing the plight of the failing consortium.

The vicissitudes of the disintegrating company were amplified by the division of its remaining holdings. True to form, the duplicitous Dumoussay continued to conduct business while simultaneously neglecting to communicate important details of his transactions to the others. In June he sold the southern half of St. Catherines to Dechenaux for £500 but applied only his name to the deed of sale even though he and Chappedelaine had invested in the property jointly. On June 14 the final agreement was drawn up between Dumoussay, Chappedelaine, DuBignon, and Grandclos Mesle—the four investors who had shares of Jekyll Island—for the dispensation of property at Sapelo and Jekyll. Transfer deeds were signed whereby Dumoussay and Chappedelaine swapped their one-fourth shares of Jekyll to DuBignon in exchange for his one-fifth share of Sapelo, which the two would hold jointly until its sale. Six years later, in 1800, DuBignon purchased the remaining quarter share of Jekyll from the holdings of Grandclos.

In the settlement Dumoussay received all of Blackbeard Island in addition to four hundred acres at Mackays Old Fields, the only land he owned on Sapelo itself at the time of his death three months later. The other shareholders divided the remainder of the island. Chappedelaine's portion was about two thousand acres on the South End, including Hanging Bull. Boisfeillet's share was High Point, Bourbon Field, and Raccoon Bluff, in all about eighteen hundred acres. The net result was that Dumoussay and Chappedelaine together now held 60 percent of Sapelo and Blackbeard, and a little over half of Sapelo itself.[14]

Like a Greek tragedy, the end of the Sapelo Company was played out with death as the principal player. Villehuchet had departed for France in the spring of 1792, never to return. That decision would have mortal consequences. The Reign of Terror erupted in full force in early 1794, and Villehuchet, even as an "ex-noble," was swept away in the turmoil. He was arrested, and then, one day after his trial before the Revolutionary Tribunal, executed by guillotine in Paris on June 20, 1794. Grandclos Mesle nearly suffered a similar fate. In December 1793 he made an adventurous escape from Brittany to London barely ahead of the arresting revolutionary authorities. At the age of sixty-five he lost his business and his fortune but nonetheless managed to elude the executioner's blade.

All that now remained was to play out the final act that occurred during a calamitous five days in the late summer of 1794. The tempestuous Chappedelaine was continuing to have differences with his uncle, Boisfeillet, over money, and they were thus in high dudgeon toward each other that summer. It did not help matters that both were having difficulties with their harvests. The cotton and corn crops were injured by cold weather in the spring of 1793 and by too much rain in the spring of 1794.

Dumoussay now managed about eighty slaves on the island, and trouble arose when some of them began stealing wood from the company's corn barns to use in their own houses. Efficient personnel management, like the sad state of their finances, was not an attribute of the partners. The white workers hired by the company, some French, were often disputatious and surly, frequently requiring company-purchased rum to encourage proclivity to work. Matters were exacerbated by the rising discontent between Dumoussay and Chappedelaine—the two supposed allies—as they began to have disagreements, each blaming the other for the company's declining fortunes. All these problems were magnified by Dumoussay's incandescent contempt for the weak-kneed, unpalatable Boisfeillet.

Dumoussay arrived at Sapelo from Savannah in mid-August. Two weeks later he fell seriously ill from fever, sank rapidly, and died on September 11, a Thursday. That

weekend, a day or two after Dumoussay's sudden demise, Chappedelaine reviewed Dumoussay's papers in the house they still shared and was appalled to discover that he had been omitted from the latter's will executed the year before. Chappedelaine thus spent a fretful, unsettled weekend while preparations were made for Dumoussay's burial. His thoughts no doubt revolved around the tergiversation of Dumoussay rather than his unexpected death, and around the fact that he had been duped, blindsided by his partner, who owed him a considerable amount of money. By now Chappedelaine must have realized that his dreams for Sapelo were unraveling and that he had lost most of his fortune.

Because of the summer heat, Dumoussay's body was buried a day or two after his death. The gravesite in the sandy soil above the marsh near the High Point house was gradually obliterated through the passage of time, ravaged by tides, storms, and erosion, eventually to disappear. A stone marker was placed at the High Point grave some years later.[15]

Four days after Dumoussay's death, on Monday, September 15, Chappedelaine had a final, fatal confrontation with his uncle. Embittered by Dumoussay's treachery, Chappedelaine was in no mood for accommodation, for he undoubtedly attributed much of his misfortune to Boisfeillet. Words could not settle an argument with his uncle this time—a bullet would do that. During a heated altercation, Boisfeillet shot and killed his nephew, an occurrence succinctly announced ten days later in the *Georgia Gazette*: "[O]n Sapelo Island, the 15th instant, was unhappily deprived of existence, by being shot, M. Hyacinthe De Chappedelaine, aged about 40 years—a gentleman who while alive was beloved by his friends, respected by his acquaintances, and esteemed as a worthy member of society by the community at large. Mr. Picot Boisfeillet, of Sapelo, is in the custody of the Sheriff of this county, being charged with shooting the above gentleman."[16]

In a codicil to his will added two days before his death, Chappedelaine stipulated that he be buried at Hanging Bull, part of his land on Sapelo's west side. No evidence of his grave has been found there, and it is more likely that he was buried near Dumoussay at High Point. Boisfeillet was indicted for murder by a McIntosh County grand jury following the sheriff's investigation. After extended legal arguments the charges were dismissed in early 1797.

As the only remaining partner on the island, Boisfeillet's subsequent activities on Sapelo are murky. Part of the confusion is the provenance of the name "Bourbon" for one of Boisfeillet's holdings. It is likely that neither Boisfeillet nor his heirs named the

Cabretta Island, looking west

tract "Bourbon" during the period of French ownership. Significantly, the use of the name "Bourbon" does not appear in any antebellum documents or plantation records that have come to light. Indeed, the name does not appear in primary documents until just after the Civil War. It has been suggested that Boisfeillet may have named the tract in respect to his supposed familial connections to the royal Bourbon family of France, but there is no evidence to support that thesis.[17]

Contrary to some accounts, Boisfeillet probably never built a house at Bourbon. While that may have been his early intent, no evidence suggests that he ever attempted to build there.[18] When he arrived at Sapelo in early 1793, Boisfeillet and his family occupied the company house at High Point. With his financial troubles and the continued availability of the High Point dwelling, particularly after the deaths of Dumoussay and Chappedelaine, it is difficult to see how Picot would have felt compelled to construct a new dwelling at Bourbon. He thus almost certainly lived at the High Point house until his death in 1800.

While Boisfeillet himself probably did not apply the name "Bourbon" to his tract, it is much more certain that he planted cotton and provision crops there for several years. Boisfeillet engaged the services of John LaFong (1759–1819) as his overseer at Bourbon and Raccoon Bluff, and LaFong continued to work for Boisfeillet's widow after Picot's death. In 1800 or soon after, LaFong acquired Patterson's Island, a large hammock near Teakettle Creek between Sapelo and the mainland, where he developed his own plantation.[19]

Of all the investors' efforts, those of Boisfeillet were the most unavailing. Debt ridden, inept as manager of his own affairs, petulant, and hypersensitive toward his colleagues, he qualifies as the partner least likely to succeed. "He expects to reap without sowing, and believes it is possible to be well off with no work . . . such a partner, born rich, having never worked, would consume the profits without producing any," was the uncharitable assessment of Boisfeillet by Grandclos Mesle as early as October 1791.[20] Unhappy and alone, Boisfeillet died on August 13, 1800, at the age of fifty-six, after having "lived out his last years prisoner to the decomposing remains of the Sapelo Company." He was buried the next day, and, although no trace of his grave is extant, he remains an unforgettable part of the French Sapelo story. Boisfeillet's death made him the last of the partners to depart the island that only a decade earlier had held so much promise. He is perhaps the saddest of the company's misguided cast of characters.

Boisfeillet was in such financial straits before his death that he sued the estates of both Dumoussay and Chappedelaine, realizing a judgment in 1797 of only three thousand dollars when balanced against money owed his late nephew. His will of March 1799 left his Sapelo property to his wife and children. His widow, Marie Anna Larmandie, died less than a year later, in March 1801, at the age of forty. Boisfeillet's one-fifth interest in the company's holdings was divided into fourths among his children, who began selling their father's properties in 1817. One of the Boisfeillet daughters, Servanne, received High Point, and her husband, John Montalet, administered the family's estate until his death in 1814.[21]

Legal complications lingered long after the company's demise. Three of the six partners were dead before the end of 1794, one by beheading and two others by sickness and mayhem on that summer weekend of chaos. Dechenaux was executor of the estates of the latter two, but soon after Chappedelaine died, a nephew discharged Dechenaux and then proceeded to sue him for what Dumoussay owed Chappedelaine. When he died, Dumoussay owned fifty-one slaves outright. Chappedelaine had only three but had been led by the skullduggery of Dumoussay to believe he had more. Dumoussay's land included Blackbeard, which because of debt litigation was sold in 1800 at public auction to the U.S. Navy Department for use as a live oak timber reserve (see box, p. 86). Some of the lawsuits by Boisfeillet and Chappedelaine's relatives involving Dumoussay's estate continued for several years.[22]

Eighty slaves owned by the French were included in the sale of Sapelo's South End to Thomas Spalding and Edward Swarbreck in 1802. By 1805 there were three co-owners who held over 80 percent of Sapelo: Spalding, Swarbreck, and John Montalet. "Despite Spalding's purchases and his fifty-year affiliation with Sapelo, he would never be owner of the entire island, nor would anyone else," notes Kenneth H. Thomas. "The French Sapelo Company had been the last to be in that unique position."[23] The legal denouement of the company came in July 1801 with the settlement of Boisfeillet's suit against Dumoussay and the sale of the company's property at Savannah.

Despite the company's breakup, Sapelo was not devoid of activity in the period from 1795 until the appearance of Swarbreck and Spalding in 1801–2. Live oak cutting under contract was undertaken on both Sapelo and Blackbeard, and small-scale planting remained active. James Charles Anthony desVergers (d. 1806), a refugee of the Haitian slave revolt, lived on Sapelo in the late 1790s, probably as an overseer for agents of the defunct company. A son was born to desVergers on Sapelo in 1799. Another French

connection emerged from a Savannah newspaper notice reporting the death of Charles Francis Chevalier on Sapelo in December 1798. While no additional details were given, it may be that Chevalier, like desVergers, was an overseer or workman in the employ of agents of the company or perhaps someone employed by the company who had remained on the island after its breakup.

There was another linkage to the company after its dissolution. Louis Harrington, brother-in-law of Grandclos Mesle, left France in 1795 and settled in Savannah. In 1797 Harrington purchased the shares of Sapelo and Jekyll held by his brother-in-law and Villehuchet, the Sapelo share including the Chocolate tract. By 1799, he had also acquired the one-fifth Sapelo share held by Chappedelaine. Harrington sold his share of Jekyll to DuBignon in early 1800, and in 1801 he sold Chocolate and other Sapelo North End land to Richard Leake and Edward Swarbreck. Harrington continued to live in Savannah until selling his remaining holdings and returning to France in 1810.[24]

The French legacies from an unsettled decade at Sapelo include surviving place names: Bourbon Field (named later), Dumoussay Field, New Orleans, and possibly Chocolate, although the latter may date from earlier than the French. Most enduring, however, is the aura of intrigue and mystery that lingers after more than two centuries in the stories told and retold, almost always embellished as in myth.

The demise of the Sapelo Company spawned yet another twist in the tale of French involvement with the island, however.

The Serendipitous John Montalet

John Montalet followed a compelling—and circuitous—path to Sapelo Island. His unusual odyssey combined good fortune and great resourcefulness. Montalet (1760–1814), born in France as Jean-Baptiste Mocquet, was a planter-aristocrat on San Domingo (Haiti) who in 1797 migrated to Savannah in the wake of the Haitian slave insurrection, apparently being one of the last of the French planters to escape the Caribbean island.[25] "He was distinguished during the trouble of the Island for his patriotism, courage and zeal in defense of his native soil and attachment to the ancient system of the French Monarchy," noted an account from 1814.[26]

In December 1798, Montalet purchased the Hermitage rice plantation on the Savannah River for $2,785.[27] Using slaves extricated from his Haitian plantation, Montalet cultivated rice at the Hermitage while settling comfortably into life among the local planters and Savannah society. According to his obituary in the *Savannah Republican* in 1814, Montalet had been "brought up amongst the most fashionable circles [and] retained the manners of an accomplished gentleman."[28] Montalet was apparently an assiduous planter as well. *Savannah River Plantations* notes that Montalet's slaves "were all called by French names [having] probably been brought from St. Domingo." In 1801, three slaves owned by William P. Montalet, brother of John, were baptized at the Hermitage and recorded in the parish register of the Church of St. John the Baptist in Savannah.

It was his local social interaction that led to Montalet's marriage in October 1802 to Servanne de Boisfeillet. The event was fortuitous for Montalet, for Servanne was the daughter of the late Picot de Boisfeillet of Sapelo Island. Unfortunately, Montalet's marriage to Servanne was all too brief: "Tragedy ended this delightful existence," and on June 14, 1805, the cathedral register recorded the interment: "in the burial ground of the City of Savannah, Mrs. Servanne Angelique Charlotte Picot de Boisfeillet, native of France, aged about eighteen years, wife of John Berard Mocquet de Montalet, planter of the County of Chatham."[29]

When her father had died in 1800, Servanne Boisfeillet inherited Sapelo High Point. After her marriage, Montalet administered High Point, Bourbon, and Raccoon Bluff for the Boisfeillet children, but he never owned the latter two tracts. In 1803, Montalet mortgaged the Hermitage and ten slaves for $6,000, indicative that his planting activity there had increased the value of the plantation.[30] Also that year he purchased from the Dumoussay estate the four hundred acres of Mackays Old Fields on Sapelo's North

Live Oaking on Blackbeard Island

Blackbeard Island was sold at public auction in 1800 for $15,000 by agents of the Sapelo Company, being purchased by the Department of the Navy for use as a timber reserve. The island had abundant stands of natural live oak (*Quercus virginiana*) on its sixteen hundred upland acres.

The trunks and lower boughs of the gnarled oaks had over time been bent by the ceaseless action of the ocean winds blowing off the Atlantic and sweeping over the exposed, low-lying island. The oaks of the sea islands of coastal South Carolina, Georgia, and northeastern Florida were viewed as ideal for the construction of wooden warships in the late eighteenth and early nineteenth centuries. The trunks and curved lower limbs of the trees were perfectly suited for shaping and molding the knees and bends necessary for the construction of the sturdy hulls, framing, and planking of sailing ships of war.

Northern shipbuilders had already discovered the desirability—and durability—of Georgia coastal live oak. When the naval architect Joshua Humphries was commissioned by Congress to design the first warships of a new U.S. Navy in 1794 he sent surveying crews to St. Simons Island and other parts of tidewater Georgia to select suitable tracts of oak for the construction of six frigates. These were fast, heavily armed, stoutly constructed ships rated at forty-four and thirty-six guns that Humphreys designed to be the best of their class in the world. These first vessels of the new republic's navy were built of oak from St. Simons, Cumberland, and Ossabaw Islands, including the most famous of them all, USS *Constitution* (Old Ironsides), which in the naval War of 1812 defeated British frigates in three separate sea actions.

Marine listings in the Savannah newspapers and other contemporary written accounts attest to the cutting and removal of live oak timber by northern contractors from Blackbeard Island for naval shipbuilding purposes from 1816 to 1818. A "Summary of Information Respecting Live Oak, 1815–1817" in the National Archives evaluating the coastal islands for their stands reported that Blackbeard "abounds with large timber as well as small."

In the fall of 1816, live oak crews from Philadelphia appeared on Blackbeard to cut timber for the navy. James Keen (1781–1860), a Philadelphia shipwright and master joiner, supervised this effort, and the journal he kept during a second trip to Blackbeard in 1817–18 provides details of the day-to-day operations of a typical live oak camp on the Southeast Coast.

While in Georgia, Keen consulted with Thomas M. Newell of Savannah, a navy agent and liaison officer for private contractors cutting timber on Blackbeard and other islands. Keen also interacted with James Shearwood of nearby Sapelo Island who was himself engaged in timber contracts with the Navy Department. In his capacity as "superintendent of Blackbeard," Newell arbitrated labor disputes between the timber-cutting crews comprised of white labor, mostly from New England, and locally leased slaves.

The crews cut and molded oak hull frames, hauled timber, and built roads for their oxen to get the timber out of the maritime forest. In sixty-nine working days during the second expedition to Blackbeard, Keen's crews cut and molded 12,061 cubic feet of live oak for the frame of a forty-four-gun frigate. Most of the work was done on Blackbeard's south end, with access to Blackbeard Creek at Brailsford's Landing at the narrowest part of the island. There are references in Keen's journal to additional activity on the north end of Blackbeard, near the cotton fields of Anthony Shaddock. A native Englishman, Shaddock (d. 1827) was a local bar pilot for Sapelo Sound who leased land on Blackbeard from the government to grow cotton. Keen was charged with maintaining discipline in the camp, not always an easy task, as noted in extracts from his journal:

December 15 [1817]. Awoke with a cry of Turnout, Turnout, we are all on Fire, the wind blowing at this time a gale from the West. The

fire caught from the Chimney of the Cook House which was soon extinguished. . . . Men employ'd all day in getting Timber.

December 17. Men employed getting Timber—at 3 a.m. went to Mr. Sherwoods to get two boards on which are the Dimensions of Stems & Stern frames of the ships—returned at 11 a.m. & went into the woods to the men. This Day killed several Snakes. Adam Much killed a large Rattlesnake with 12 Rattles. On opening it found it had swallowed a full grown Rabbit.

February 28 [1818]. W. Clinton went to T. Spalding Esqr. with the report to the Commissioners . . . all hands employed washing [laundry] & James Hart & Wm. Naylor fighting in the Cook House. The frame of the 44 is now complete. . . . The weather windy & Cold. Wm. Clinton went to Darien with the weekly report. Timber moulded up to last evening 11,125 feet. This morning Lieut. Newell told me he was informed by the Danish Consul at Savannah . . . to ascertain what Live Oak timber could be got on the coast of South Carolina, Georgia and W. Florida. . . .

21st March. Wind blowing a Gale from N.E. This morning John G. Woodward informed me that Lieut. Newell sent his Black man to draw Molasses for three sick Black men in place of their Whiskey—This being contrary to a standing rule among the White men; he refused to give it. . . . The reply of Newell was that he did not care a damn for any White man on the island. He Woodward informed me that Newell sent two of Shaddock's Neagros [sic] to him to get a weeks provision to take to the N end of the island to make roads [and] that he went the next day & found the above Neagros making fence around their Masters cotton field—while in the pay of the Government & eating the provisions of the same.

March 29th. This evening a Fight between Crest & Henry all drunk as usual.

March 30th. This morning Rider, Hartford & Loyd refused to go to work unless they got their Whiskey, they having been drunk all night disturbing by their noise the Sober men. I refused to let them have any & they refused to go into the woods to work.

SOURCE: "Journal of James Keen, November 27, 1817–April 5, 1818," entry 346, Records of Boards and Commissions, 1812–1890 in record group 45, Naval Records Collection of the Office of Naval Records, National Archives and Records Administration.

End. However, his legal ownership of the tract is open to interpretation since deed records indicate that Montalet had not actually paid for the property at the time of his death in 1814.[31]

After his wife's death, and with the Hermitage having been mortgaged, Montalet relocated to High Point, residing in the house overlooking Sapelo Sound occupied earlier by the Sapelo Company partners. He made improvements to the residence, adding a piazza with an expansive view of the Sound, and planted crops using slaves brought to the island from Savannah. Montalet grew sea island cotton at the Old Fields and is said to have possessed about one hundred slaves. During this period Montalet interacted with his Sapelo neighbors, Thomas Spalding on the South End and Edward Swarbreck at Chocolate.[32]

There is a connection between Sapelo and Cumberland Islands that involves Montalet and yet another of the seemingly ubiquitous Frenchmen of this period in coastal Georgia. Peter Bernardey (1784–1827) spent part of his childhood on Sapelo during the French ownership, later migrating to Cumberland where he planted cotton. In a promissory note dated December 19, 1810, Montalet agreed to pay Bernardey $400 from his next cotton crop; then a month later he promised to pay an additional $100 from his current harvest. Although unspecified, the transaction was presumably repayment of a loan provided Montalet by Bernardey. Recompense was never made for in 1816 Bernardey successfully brought suit against Montalet's estate for recovery of the two sums of money.[33]

Montalet never remarried, living in domestic tranquility on Sapelo until his death in June 1814. Noted the *Savannah Republican*: "Died on the 3rd instant at his plantation on Sapelo, Marquis de Montalet, aged [fifty-four] years. This gentleman was esteemed and respected by his friends and acquaintances. . . . Poor Montalet! May thy soul rest in peace is the prayer of one who loved thee sincerely."[34] Like his French countrymen who preceded him to Sapelo, Montalet died having very little of his own and was encumbered by debt. He was ten years delinquent on his local property taxes, and Chatham County records show that he had a debt of $5,369, which the auction bid for the sale of Hermitage failed to cover. Francis Hopkins, an executor of Montalet's estate, acquired "Montalet's Point" (High Point) shortly after Montalet's death and owned the tract and the house at the time of his own death in 1821.[35]

A footnote to the Montalet story emerged a century later. In 1912, several litigants claiming to be Montalet descendants attempted to sue for land comprising a portion of the town of Nancy, France, in the name of the family of Leopold LeFils.

The suit claimed that the property had been owned by Montalet at the time of the French Revolution. This unusual action was filed by, among others, James A. LeFils of Omaha, Nebraska. James LeFils was the son of Armand LeFils (1790–1875), a long-time McIntosh County, Georgia, civic official—he was county clerk of ordinary (probate judge) in 1870 at the age of eighty. The younger LeFils argued that his supposed grandfather, Montalet, "acquired Sapelo Island by purchase and established a French colony on the north end of it. Walls of ruined buildings now mark the residence of this famous refuge." A brother, William W. LeFils of Jefferson County, Alabama, claimed in a separate deposition that he was "the lawful son of Armand LeFils, who was a son of Marquis de Montleley [sic] . . . . That affiant [William W. LeFils] was born December 12, 1832 and when about fourteen years of age accompanied his father Armand LeFils to Sapelo Island and on the north end of that island, at what is known as Sapelo High Point, his father pointed out to him the grave of affiant's grand-father, the Marquis de Montleley. That affiant's grand-father lived on said island and was buried near his residence, his being the only grave of a white person buried on the island."

There is no small degree of ambiguity here. Armand LeFils was clearly not the son of Montalet but rather that of Bernard Robert LeFils and Elizabeth LeFils, the former a Savannah merchant and factor. The LeFils-Sapelo connection is established by virtue of the elder LeFils being a business associate of Christophe DuBignon and Dumoussay de La Vauve of the Sapelo Company. As noted earlier, LeFils had traveled on the same vessel that conveyed the two Frenchmen from Brittany to Savannah in early 1791.[36]

Three of the French investors were interred on Sapelo—Dumoussay, Chappedelaine, and Boisfeillet. The grave referenced in the affidavit could as easily have been that of Dumoussay, marked by a stone tablet at the time, rather than that of Montalet. This story assumes additional mystery when, in an April 1912 deposition, several McIntosh County residents

> say that they are thoroughly familiar with Sapelo Island and know of their own knowledge that there are two and only two graves of white people on that certain portion of Sapelo Island known as Sapelo high point, or within four miles thereof, and that one of these graves contains the remains of Frances Maria Lois Demossey [sic], and the other grave, now unmarked by a stone, contains the remains of the Marquis de Monteley [sic]—as shown by a certain head stone known to deponents to have been in place at the grave—but which has now disappeared—its location being unknown to deponents—but is supposed by them to have been buried by the great gale of October 2nd 1898, which said storm did great damage to the

burying place, so much so that the bones of the said Marquis de Monteley had to be removed quite recently to another place for re-interment.[37]

In his 1914 memoir, Charles Spalding Wylly notes that in the 1830s Charles Rogers placed a marble slab from Montalet's grave over his barn at Chocolate, "and for years there was nothing to mark the lonely grave on High Point as Montalet's save tradition. In the tidal wave of 1898, the sea encroached, tore open the grave, and scattered the bones upon the shore." The Wylly reference is conjectural, for the "scattered bones" could have been those of Dumoussay or Boisfeillet. Concomitantly, there may be some veracity to Wylly's account. A marble slab from Montalet's grave could have found its way to Chocolate, several miles south of High Point. Embedded in the façade of an outer wall of the tabby barn, which still stands, is a marble block on which is inscribed the date of the building's construction, 1831, and Rogers's initials. Could this have come from a Montalet gravestone at High Point? Possibly, perhaps even likely.

The location of the graves of Montalet and his three French predecessors is unknown, although Montalet was likely buried near his High Point house. Unless his marker is a part of the Chocolate barn, the question remains as to why no headstone has been found for Montalet, even though one was discovered for Dumoussay. Montalet was held in regard by many, not least his Sapelo neighbors, Spalding and Swarbreck. If Spalding or someone else had a headstone made for Dumoussay, then it could be assumed one was made for Montalet as well. It is plausible that someone had markers erected for both and that Montalet's has simply never been located, perhaps as a result of storms and erosion as suggested in the deposition. This possibility gets credence if, indeed, Montalet's remains were moved and reinterred after the 1898 hurricane, but that opens the equally plausible possibility that the "removed remains" were Dumoussay's or those of the two other deceased Frenchmen. Some of these questions may never be satisfactorily answered.

The affidavit's reference to "ruins" is probably to the tabby foundations of a house built at High Point just after the Civil War, not to a structure built or rebuilt on the same site by the Sapelo Company. Neither Patrick Mackay nor the French used tabby, but Montalet may have done so on the counsel of Spalding, who was using tabby in his South End structures at the time Montalet came to Sapelo. The tabby remains (still visible) are more likely the foundations of the house built on or near the original house site by postwar North End owner John Griswold. That being the case, a good argument could be made that the tabby came from blocks sawn at Chocolate for Griswold.

CHAPTER IV   Agrarian Sapelo

The Apotheosis of Thomas Spalding

THOMAS SPALDING, antebellum planter of Sapelo Island, was one of the preeminent agriculturists of his day. Devoting great energy and resourcefulness to the management of his island plantation, he cultivated cotton, introduced the manufacture of sugar to Georgia, and promoted the commercial prosperity of the coast. Spalding's scientific approach to crop management through innovation and experimentation had consequences that lasted well beyond his life. His contributions to agrarian advancement were recognized by the Georgia state legislature, which named a new county for him following his death in 1851. It may be said without exaggeration that Spalding was one of the genuine renaissance men of his time.

Who was this singular planter of the tidewater, a person who despite the importance of his contributions has been consistently underappreciated by many historians? Spalding's life spanned most of Georgia's history from statehood to the national trauma of 1861, and his legacy extended far beyond that. One thing is immutable: Spalding, and the Spalding name, will always be associated with Sapelo, the scene of his crop experiments, his tabby buildings, and his enduring sense of Jeffersonian localism and

Thomas Spalding, antebellum planter
of Sapelo Island. (Courtesy of Georgia
Historical Society, A-0750-001)

regionalism. Ironically, Spalding came to the island almost by accident. It was only a series of unforeseen circumstances that led him to Sapelo, the scene of his greatest contributions.

Spalding was born at Frederica, St. Simons Island, on March 25, 1774, the only child of James and Margery McIntosh Spalding. He was descended from the Spaldings of Perthshire, Scotland, who held title to the Barony of Ashantilly, and the McIntosh family (Mohr) of Inverness, Scotland. James Spalding (1734–94) came to America about 1760 and soon thereafter entered into a partnership with Donald Mackay of Savannah to open trading houses in Georgia and East Florida. Following Mackay's death in 1768, Spalding collaborated with Roger Kelsall and established a trading post at Frederica, living there in a house, Orange Hall, originally built for James Oglethorpe. In 1772, Spalding married Margery McIntosh (1754–1818), daughter of William McIntosh of St. Andrew Parish. Her grandfather was John Mohr McIntosh, leader of the Highland Scots at New Inverness (Darien, Georgia) in 1736.[1]

To protect his interests, Spalding remained loyal to Britain during the Revolution, moving his family to a home on the St. Johns River in British East Florida where he and his associate, Kelsall, operated five trading posts. As was the case with many Loyalists, Spalding's property and assets were liquidated near the end of the war, "all being sold for the credit of the State of Georgia."[2] Despite being almost ruined financially, Spalding in July 1783 successfully petitioned the Georgia legislature to be removed from the confiscation list of Loyalist properties, and thus he retained many of his prewar holdings.[3]

In 1786, Spalding acquired 800 acres on the south end of St. Simons, which he named Orange Grove (later Retreat), and by 1790 he possessed an aggregate of 5,550 acres and ninety-four slaves. He was among the first to cultivate sea island cotton after the Revolution, and by the time of Spalding's death in November 1794 at the age of sixty, Orange Grove was heavily invested in the production of the staple.[4]

In the late 1780s, Thomas Spalding acquired his formal education in Massachusetts, after which he studied law at Savannah under the tutelage of the prominent jurist Thomas Gibbons.[5] He was admitted to the

Georgia bar in 1795. Later that year, Spalding married Sarah Leake (1778–1843), the only child of Richard and Jane Martin Leake. A surgeon from Cork, Ireland, Leake (1747–1802) successfully planted cotton at Jekyll Island, for which he had become administrator in 1784. (Leake's father-in-law was Clement Martin Sr., who had been granted Jekyll Island in 1768).

In 1791, Leake sold Jekyll to the Sapelo Company. He also owned the Gascoigne Bluff tract at St. Simons before selling it to James Hamilton. Leake moved to Belleville on the Sapelo River, where he leased land from the Troup family before purchasing the tract in 1795. There he cultivated cotton, provision crops, and citrus.[6] The Spalding-Leake union at Belleville was a significant social event, the ceremony being performed by Rev. William McWhir.[7]

The newlyweds resided briefly at Orange Grove, where Spalding managed the legal affairs of his late father as well as continuing cotton operations. The father-in-law, Leake, occasionally expressed frustration with Spalding's St. Simons activity, apparently due to the displacement of his daughter some distance from Belleville. In a rather churlish epistle to Spalding in 1797, Leake complained, "It is somewhat astonishing that you can be so blindly partiall [sic] to the spot you are on as to make it a residence when you must experience the want of everything that can make a family happy." Leake's petulance was founded on selfish motives—he was weary of commuting by water between Belleville and Orange Grove for visits.[8]

In his younger years Spalding was politically active, being a member of the Georgia Constitutional Convention in 1798 and elected to the Georgia senate. In 1800 and 1801, he and Sarah spent a year and a half in England and France, during which time Spalding made several important London financial connections. In 1803–4, Spalding again served in the state senate and then won a disputed election to the U.S. House of Representatives for 1805–6 but lost his bid for reelection in 1806. Merton Coulter, Spalding's biographer, notes that Spalding "was never an ambitious man for personal glory. The national political scene, he had now found out, was not more attractive to him because it was bigger than the Georgia scene; in fact, he liked the Georgia scene better, and was never, throughout the rest of his life, to wander very far away from it. He was a broad-minded localist in the most refined Jefferson sense."[9] Spalding served two more terms in the state senate, 1808–10 and 1812–14.

Spalding's passage to Sapelo Island rested upon an unforeseen concatenation of circumstances. It originated with his father-in-law's 1791 sale of Jekyll Island to the French consortium and Leake's subsequent interaction with several of the French investors. In

1801, while the Spaldings were in England, Leake and Edward Swarbreck began negotiations with Louis Harrington of Savannah for purchase of the latter's land on the South End of Sapelo formerly owned by the French company, and tracts on the North End, including Chocolate. The Chocolate transaction was completed in 1801.

In March 1802, after the Spaldings' return from Europe, Leake died unexpectedly in Savannah of an undisclosed "short but severe illness of five days." He left his estate to his daughter Sarah to be administered by her husband.[10] This gave Spalding a half-interest in Chocolate with Swarbreck (the two were previously connected, having exchanged correspondence as early as 1799).

After Leake died suddenly it was left for Swarbreck and Spalding, as executor of his father-in-law's estate, to complete the negotiations with Harrington for the purchase of about five thousand acres of upland and marsh on Sapelo's South End. Leake's demise thus unexpectedly gave Spalding a half-interest with Swarbreck in the South End before the end of 1802, as well as Chocolate earlier. When these were combined with a later purchase of additional South End land from Harrington, Spalding became owner of a sizeable amount of property. By 1804 he was owner or co-owner of about three-fourths of Sapelo.

The 75 percent ownership is calculated thusly by historian Kenneth H. Thomas: Spalding was co-owner with Swarbreck of the South End (one-fifth) and the Chocolate tract (one-fifth). Spalding was also probably sole owner of the former DuBignon tract (one-fifth), "which would be sixty per cent of the Sapelo Company's holdings. Since only 400 acres was given to Dumoussay [Mackays Old Fields], Spalding's theoretical 6,000 acres out of the eighteenth century estimate of 7,800 acres would then be seventy-five per cent." It should be noted that the 1760 Yonge and DeBrahm survey actually listed 7,700 acres of high land on Sapelo, and 220 acres on Little Sapelo Island and adjoining hammocks.[11]

A loan from British bankers enabled Spalding to finance his South End acquisitions, with additional funds coming from the sale to William Page in 1804 of his Orange Grove house and three hundred acres on St. Simons for $10,000. (Page later expanded his holdings on the south end of St. Simons, renaming the Spalding tract Retreat).[12]

There is no surviving documented confirmation, but Spalding and Swarbreck presumably later swapped their respective half-interests, giving Spalding sole possession of the South End and Swarbreck ownership of Chocolate. Whether this occurred in the 1804–6 time frame is unclear. It could be that the agreement between the two occurred later, based on the ambitious construction of buildings at Chocolate around 1815–20, in which Swarbreck and Spalding apparently collaborated.

Spalding thus began building his antebellum plantation empire, the only period in Sapelo's history in which the island was profitable to its owner. He never owned the entire island, but by the time of his death in 1851 Spalding held everything but Raccoon Bluff in the east-central section of Sapelo, nearly one thousand acres of upland and marsh. Other acquisitions were Black Island near Darien, Sutherland's Bluff on the Sapelo River, and Cambers Island in the Altamaha delta.

The 1825 McIntosh County tax digest shows Spalding as the largest local landowner, with 7,910 acres of cultivable land, this being before he acquired additional acreage on Sapelo's North End in 1843. He was the second largest slave owner in the county to the Pierce Butler estate, and he paid $199 in taxes in 1825, compared to the Butlers' $257.[13] Spalding brought "slaves, sea island cotton, rice and sugar cane to Sapelo Island, along with considerable organization and energy . . . and placed great emphasis on the permanence of his empire."[14]

Spalding as the Scientific Farmer

Thomas Spalding was a remarkable man. He possessed the essential qualities to be a successful planter: finely tuned agricultural sensibilities, procedural discipline, and a thorough understanding of his local environment. Spalding was imbued with an unusually strong sense of place, with a concomitant belief in the *permanency* of place, a philosophy that equipped him with the insights that underlay his inquisitive nature and predilection for innovation. His localist perspective enabled him to make the ecology of the tidewater work for him. Spalding fully understood the salutary effects of his local environment: temperate climate, river hydrology, and ideal soil conditions for cotton, cane, and rice. He was possessed of great capacity for interpreting local weather, reflected in a sagacious awareness of the cyclical nature of temperature variations, and the effects of soil conditions, wind, water, and tides on his planting systems. Spalding usually correctly anticipated the first and last frosts of the season, and he made distinctions between rainstorms, northeasters, and hurricanes. His propensity for sensing relative humidity, the degree of barometric pressure, and other conditions was

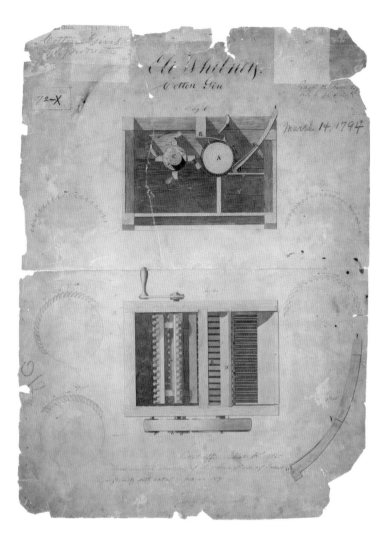

Whitney's application for a patent on his cotton gin, dated March 14, 1794. (Courtesy of the Records of the Patent and Trademark Office, record group 241, National Archives)

an important component in the efficacy of his crop management. Spalding was thus the consummate scientific farmer and ipso facto one of the most efficient plantation owners on the tidewater.

To know Spalding it is necessary to understand the exceptionalist approach he took in implementing his farming methods. In his era he was often considered different, occasionally even radical, in some aspects of his techniques. His experiments resulted in successful implementation of crop rotation and diversification, and his planting of sugarcane enabled him to be the first Georgian to manufacture sugar commercially.

Concurrent with his sugar making, Spalding established a technological paradigm for the use of tabby in the construction of his mill works. The promulgation of his cane and tabby methods was such that they were emulated by many of his contemporaries. The remains of tabby buildings at Sapelo and elsewhere in coastal Georgia are testimony to Spalding's resourcefulness. These ubiquitous monuments to his vision serve as tangible reminders of the influence he had on his times. He delighted in sharing his successes with his contemporaries but did so only after a suitable period of experimentation to determine that his concepts were sufficiently sustainable within the fabric of local environmental conditions.

Spalding was a leader in the cultivation of sea island cotton, setting enduring standards for the production of that staple. He pursued an agrarian philosophy predicated not only on the cultivation of his moneymaking staples—cotton and cane on Sapelo, and rice in the Altamaha delta—but also on the secondary provision crops by which he sustained his labor force and livestock.

Spalding's agrarian reasoning is expressed in his frequent contributions to farm journals, through which he freely shared the conceptualization of his ideas. He helped organize the Union Agricultural Society, a forum by which the cognition of the local planting establishment could be advanced through exchange of information. It is no exaggeration to say that Spalding was a philosopher, argues Coulter. Spalding "had a pattern for living, and the fundamental elements in that pattern were permanence and unity . . . his great common denominators were localism, regionalism, state rights . . . he never talked in generalities—he read his philosophy of life into everything he was doing."[15]

Spalding's philosophy, not unlike that of the ancient Greeks, was embodied in his understanding of the linkage between profitability and environment—that is to say, the benefits to be realized from the proper use of the local subtropical weather, soils, tides, and river hydrology. This understanding was joined with knowledge of which crops prospered and which ones did not. The fundamental expression of Spalding's ecological intuition, and therefore of his acute awareness of place, was elucidated in May 1824 in an address before the Union Agricultural Society. Using his knowledge of the classics, Spalding tendentiously paralleled the Georgia coast with the ancient agricultural kingdoms of the Mediterranean and Mesopotamia:

> Gentlemen, we are in the climate of Chaldea and of Egypt, of Greece, of Tyre, and of Carthage. We are in a land where rice, wheat and cane, indigo, cotton and silk, where the olive and the vine not only grow but will find their favorite home if man will only lend his aid. . . . Let us turn with renovated energy, let us turn with renewed exertions, to the repairing of the past, and the improvement of the future, remembering, that when God abandoned man in paradise, to save him from despair, he plucked from Eden's bower one Flower and planted it in his bosom; watered by love divine, it grew, and grows there still. It is Hope.[16]

Despite his innovative proclivities, Spalding cannot be considered an iconoclast insofar as proven practices in coastal agriculture were viewed in his time. He might be better described as a risk taker. He was rarely averse to accepting the consequences of his agronomic experiments or business ventures. This is manifested in his being $100,000 in debt from 1808 to 1815 (about $1.5 million in 2016 dollars), in large measure because of mainland acquisitions and the purchase of about one hundred slaves. Yet by 1818 Spalding had satisfied the obligation through his prudent agricultural and marketing practices.[17] This was hardly an aberration. In 1822 Spalding was so financially stable that he was able to purchase from William Mein six hundred acres and 125 slaves on Hutchinson's Island opposite the city of Savannah. By the early 1830s, this debt too had been fully repaid with interest.[18]

At the basis of Spalding's practices was his conviction that crop diversification was advantageous, even necessary, for tidewater planters. Dependence on cotton alone, he

Preparing fields for planting staple crops. (Courtesy of Bill Jones III)

reasoned, could lead to financial ruin. Thus the paradigmatic expression of Spalding's philosophy was found in his adherence to maximizing the growing cycles of his staple crops in tandem with his secondary crops (corn, peas, sweet potatoes), almost always in rotation.

Besides experimenting with sugarcane, Spalding occasionally cultivated various irregular crops: indigo, silk, olives, dates, oranges, and native and exotic grasses for livestock forage. Along with Spalding's theoretical competence was the Georgia coast itself, which he was convinced was one of the most ideally suited regions of America for agriculture.

"It is upon this ground," he wrote, "that our most valuable plantations are situated, for man has stepped in and said to the waters of the sea and the rivers, this land is mine: I will raise dikes upon it, and bound you out, I will place trenches in it, and place water-gates upon them, so that if the rains fall, they shall flow off; but when droughts come, I will lift my water-gates, and let you in to flow my rice, and my sugar cane, my cotton, and my corn, and there will be health, and healing, and fertility, in your floods."[19]

Spalding publicized the efficacy of his innovations, enthusiastically communicating developments with characteristic vigor and promptitude. In a 1940 review of Coulter's *Thomas Spalding of Sapelo*, Margaret Davis Cate shared the perspicacity of Spalding's biographer: "In one short sentence Dr. Coulter sums up the bigness of the man: 'If Thomas Spalding had invented the cotton gin, he probably never would have patented it . . . [Spalding] despised people who kept agricultural secrets.' It was his duty, so he thought, to tell people about new plants, crops, methods or devices." Farm journals such as the *Southern Agriculturist* and the *Southern Cultivator* were filled with Spalding's essays covering an array of topics.

Spalding wrote, for example, on the culture of perennial grasses for their utility as livestock fodder. He approached the matter with characteristic energy and experimented with gama grass at Sapelo, eventually finding it to be "utterly worthless." His favorite was Bermuda, or "brama" grass, which he believed originated in India, not Bermuda. The grass was excellent for the maintenance of cattle, horses, and sheep, and it acted as an effective binder to prevent erosion. Salt production also interested Spalding. He examined the possibility of making salt from seawater, proposing to build vats close to the shore to be filled by the tides sufficient to produce three thousand bushels of salt annually.[20]

This Sapelo Island field was once the scene of extensive cotton and sugarcane cultivation.

His creativity was not confined to Sapelo. For his planter contemporaries who grew rice in the nearby Altamaha delta, including his son Charles who cultivated the commodity at Cambers Island, Spalding devised in 1835 an efficient means of transporting rice bundles from the fields to the threshing works. He designed a system that called for building wooden rollers, carts, and rail tracks with planks over the rice canals and ditches, "to render great and important benefits, as well to the servant as to the master of the plantation."[21] It was typical Spalding calculation—thinking to ease the labors of his slaves while simultaneously enhancing operational profitability.

Spalding cannot be said to be a polymath of the refined intellect of his friend James Hamilton Couper (1794–1866) of Hopeton. Yet he was certainly an intellectual in his own way. His inquisitive nature, his constant inquiry into the nuances of his profession, and his scientific connection of the environment to the facilitation of his economic aspirations are a testament to his intellect. Spalding's writings were the formal exposition of his vision, the distillation of the ideas of his fertile mind. His tracts were imaginative and individualistic, and, as Coulter says, "he wrote with decision and with authority."[22]

Assigning a specific year for sea island cotton introduction into the United States is arbitrary due to differing, often contradictory, accounts, although most agree that it took place in Georgia first. Some accounts erroneously credit Spalding with introducing the staple. However, Spalding was twelve in 1786 when his father was among the first to grow the staple.

Lewis Cecil Gray describes how, in 1785, black seed from Anguilla, where the best long-staple cotton in the West Indies was grown, came to the Bahamas. There Georgia Loyalists who had moved to those islands transformed it to a perennial plant, refining it from coarse fiber to the long, silky fiber that characterizes sea island cotton. They sent the seed to their friends in Georgia—James Spalding received Anguilla seeds from his former business partner, Roger Kelsall, who was cultivating cotton on the Bahamian island of Exuma. Spalding, Richard Leake, Francis Levett, and Nicholas Turnbull harvested their first cotton crops in 1787. Levett had received "three large bags of cotton seed" from a Loyalist friend in Pernambuco, Brazil, in 1786, and in the spring of 1787 he had cotton sprouts at his plantation, Julianton, at Harris Neck.

Some accounts have the first sea island cotton being produced earlier. Writing in the *Southern Agriculturist* in 1844, Spalding himself noted,

The first bale of Sea-Island cotton that was ever produced in Georgia was grown by Alexander Bissett, Esq., of St. Simons Island, I think in the year 1778. In the winter of 1785 and 1786, I know of three parcels of cotton seed being sent from the Bahamas, to friends in Georgia; Col. Kelsall sent to my father a small box of cotton-seed; the surveyor Genl. of the Bahamas, Col. Tattnall, sent to his son, afterwards Governor Tattnall of Georgia, a parcel of cotton-seed; Alexander Bissett's father, sent a box of cotton-seed to his son in the year 1786; this cotton gave no fruit, but the winter being moderate, and the land new and warm, both my father and Mr. Bissett had seed from the rattoon, and the plant became acclimatized.

Nicholas Turnbull, in a November 1799 letter to the *Georgia Gazette*, made no mention of Spalding, Bissett, or Leake, averring instead that the first sea island cotton was cultivated by John Earle of Skidaway Island in 1767. Turnbull added that he had grown black seed cotton at Whitemarsh Island in 1787 and shipped it to England, adding further that "Old Mr. Patrick M'Kay, on the Island of Sapelo, planted cotton as a crop. These are facts well known."[23]

Various claims to be the first to cultivate cotton were made, chiefly by Levett. These were disputed by Spalding, who asserted that no single individual could claim the distinction. Writing in the *Savannah Georgian* in June 1828, Spalding noted, "[T]he winter of '86 brought several parcels of cotton seed from the Bahamas to Georgia . . . and the cotton adapted itself to the climate and every successive year from 1787 saw the cotton extending itself along the shores of Georgia where an enlightened population [previously] engaged in indigo cultivation, readily adopted it."

It is unclear when Levett first grew cotton. Spalding's argument that Levett was not among the first planters receives some validation in the November 1799 letter by Nicholas Turnbull. Turnbull was rebutting a claim apparently made on behalf of Levett in the *Columbian Museum and Savannah Advertiser* in October 1799 by an anonymous "Inhabitant of Chatham County" that stated that "planters were . . . were encouraged by a crop of black seed cotton from seed procured for Major Barnard on Wilmington Island which was raised on the Island of Skidaway, 10,000 lbs. of which crop was shipped to England in the spring of 1791 by Messrs. Johnston and Robertson on account of Francis Levett, Esq. which established the character of Georgia sea island cotton; being the first shipment of any consequence; and to him [Levett] the state is indebted for having it entered as an article of commerce in the British prices current."

Levett's correspondence indicates that he grew his first cotton at Julianton in 1787 from Pernambuco seed.[24] Parenthetically, Joseph Eve invented a working cotton gin in

Rice cultivation on the Georgia coast, 1850s. (Author's collection)

the Bahamas in 1785, eight years before the more famous gin contrived by Eli Whitney at Mulberry Grove plantation near Savannah. Eve's "roller gin" was designed to process the delicate strands of sea island cotton fibers, while the Whitney gin revolutionized the upland cotton economy of the South. Spalding was the Savannah agent for Eve's gin and noted that it could produce "three hundred pounds of clean cotton in a day" and could be operated "by a small impelling power of wind, of water, or of horses."[25]

In time, Spalding's own contributions to the coastal cotton industry attracted world-wide notice. Typically, he refused to promote himself: "Although he and his family were closely identified with the introduction and development of this important article of commerce, [Spalding] never claimed for himself any of the credit," Coulter notes.

The rationale for adopting cotton production was the precipitous decline in indigo markets due to competition from India. As in rice production, the coastal environment established the desirability of planting long-staple cotton from South Carolina to northeast Florida. The islands, with their temperate climate and exposure to salt air, were conducive to the variety, with its silky, delicate strands that brought a higher price on the markets than upland short-staple cotton. Like rice, cotton production was labor

View of Butler's Island looking south, circa 1928. (Author's collection)

intensive and required a heavy investment of capital. Unlike rice, however, cotton was a dry-culture crop, flourishing in the porous, sandy soils of the islands. Excessive soil moisture caused deterioration of the plant roots. Paradoxically, long-staple cotton was grown at Butler's Island, a wet, low-lying rice tract. Cotton was cultivated there as a rotation crop in the rich delta soil where Spalding's average allotment of cotton land to one slave was five acres, with the average yield per acre varying between 150 and 250 pounds. In January 1844, Butler's Island shipped thirty-five bags of cotton to a Charleston factor. The same month saw the sizeable shipment of 248 tierces (about eighty-three thousand pounds) of rice, presumably consigned to the same factor. These figures demonstrate that while cotton was an important crop, it remained subsidiary to rice for the Butlers.[26]

Spalding was cultivating high-grade cotton at Sapelo Island by 1804, usually experimenting by varying his seed selection until achieving the results he wanted. Seed quality was important, often making a difference in market price. Several varieties were planted, with a general preference for the translucent black, green, and brown seeds. Planting began in mid-March, followed by the hands periodically removing weeds and grasses by hoeing, and thinning the maturing plants to prevent their coming into contact. Early thinning was "the true principle of cotton planting" and led to earlier development of the pod.[27] Pods began to bloom in July after several hoeings, with the first bolls opening by early August. Spalding was systematic in his methods, planting his cotton in linear rows on cleared flat land using the sandy, well-drained Sapelo soil that was most conducive to cultivation. With his economical employment of the task labor system in which workers were assigned "tasks" commensurate with their age, skill, and physical ability, Spalding found that a prime field hand could work three to four acres in a good harvest, yielding up to 350 pounds of cotton per acre.[28]

Cotton required specialized fertilization, chiefly a variety of manures. Spalding made use of the ecosystem for fertilization, employing marsh cordgrass and nutrient-rich marsh mud. The routine work of slaves included carting salt marsh cuttings and mud for spreading in the fields, particularly on the island plantations. Spalding alternated between fertilizing his fields with manure, marsh mud, and crushed oyster shell.[29]

Sea island cotton was vulnerable to weather changes, particularly heavy rains produced by summer thunderstorms. To alleviate overwatering, small ditches were placed between the plant ridges to drain excess moisture. Little or no hoeing was done following the appearance of the pods to avoid damaging the plants.

After the bolls appeared, a staggered series of pickings began. Cotton was picked according to task, or "task-row," the harvest being gathered and stored at the plantation complex where it was dried. On the river plantations, cotton harvesting usually ran in tandem with that of rice, although cotton continued to be picked well into the winter after all the rice was in.

From late summer into fall the cotton was sorted, ginned, and moted. Hand-moting entailed the removal of cracked seeds and yellowed bolls. After ginning, cotton was sorted by quality and then packed in three-hundred-pound bags for shipment. Some coastal planters baled their cotton, although bagging remained the preferred method since damage was more liable to occur to sea island cotton pressed or packed into bales. Screw presses commonly used in baling upland cotton are rarely mentioned in the records of the coastal planters.

Market prices fluctuated, but by the mid-1820s long-staple cotton was bringing $1.25 to $2 per pound, compared to upland cotton that brought twenty-five to forty-five cents.[30] During uncertain market cycles Spalding devoted acreage to short-staple (petit) cotton.

In late 1832, John D. Legare of the Charleston *Southern Agriculturist* toured several Georgia plantations. Legare promoted coastal agriculture, encouraged the sharing of ideas and methods, and recommended the organization of local agricultural societies to broaden technical knowledge, all reflecting approaches advocated by Spalding. His comments about Sapelo provide useful contemporary insight into the acuity of Spalding's techniques:

> This island contains about ten thousand acres above the flowing of the tide, made up of hummock lands, covered with live oak and pine, to the extent of two or three thousand acres, and at least three thousand acres of prairie lands, which are considered fertile and are cultivated in cotton and corn. This land appears to be made up of what appears to be a rich vegetable mold, in some places six feet deep, resting on white sand. In its uncultivated state, it is thickly covered with various grasses and affords fine pasturage. . . . In our morning ride, we passed through a considerable portion of prairie land and visited the fields of sugar cane and cotton. . . . These are all at a distance of at least three miles from the mansion, with the exception of a small cotton field near the house. . . . Having been an eyewitness, although very young, to the first introduction of long-staple cotton into the United States, the changes the cultivation has gone through, are distinctly in remembrance. . . . The cultivation on Sapelo does not differ materially from the course pursued on St. Simons. The only novelty in the cultivation has been in making the ridges in prairie[,] or low lands, permanent and unchangeable for a series of years. . . . On the prairie lands, the growth of the cotton is from four to eight feet high—it is lower on the hummock lands, which are quite sandy. The finest quality is produced on the former.[31]

The cotton and sugarcane fields Legare viewed were at Long Tabby. The reference to the "small cotton field near the house" was probably in the open tract adjacent to the present Azalea Cottage near the Spalding mansion.

The worst misfortune that could befall a coastal planter was the hurricane. With his scientific curiosity, Spalding was interested in all weather phenomena but particularly tropical storms. "Spalding believed that hurricanes were becoming more frequent in his times," notes Coulter, "and he had great cause to fear them, for he suffered their destructive effects more than once." The early 1800s saw an unusually high number of local hurricanes: an 1804 storm struck St. Simons and Sapelo and killed eighty-five slaves on Broughton Island in the Altamaha delta; St. Simons was badly injured by a hurricane in 1813; and a storm in 1819 caused damage in Darien and the nearby islands.

The hurricane that "might well have taken the heart out of Spalding" was a catastrophic one that made landfall on the middle Georgia coast in September 1824, causing extensive damage to crops, structures, and livestock as well as exacting a human toll. On Sapelo, Spalding reported the loss of his entire cotton crop, 250 head of cattle, all of his sheep, and twenty-seven horses and mules. Eight slaves died, but Spalding's overseer, Muhammad Bilali, was responsible for saving many slaves at the height of the storm. Spalding estimated his financial loss at between $40,000 and $50,000.

Despite these natural calamities the coastal cotton industry recovered, and it prospered for most of the antebellum era. The most productive period was the earliest phase, from 1790 to about 1825, after which markets gradually declined, with increasingly depressed prices. Long-staple production came to require increased investment and eventually exceeded its profitability.

Rice, cotton, and molasses were transported to market along the inland waterway on coasting vessels built to navigate the shallow estuaries, tidal mudflats, and creeks of coastal Georgia and lower South Carolina. These vessels regularly called on the island and river plantations to load commodities for shipment to Savannah and Charleston. Freighting crops played an important role in the tidewater economy.[32] Staples were shipped to the market factors in the fall and winter, with cotton shipments extending into spring. The leading Savannah factor was Robert Habersham & Son. The Habersham family

The brick chimney of the Butler's Island rice mill remains as a visual testimony to slavery and the once-flourishing rice industry on the Altamaha River near Darien.

was among the most influential of coastal Georgia, and the factor was an important element in the plantation economy, managing the interests of his planter clients and providing a variety of financial and marketing services, including the advancement of funds to planters against their next year's crop.

Coasting vessels operated between Charleston, Savannah, and the smaller market hubs of Beaufort, Riceborough, Darien, Brunswick, St. Marys, and Fernandina. Savannah port activity reported in the winter of 1843 provides details of agricultural shipping, with lists of vessels, their owners or masters, cargoes transported, and their origination points. In January, for example, arrival at Savannah was noted for the sloop *Eutaw* with a cargo of thirty-one bales of sea island cotton from Sapelo Island. In February the *Daily Georgian* reported the arrival of the sloop *Splendid*, Captain Stevens, from Sapelo Island with 102 bales of sea island cotton consigned to several Savannah factors. Stevens later had the *Northern Belle*, as noted by his arrival at Savannah in 1859 with a cargo of 124 bales of Sapelo cotton consigned to Habersham & Son.[33] Sapelo's main loading points were docks at Barn Creek and High Point.

The splitting of households between Sapelo and Ashantilly on the mainland (see chapter 5) conveniently accommodated Spalding's business and political activities. Sarah Spalding had a distinguished visitor at Ashantilly in February 1839, the English actress Frances Anne Kemble, then on a Georgia sojourn from Philadelphia with her husband, Pierce M. Butler, at his nearby Butler's Island plantation. Kemble described a visit to Mrs. Spalding in her published *Journal* in rather uncomplimentary terms, referring to Ashantilly as "large and not unhandsome, though curiously dilapidated, considering that people were actually living in it." Apparently the call on Mrs. Spalding was made unannounced and without invitation during one of Kemble's frequent rambles around Darien and the delta. "The old lady mistress of this most forlorn abode amiably inquired if so much exercise did not fatigue me; at first I thought she imagined I must have walked through the pine forest all the way from Darien," Kemble noted, obviously not realizing that the "old lady mistress" of Ashantilly, who was sixty-one, was the spouse of one of the most prominent men of coastal Georgia.[34]

In 1828, the St. Andrews Society was organized, with John Couper as the first president and Spalding as vice president. The society comprised planters and businessmen of the section who were of Scottish ancestry. In March that year the *Savannah Republican* reported that the clans had gathered in Darien with bagpipes and highland dress, including their "haggis prepared by two of the fair daughters of Andrews. . . . Toasts passed gaily round the jovial board; and the health of the ladies who made the haggis was toasted in full bumpers."[35]

Spalding had numerous local friends: John Couper, Couper's son James Hamilton Couper, Christopher DuBignon, William Brailsford, William Carnochan, John Kell, Gilbert Gignilliat, Roswell King, Ebenezer Rees, James M. Troup, George Street, Francis Hopkins, James Nephew, and John Hudson. Three of Spalding's sons-in-law were planters: Alexander W. Wylly (1801–72), married to Elizabeth Sarah Spalding (1806–76); William Cooke (1796–1861), married to Hester Margery Spalding (1801–24); and Daniel Heyward Brailsford (1797–1833), married to Jane Martin Leake Spalding (1796–1861). The Wyllys were the parents of Charles Spalding Wylly (1836–1923).

A. W. Wylly planted cotton at the Forest plantation on the Sapelo River, and William Cooke owned the Shellman plantation on Bruro Neck north of Sutherland's Bluff. In 1838 Cooke purchased Creighton Island from Patrick Gibson for $13,500, and he was planting cotton on the north end of that island at the time of his death in 1861. As a wedding gift, Thomas Spalding awarded Daniel H. and Jane Spalding Brailsford one of his mainland properties, Sutherland's Bluff, on the Sapelo River.

Brailsford became a successful cotton planter, but in August 1833 he was murdered by a shotgun blast to the groin by his former overseer, John Forbes, at Sapelo Bridge (later Eulonia) in broad daylight and in the presence of witnesses. The incident, which was a sensation throughout the region because of the prominence of Brailsford and the methodology of the crime, was supposed to have been precipitated by Brailsford's dismissal of Forbes as his overseer. But less publicized were the former's alleged indiscretions with Forbes's wife, Margery, which may have been the real impetus behind the murder. Forbes was arrested, tried, convicted by a McIntosh County jury, and hung at the courthouse in Darien in November.[36] One of the Brailsford children was William Brailsford (1826–87), who continued his father's planting at Sutherland's Bluff up to the Civil War. William was closely bonded socially with his uncle Randolph Spalding of Sapelo Island, the latter being only four years his nephew's senior.

A noted guest at Sapelo was clergyman-author Francis R. Goulding, who would later write the well-received book *The Young Marooners*. Goulding described his Sapelo visits with obvious fondness: "Between Baisden's Bluff and the sea is a dead level of

Abandoned rice fields in the Altamaha delta are now state-owned waterfowl management areas.

green marsh, beyond which, at a distance of eight miles, is a blue streak of woodland. That is the beautiful island of Sapelo, so famous in those days for the princely hospitality of its chief proprietor."[37]

Transportation around Sapelo was necessarily by water. Plantation boats were an essential means of conveyance both socially and commercially. Most planters had dugout canoes manned by their ablest slaves, and regattas were conducted with all sizes of craft competing, "from the ducking canoe, whose skillful paddler urges her with noiseless speed, spectre-like through the marshes, to the ten-oared family barge."[38] The boats had names reflecting speed or the spouses of their owners—*Lightning*, *Spitfire*, *Blue Devil*, *Sarah Morris*, *Anne Boyd*, and *Fanny*. Occasionally the planters would race the boats themselves. The planter rowed, and "with ladies as coxswains" the *Thomas Spalding*, a four-oared boat, won a race on the Altamaha in the spring of 1849. A one-day gathering featured planters, their families, and many of their bondsmen from Sapelo, Darien, and St. Simons, typical of events of this type. As the day ended, "each party gathered to its boat, goodbye was said, and soon the rattling of distant oar-locks was all the sound that could be heard."[39]

Besides the use of dugouts, most travel was by sailboat and commercial steamboat via the inland waterway. There were no railroads in McIntosh County until the mid-1850s. One of the steamboats was named in memory of the late Mrs. Thomas Spalding, the *Sarah Spalding*, said to be a "pretty little steamer, accommodating twenty-six passengers."[40] Spalding's business required his frequent transit from Sapelo to Darien, crossing Doboy Sound through the Ridge River to Blue and Hall's Landing, and thence a three-mile ride to Darien. A trip from Sapelo to Savannah was usually on the inland waterway northward past St. Catherines, Ossabaw, Wassaw, and Skidaway Islands to the Wilmington River. Alternatively, Spalding could go to High Point, cross Sapelo Sound, and land either at Sutherland's Bluff or farther upriver at Mallow to take the stagecoach to Savannah.

Watercraft were a necessary part of any island plantation's equipment, required for shipment of supplies from the mainland as well as for transportation.[41] They served other purposes too. In 1817 after an American brig laden with cotton was wrecked on the north breakers of Doboy Bar less than a mile off Sapelo South End, Spalding's boat crews responded, reaching the scene and salvaging seventy-five bales of cotton. As was customary in these circumstances, Spalding received a settlement for the salvage as determined by a Savannah admiralty court.[42]

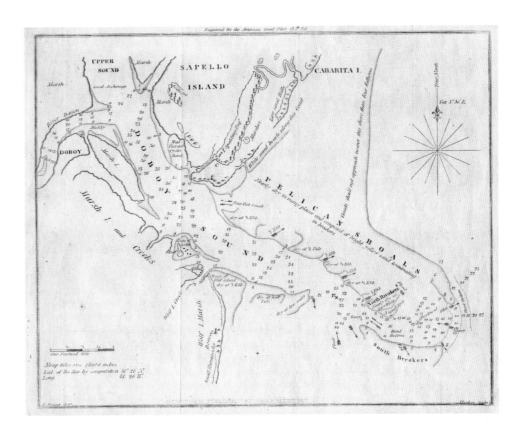

An 1850 navigational chart of Doboy Sound, from G. W. Blunt's *The American Coast Pilot*, 16th ed. (New York: G. W. Blunt, 1850). (Author's collection)

Sapelo Island lighthouse with its distinctive alternating stripes (which were red and white) and keeper's dwelling as it appeared in the nineteenth century. (Author's collection)

OPPOSITE PAGE: In 1998 the State of Georgia restored the Sapelo light, and it once again became a working aid to navigation.

Commensurate with his maritime awareness, Spalding promoted Darien as the agricultural entrepôt of tidewater Georgia (see box, p. 116). He used his political and business acumen to advance the economic interests of the coast and aspired to develop Sapelo Sound as a southern naval base, promoting the deepwater natural harbor there. A British naval captain once told Spalding that he could bring the entire British fleet safely across the bar to the deep anchorage between St. Catherines and Sapelo islands. Coulter notes, "The two islands afforded protection from the fury of any storm. . . . The whole United States navy could ride in safety on Sapelo waters, free from danger of storms . . . and the giant live oaks for ship-building were to be found everywhere."

Engineers surveyed the anchorage in 1839 and reported that there was no equal to Sapelo Sound as a natural harbor between Norfolk and Florida, with its nineteen feet of depth at low water and twenty-seven feet at flood tide. A local source was even more effusive, noting that the sound was "a bay sufficiently capacious for five hundred vessels to ride at anchor in six fathoms water under the lee of Sapelo Island. What better can you desire?"[43] The idea was never seriously pursued, but it took a long time to die because of Spalding's persistence. A great commercial city on the sound was envisioned by some, but ultimately "the navy yard was never established, the great city died before it was born, and Darien was left with one less trouble to disturb her."[44]

Spalding's advocacy for a lighthouse on Sapelo's South End was another step toward realizing his commercial aspirations for Darien, and to this end in 1816 he deeded five acres on a spit projecting into Doboy Sound. In September 1819, Winslow Lewis of Boston was contracted by the U.S. Lighthouse Establishment to construct a circular, eighty-foot brick tower topped by an iron lantern containing sixteen-inch reflectors, to Lewis's speci-fications. The $14,500 contract stipulated that "the Tower be built of hard brick, the form round . . . the height of the Tower to be sixty-five feet from the surface of the ground [not including the lantern room and cupola], the diameter of the base to be twenty-five feet, and that of the top to be twelve feet . . . Also a Brick Dwelling house, thirty-four feet by twenty, the house to be divided into two rooms, a fire place in each."[45]

Spalding, Darien, and Local Politics

Thomas Spalding's ambition was to make Darien the commercial center of coastal Georgia, which paralleled his advocacy for a naval base in Sapelo Sound. Because of its geography, Darien became an important outlet for upland cotton shipped to U.S. and European markets in the 1820s. It was a decade of rapid growth that saw cotton conveyed from the interior via the Altamaha River to Darien, the only port at its mouth and the terminus for a watershed that drained roughly the eastern third of Georgia when including the Ocmulgee and Oconee. By 1830, Georgia was the world leader in cotton exports, and over one-third of that cotton was being shipped from Darien.

Spalding's hopes never materialized. Owing to the inconvenience of its harbor, Darien had a history of navigational problems, and masters of deepwater vessels were often reluctant to venture there. Doboy Inlet was notorious for its shifting shoals and sandbars, leading to frequent groundings and shipwrecks.

Darien was eleven miles inland, and the river approaches to its waterfront were shallow, with exposed mudflats at low tide, allowing only smaller vessels ease of access to the town.

The most serious setback to Darien's aspirations was its being bypassed by the state's early railroads. When the Central of Georgia Company built a railroad from the middle of Georgia to Savannah in the mid-1830s, Darien's economic dynamic completely changed. Almost overnight most upland cotton was rerouted to the larger city, inland planters eschewing the river route for the speed and efficiency of rail shipment. The railroads bypassed Darien for another sixty years due to the deficiencies of its harbor and the fact that the town was enclosed on three sides by malarial rice fields, factors not conducive to sustained commercial progress. The first railroad in McIntosh County was the Savannah, Albany & Gulf, built 1855–61 from Savannah to southwestern Georgia. It traversed

Sketch of the Darien waterfront, circa 1835. (Courtesy of Bryan B. McDonald, Water and Air Research)

the western part of the county, through Johnston's Station (later Ludowici), too remote to be of benefit to Darien. (The town's first rail link did not come until 1895.)

The national Panic of 1837, combined with the decline in its cotton business, led to the state's revocation of the Bank of Darien's charter in 1842, and the town's commercial success was only marginal for the remainder of the antebellum period, exports chiefly being rice, naval stores, and lumber.

Reflective of his ambitions for regional economic development, Spalding advocated railroad and canal development. One of his proposals was to link the Ocmulgee River in the middle of the state (which merged with the Altamaha) to the Flint River in southwestern Georgia by a canal or railroad. Implementation of the plan would have linked the Gulf and Atlantic coasts, with Darien as the terminus on the Atlantic end. Spalding obtained charter rights to connect the Ocmulgee to the Flint by railroad, and in 1827 he and other investors received legislative approval to build the link. Work was begun, but the project eventually failed financially.

As a prominent planter, Spalding wielded considerable political influence. He had several partisan rivals, particularly Darien contemporaries Jacob Wood and Allen Beverly Powell, who disputed with Spalding on issues of local and state concern. Spalding and Wood had memorable debates in the 1830s over tariffs, trade regulation, and agricultural resolutions.

Family connections were important. A coalition revolved around Spalding, his sons James, Charles, and Randolph, and his sons-in-law Alexander Wylly, Daniel Brailsford, and Michael Kenan, along with James Troup and his brother George Michael Troup. Antebellum politics coalesced behind opposing factions led by Georgia governors John Clarke (1819–23) and George Troup (1823–27). Spalding naturally allied himself with the Troup faction.

While an ardent sectionalist in his support for the South's agrarian and economic policies, Spalding was also a Unionist, placing the preservation of the nation's unity even over that of preserving slavery if it came to a choice. Espousing Spalding's Unionism, McIntosh County usually sent Democratic candidates to the state legislature, while Darien was more inclined to strong Whig sentiments. With Charles Spalding serving in the senate in the 1840s, and Randolph Spalding elected to the state house, the Spaldings made McIntosh County a Democratic stronghold. A bitter political and personal rivalry developed in the 1840s and 1850s between the Spaldings and transplanted New Englander Thomas Butler King of St. Simons, a Whig.

McIntosh County leaders played prominent roles in the Democratic state convention at Milledgeville in December 1850 to ponder the question of states' rights, secession, and Unionism. Thomas Spalding and John Demere were the elected local delegates as they outpolled William J. King of Harris Neck, a southern rights advocate. Spalding's impassioned address to the convention urging preservation of the Union was one of the singular moments in antebellum state politics.

SOURCES: *Darien Gazette*, 1818–25; E. Merton Coulter, *Thomas Spalding of Sapelo* (Baton Rouge: Louisiana State University Press, 1940).

In October 1819, the state of Georgia ceded Wolf Island, across the sound from Sapelo, to federal jurisdiction to build a fifty-five-foot wood-frame beacon that, with the Sapelo light and its own beacon east of the brick tower, would establish a triangular range to facilitate the navigation of ships entering the harbor. The Wolf Island lighthouse was completed by late 1820, and its beacon was lit in 1822. One of the Sapelo light's antebellum keepers was Alexander Hazzard, appointed in 1853 at an annual salary of $600. A fourth-order Fresnel lens was installed in 1854, a marked improvement over the original fifteen lamps and reflectors built by Lewis.

Spalding and Slavery: Life and Conditions

Even with ownership of over four hundred slaves at the peak of his holdings in the early 1840s, Spalding had misgivings about slavery, exemplified by his reputation as a benevolent slave owner. To the extent that his livelihood depended on slavery, Spalding engaged in it, but he regarded the institution with increasing distaste and often predicted it would eventually end. "His response to such a fixed institution in the social and economic order of the time was to moderate it as much as possible."[46] An aversion to slavery ran in Spalding's Scottish ancestry. In 1739, his great-grandfather, John Mohr McIntosh, was instrumental in writing the "Darien Petition" in which the Georgia Scots protested to the provincial Trustees against a proposal to allow slavery in the colony. This was the first antislavery protest in Georgia. One passage in the petition was particularly prescient:

> It is shocking to human nature that any Race of Mankind and their Posterity should be sentenced to perpetual Slavery; nor in Justice can we think otherwise of it, than that they are thrown in amongst us to be our Scourge one day or other for our Sins. And as Freedom must be as dear to them as to us, what a Scene of Horror must it bring about! And the longer it is unexecuted, the bloody Scene must be the greater. We therefore . . . beg that instead of introducing Slaves, you'll put us in the way to get us some of our Countrymen who, with their labor in time of Peace . . . will render it a difficult thing to hurt us, or that part of the Province we possess.[47]

Spalding was as systematic in the governance of his labor force as he was in his crop management. As areas of Sapelo were cleared, settlements were built in proximity to the seats of labor: Behavior and New Barn Creek (Bush Camp Field)—both near

Long Tabby, Hog Hammock, South End, Kenan Field, and Chocolate, with smaller, transitory settlements at Bourbon and Little Sapelo. The surviving records reflect this distribution.[48]

Spalding purchased slaves from Charleston, Savannah, and the West Indies. An early acquisition was eighty formerly French-owned slaves upon his acquisition of the South End in 1802. He consciously built his labor force with equal numbers of men and women and was known for keeping his slaves together, rarely selling them unless he had occasion to include them in the sale of land. For example, in 1806, he advertised in the *Columbian Museum and Savannah Intelligencer* the sale of Black Island, including "one hundred seasoned slaves." Since Spalding still owned Black Island in 1824, either he did not find a buyer or he took it off the market. In 1841 Spalding deeded the island to his son, Charles Spalding, with the transfer including one thousand acres of high ground, marsh and hammock land, and "One Hundred and eleven Negroes . . . now upon the said Island."[49] Charles Spalding Wylly (Charles Spalding's nephew) later noted (without attribution) that Thomas Spalding never sold a slave and did not buy any slaves after 1810.

"It was Spalding's hope that his slaves might progress through serfdom to a measure of liberty and independence," Coulter wrote. "They should be attached to the land, and they should not be sold away from it."[50] This approach is exemplified by the infrequency of Sapelo slaves attempting to run. Apparently, few tried to flee: "when a slave had been with him long enough to learn his plantation methods, [the slave] had learned enough to want to stay."[51] Prime slaves at the peak of physical strength and skill represented a substantial investment for a planter, and the loss of one through accidental death, injury, or escape was significant. An item in the Savannah press not long after Spalding acquired the South End demonstrates the lengths planters went to retrieve runaway slaves:

> 20 Dollars Reward. Ran away from the subscriber, on the island of Sapelo, a Negro Man of the name of Landau, about five feet, nine inches high, stout and well made, pleasing countenance, speaks both French and English, about forty-five years of age. This fellow was the property of the late Francis Dumoussay. . . . He is supposed to be lurking about the city of Savannah or Sapelo Main.—Any person delivering this fellow to Thomas Decheneaux in Savannah, or the subscriber at Sapelo Island, shall receive the above reward. Thomas Spalding.[52]

Spalding provided his slaves freedom to pursue domestic farming, fish Sapelo's creeks, and raise their own chickens and hogs. The more privileged were permitted to own cattle and horses. Home-cultivated food not used for domestic purposes he allowed the slaves to sell at the Darien market. Spalding's reasoning here was simple: he wished to instill a sense of self-reliance and independence among his slaves. These attitudes, in tandem with his use of the task labor system and the liberalities allowed his slaves, often led to criticism of Spalding by his more constrained contemporaries.

The task system, while employed to achieve maximum efficiency, allowed slaves free time for personal pursuits after completing a day's work assignment, usually issued by the head driver. The younger men were employed in the more arduous tasks—ditching, plowing, construction, boatbuilding, and operating gins and threshing mills—while women were assigned somewhat lighter tasks: hoeing fields, and picking and sorting cotton. Fields were planted in sections of varying size and the hands given tasks matching an amount of acreage with their proficiency. The work was designated as a "full task," "half task," or "quarter task," depending on the degree of capacity and volume of work performed.[53]

Spalding was evidently concerned about poor health conditions associated with the river rice tracts. C. S. Wylly relates that Spalding told his son Charles H. Spalding, amid their discussions of the potential profitability of rice cultivation at Cambers Island, "I will never subject any dependent of mine [slave] to such climatic dangers, nor can I think it right to exact the increased amount of labor that would be necessary. . . . If you cannot get men of their own choice to undertake the danger of sickness and malaria, I will have nothing to do with it, and you can have the island to do with it as may seem just and proper to yourself."

Spalding established a six-hour workday, excepting occasions when additional time was required for harvests in late summer and fall. He also refused to employ his slaves in dangerous work. Sapelo had the reputation as one of the most competently managed plantations on the tidewater, and the task system was partly responsible. His method was based on the ability of his workers proportional to the types and acreage of crops being planted, and the planting procedure used. At Sapelo, the acreage of crops planted in any year was based on the yield realized from the previous crop, while taking into account late frosts, extended droughts, and excessive rainfall. "The task in listing the fields being previously cleared up and the remains of the former year burned off, was half an acre," Spalding noted. "The laborer [is] required to ridge afterwards, when carefully done, three-eighths of an acre; and in hoeing, half an acre was the task, depending, however, much upon the season and the condition of the field."[54] The task method was also used in preparing cotton for market: "It requires 1,000 lbs. of seed cotton to produce 300 lbs. of clean white cotton wool . . . requiring 38 good and steady persons for the cotton about to be ginned upon the drying floor."[55]

Planters held differing opinions on slave discipline. The views of Butler manager Roswell King Jr., while sometimes antithetical to those of Spalding, reflect a degree of consensus among tidewater planters. King noted in the *Southern Agriculturist* that

> the grand point is to suppress the brutality and licentiousness practiced by the principal men, say the drivers. . . . More punishment is inflicted on every plantation by the men in power, from private pique, than from neglect of duty. . . . When I pass sentence myself, various modes of punishment are adopted, the lash least of all.— Digging stumps, or clearing away trash about the settlements, in their own time; but the most severe is confinement six months or twelve, or longer. . . . No intercourse is allowed with other plantations. . . . The lash is unfortunate and too much used; every mode of punishment must be devised in preference to that.[56]

For the farsighted owner a degree of benevolence usually resulted in greater operational efficiency. It cannot be a coincidence that the productivity and profitability of plantations that adhered to the management principles of Spalding and the Coupers usually exceeded those of their less humane colleagues. John D. Legare concluded that James H. Couper's plantation was one of the most efficient he had seen in his travels in the South, a determination that could not have been reached without insights into Couper's labor management. "We hesitate not to say *Hopeton* is decidedly the best plantation we have ever visited," Legare wrote, "and we doubt whether it can be equaled in the Southern States."[57]

Food and housing for slaves also varied. On the rice tracts slave diets were somewhat better than those at the island plantations. Variables depended on the attitudes of the owner or overseer, proper care of the labor force being essential to productivity. "Slave owners cannot be too particular to whom they intrust [*sic*] the health (I may say life) and morals of what may justly be termed the sinews of an estate," King observed. "A master, or overseer, should be the kind friend and monitor to the slave, not the oppressor."[58]

King's views on the handling of different age groups are revealed in the feeding of younger people. In 1828, he reported, "Everyone knows they do not increase in proportion to a large gang, as in a small one, with the same attention. I cannot exemplify in too strong terms the great advantage resulting from preparing the food for Negroes—They will object to it at first, but no people are more easily convinced of anything tending to their comfort than they are." King reported satisfaction with the results of his program of feeding the younger slaves, though in somewhat unusual terms: "During the summer, little Negroes should have an extra mess. I find at Butler's Island, where there are one hundred and fourteen little Negroes, that it costs less than two cents each in giving them a feed of Okra soup, with Pork, or a little Molasses, or Hominy or Small Rice. The great advantage is that there is not a *dirt eater* among them—an incurable propensity produced from a morbid state of the stomach, arising from the want of the proper quantity of wholesome food."[59]

Had more Spalding documents survived they would doubtless reflect the views of James Couper, whose surviving records are extensive. For example, Spalding's papers would likely reveal that his standards for slave diets exceeded those of most planters. Rations for a Sapelo slave family typically consisted of corn, rice, sweet potatoes, peas, pork, salted fish, and molasses, supplemented by food the slaves grew or otherwise acquired for themselves. Acreage at Sapelo was set aside for growing provision crops for the sustenance of the workforce.

Slave diets at Sapelo were supplemented by finfish and shellfish: mullet, croaker, sea trout, crabs, oysters, clams, and shrimp were abundant, and easily obtainable in the tidal creeks. There were seasonal allocations of clothing for the men and women, outlays of work clothes, shoes, blankets, and sewing cloth supplied from stocks imported from Savannah. Spalding provided his slaves with extra clothing and farm implements, as well as cookware, crockery, and other items no longer needed from the main house, standard practice at many island plantations.

Most of Spalding's records have been lost, making it difficult to ascertain the details of his management. Fortunately, there is surviving documentation of Muhammad Bilali, Spalding's highly skilled black overseer (see box, p. 126). An educated man, Bilali left a series of Arabic writings that reflect his Muslim religion and philosophy. Due to Bilali's management, and Spalding's unequivocal trust in him, conditions for Sapelo's enslaved people were probably better than at most plantations.

Everything considered, however, it is impossible to characterize slavery at Sapelo, or anywhere else the institution was practiced, without using the worst of pejoratives. Slavery was toilsome, burdensome, onerous, and arduous. "There is no way to romanticize the back-bending labor these workers were forced to perform," notes William

McFeely. "Among the many recorded reminiscences of Bilali nothing tells us what these people who were doing [Sapelo's] labor thought about their work and all of the other aspects of their lives."

In her *Journal* Fanny Kemble described the squalor seen in the slave settlements at Butler's Island: "These dwellings were filthy and wretched in the extreme. There was the careless, reckless, filthy indolence which even the brutes do not exhibit in their lairs and nests." Kemble observed the lack of personal hygiene among the slaves while assisting a female so "begrimed with filth that it was no really agreeable task to examine her. The first process, of course, was washing, which, however, appeared so very unusual an operation [to her], that I had to perform it for her myself." Kemble noted that some slaves wore the same clothing without once washing the garments between the twice-yearly distributions of new clothing. She attributed the poor conditions to low morale and self-esteem and the exhaustion of laboring in the fields six days a week, rather than the slaves not having been taught the virtues of cleanliness.

Kemble's observations reflected conditions at a rice plantation, one with considerably less sensibility demonstrated in its slave management than that of Spalding. There is no evidence that similar conditions existed at Sapelo. It would be surprising if such conditions did exist, and they certainly did not to the degree of those described by Kemble.[60]

Slave quarters at Sapelo varied in style and construction. Duplex tabby dwellings were built at Behavior, South End, Hanging Bull, and Chocolate, reflecting Spalding's tendencies toward permanence and stability. The use of tabby for housing was common on the island plantations where the natural materials (oyster shell, sand, water, and lime) were available from Indian mounds and creek banks. Besides Sapelo, there are tabby remains at Cumberland, St. Simons, St. Catherines, and Ossabaw. Concomitantly, evidence of slave dwellings at the river plantations is almost nonexistent due to their wood construction. Wooden structures deteriorated quickly in the damp conditions, and little evidence of them remains. Remnants of brick chimneys and foundations are occasionally seen in the Altamaha delta, but because of its instability in the marshy bottomlands tabby was unsuitable on the river tracts.

Sapelo's slave settlements were Chocolate, Hanging Bull, New Barn Creek, and Behavior, the latter two being contiguous to the fields at Long Tabby. *Topographical Reconnaissance of Sapelo Island, Georgia*, prepared by H. S. DuVal for the U.S. Coast Survey in 1857, is useful for determining the sites of antebellum structures on

Tabby ruins on the Darien waterfront attest to the town's economic prosperity as a cotton, rice, and lumber port before the Civil War.

Sapelo. The map delineates several buildings at Long Tabby, labeled "Mr. Spalding's Plantation," including the sugar mill and what is likely a cotton barn. To the east near a forested oak grove are symbols for a cluster of slave dwellings within and contiguous to Behavior. Seventeen structures are shown, some enclosed by fences.

Archaeological investigation has uncovered remains of two small (six feet by twelve feet) tabby slave houses, one at Behavior proper and the other just north of Behavior at New Barn Creek (Bush Camp Field). The 1857 survey shows a layout of thirteen houses at Behavior over an area of roughly sixty acres, with four additional houses north of the main group at New Barn Creek, three of which are situated parallel to the High Point road. Based on the layout of the dwellings, and assuming full occupancy, there would have been just over one hundred slaves in the Behavior settlement.[61] The 1868 Coast Survey topographic map, *Doboy Sound and Vicinity*, shows additional structures at Behavior, indicating construction of houses by returning freed people.

Behavior was home to the earliest of Spalding's enslaved people. Bilali and his wife Phoebe probably lived at Behavior; they were among the first of Spalding's acquired slaves, as were Carolina and Hannah, who later adopted the surname Underwood. Bilali, Phoebe, and their daughters, along with Carolina and Hannah, were likely

Muhammad Bilali: Black Overseer of Sapelo

Muhammad Bilali was Sapelo Island's most famous slave. He was born in Timbo in what is now Guinea in West Africa, probably in the mid-1770s, although it is impossible to ascertain the exact year of his birth. Estimates range from 1760 to 1779, with the later date being more likely. According to a 1931 affidavit by Benjamin L. Goulding, then the custodian of Bilali's diary, Bilali "was about 80" when he died in 1859.

Bilali apparently spent about ten years as a slave in the Bahamas before being brought to Sapelo. There are conflicting accounts as to how he came to Georgia. C. S. Wylly states that he was purchased in Charleston by Thomas Spalding either in 1802 or 1803. William S. McFeely in *Sapelo's People* (W. W. Norton, 1994) asserted that Bilali was encountered by Spalding in the Bahamas, and because of Bilali's knowledge about sea island cotton, Spalding brought Bilali and his family to Sapelo.

Among Spalding's views on slavery was that supervision of labor and plantation operations in general were more efficient when conducted by black managers and drivers rather than the typical white overseer. After his first several years at Sapelo, Spalding never hired a white overseer. In one of his agricultural tracts he noted that he managed his plantations "without the intervention of any white man." Farming operations were supervised either directly by himself or by his black drivers. The most prominent of these was Bilali, Spalding's overseer for much of the antebellum period. An educated Muslim, Bilali was the patriarch of the Spalding slaves and, next to Spalding himself, the most powerful man on Sapelo Island.

Bilali's expertise raising long-staple cotton in the Bahamas led to his being appointed head driver at Sapelo not long after he came to the island—essentially the plantation overseer in charge of day-to-day farming operations. Because of his responsibilities, Bilali was privileged. Literate, skilled, and possessed of a complete understanding of Spalding's agricultural ideology, Bilali effectively supervised planting and managed the labor force. Spalding placed complete trust in him, and on the frequent occasions that Spalding was away from Sapelo, Bilali was left in charge of the island. He was a plantation manager in every sense, tasked with far more responsibility than would be found among slaves at other plantations.

Bilali had a large family of twelve sons and seven daughters. Phoebe, his wife, may have been born in the West Indies. According to Cornelia Walker Bailey, the great-great-great-granddaughter of Bilali, Phoebe was "from the islands" in the Caribbean. It is likely that some of the couple's children were born in the Bahamas before they came to Sapelo, and possibly all seven daughters. Bilali's Sapelo legacy cannot be overstated. It extends from the family's arrival on the island to the present day.

When interviewed in 1939 by the Georgia Writers' Project, Katie Brown (1853–1940) of Sapelo, "one of the oldest inhabitants" of the island at the time and great-granddaughter of Bilali, told of his daughters' names being "Magret, Bentoo, Chaalut, Medina, Yaruba, Fatima, and Hestuh," several of which are distinctly Muslim names. The name of "Bentoo" (Bintu), Katie Brown's great-aunt, evolved to Minto Bell when she married. Minto's gravestone is in Behavior Cemetery.

Bilali and his family "all worshiped Mahomet" according to Lydia Parrish in *Slave Songs of the Georgia Sea Islands* (1942). Katie Brown described in detail her ancestors' disciplined approach to their religion and their daily prayers to Allah: "Magret an uh daughter Cotto use tuh say dat Bilali and he wife Phoebe pray on duh bead. Dey wuz bery puhticulah bout

Journal of Muhammad Bilali.
(Courtesy of Hargrett Rare Book and
Manuscript Library, University of
Georgia Libraries)

duh time dey pray and dey bery regluh bout duh hour. Wen duh sun come up, wen it straight obuh head an wen it set, das duh time dey pray. Dey bow tuh duh sun an hab lill mat tuh kneel on." Magret, who became Margaret Hillery on her marriage, made rice cakes in observance of Muslim holy days, according to Brown. Rice was an important staple in the slaves' diet on Sapelo and was grown at Hog Hammock and Raccoon Bluff for much of the nineteenth and twentieth centuries. In a style adopted from their African roots, Margaret's rice cakes were made of moistened grains mortared into a paste with a wooden pestle, then flattened and spiced with sugar and honey.

Wylly states (without attribution) that Spalding assigned to Bilali the defense of Sapelo late in the War of 1812, when British naval forces were raiding plantations on nearby islands. Spalding, according to Wylly, obtained a consignment of muskets from the state militia and had Bilali drill a number of reliable slaves to challenge the British should they attempt to land. The British never threatened Sapelo, whether because of the rumors of Spalding's slave defenders or not. Though the story of "slave militia" has never been fully substantiated, it nonetheless has the ring of truth based on an understanding of Spalding's methods and those of his trusted black overseer.

Bilali outlived his owner by several years, being given his papers of manumission upon Spalding's death, as stipulated in the latter's will. In declining health, Bilali moved to Darien where he died in 1859. In Darien, he was befriended by Rev. Francis R. Goulding of the Presbyterian church to whom Bilali gave his "diary" of thirteen pages for safekeeping. This important record reflects Bilali's devotion to his religious beliefs and is one of the rarest and most significant of antebellum slave documents because of its uniqueness as an original Arabic manuscript. Goulding's son Benjamin donated the document to the Georgia State Library in 1930, and it was transferred to the Hargrett Rare Book and Manuscript Library at the University of Georgia in 1992.

St. Simons folklorist Lydia Parrish was one of those showing an early interest in the diary, providing copies to Melville Herskovits, an anthropologist, and linguist Joseph Greenberg in hopes of obtaining an accurate translation. Although only able to read a portion of its Arabic text, Greenberg was the first to analyze the manuscript and assess it as a religious lay document. Over the years other scholars have attempted to produce a translation. Most of the diary appears to be a compilation of religious sentiments and the performance of prayer. The paper on which the diary was written is probably of Italian origin, manufactured for the Islamic trade, and only available on the African continent. Thus it is possible that Bilali brought the paper with him on a slave ship from West Africa, although slaves were rarely allowed to take personal possessions with them when placed in bondage. Conversely, he may have obtained the paper for his diary in the Bahamas prior to coming to Sapelo. In summary, some mysteries continue, and much remains to be learned about Bilali and his manuscript.

SOURCES: Georgia Writers' Project, Savannah Unit, *Drums and Shadows: Survival Studies Among the Georgia Coastal Negroes* (Athens: University of Georgia Press, 1940); B. G. Martin, "Sapelo Island's Arabic Document: The Bilali Diary in Context," *Georgia Historical Quarterly* 78 (1994): 589–601.

among the slaves Spalding purchased during one of his trips to the Bahamas in 1802–3. The 1870 census showed the Underwoods both to be about ninety-five years old; they died in 1873 in a house fire on Sapelo. Bilali died a freedman in 1859, and the year of Phoebe's death is unknown.

East of Behavior, at a settlement labeled "Hog Hammock" on the 1857 map, were three more structures near the marsh. The map reveals another settlement of a dozen dwellings just northwest of the Spalding house, indicating that about eighty slaves lived there working a nearby cotton field, tending livestock at Root Patch and Flora Bottom, and serving as domestic servants at South End House. The DuVal map identifies several larger structures near the mansion, possibly a barn and other outbuildings, and a dock at South End Creek. Taken together, the number of slave dwellings

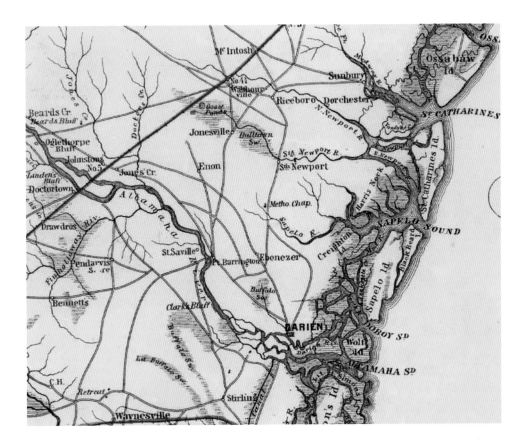

McIntosh County in 1860, depicting islands, waterways, and roads. (Author's collection)

mapped at South End, Behavior, Hanging Bull, and Chocolate would have accommodated over 350 people.

The 1837 McIntosh County tax digest listed Spalding's ownership of 421 slaves, the majority of whom were at Sapelo. Despite the large number, Spalding was not the leading slave owner in the county that year. Pierce and John Butler had 678 slaves at Butler's Island in 1837.

The 1860 census enumerated 370 Sapelo slaves living in almost sixty dwellings. The reduced total from 1837 reflects the sale of some of Spalding's mainland properties before and after his death. The 1860 count included 252 slaves on Randolph Spalding's Sapelo plantations inherited from his father and 118 attached to his brother-in-law Michael Kenan's plantation (Hanging Bull).[62]

Chocolate, Kenan Field, Bourbon, and Raccoon Bluff

"Chocolate" is perhaps Sapelo Island's most misunderstood place-name. Chocolate, a tract three miles south of High Point, fronts on Mud River on the northwest shore of the island. In 1914, C. S. Wylly related a story perpetuated in books, articles, and island lore that the name originated as an antebellum slave corruption of "Le Chatelet." "Chocolate," however, was the actual designation of the tract, a place name that originated earlier, either from the French ownership of Sapelo or from the colonial era. It was not a name that evolved from the enslaved people of antebellum Sapelo.[63]

After the French acquisition of the island in 1789, Nicolas-François Villehuchet and Pierre-Jacques Grandclos Mesle jointly owned Chocolate as part of their one-fifth holdings, but neither ever lived there. The earliest documented use of "Chocolate" occurred in 1797 correspondence by Louis Harrington upon his acquisition of the tract from the estate of his brother-in-law, Grandclos. It is possible the name predates even the French. As related in chapter 2, Isaac Levy had agricultural operations on Sapelo in the 1750s. The 1760 Yonge and DeBrahm survey delineated buildings and a farm plot on the site indicating that someone, likely Levy, was planting crops at Chocolate.

The name likely relates to pre-Columbian occupation of Sapelo. Spanish documents referenced two Guale towns on the island, *Espogue* and *Chucalate*. The location of both is undetermined, but archaeologists speculate Chucalate was probably near Chocolate.[64] Shell mounds and middens at Long Row Field immediately south of Chocolate provide a valid argument for that area being the site of the Chucalate village. Could Levy have used "Chocolate" as the name for his farm based on his connections with Creek Indian interpreter Mary Musgrove, who would have known of a Guale settlement on Sapelo called Chucalate and might have conveyed that knowledge to Levy? Whatever the case, historians have consigned Wylly's slave corruption of "Le Chatelet" with the naming of Chocolate to the category of myth. Parenthetically, Le Chatelet was the name of John Montalet's home at High Point, around which have emerged several other highly speculative stories.

After purchasing Chocolate in 1797, Harrington farmed there with sixty-eight slaves for several years before selling the tract to Richard Leake and Edward Swarbreck in 1801. Soon after, Thomas Spalding, as Leake's executor, acquired a half-interest in

Aerial view of Chocolate plantation on Sapelo's North End. The cleared areas were once the site of the slave settlement and cotton fields.

The waterfront at Chocolate
overlooking Mud River, circa 1925.
(Courtesy of Bill Jones III)

Chocolate. He and Swarbreck later negotiated the acquisition of Sapelo's South End from Harrington. With his maritime activities, Swarbreck (1760–1844) was a conduit for shipping supplies down the inland waterway from Savannah to Spalding at South End and Montalet at High Point.

From 1805 to 1808, Francis Hopkins (1772–1821) leased Chocolate from Swarbreck and Spalding, probably continuing the agricultural operations begun by Harrington. Unhappy with the inconvenience of island living, Hopkins moved to the mainland in 1808 upon purchasing Belleville from Spalding. Later Swarbreck and Spalding exchanged their half-interests in the sections of the island they jointly held, with the former establishing himself at Chocolate, and Spalding at South End.

Swarbreck is one of the most interesting players in the complicated antebellum history of the North End. Details of his activities lack clarity, but it is known that he developed Chocolate into a profitable enterprise, growing cotton as his commercial staple. Wylly notes that he "replaced all the earlier buildings, including the slave quarters," among his various improvements to the plantation.[65] Benefiting from Spalding's expertise with tabby, a complex of buildings was constructed circa 1815–19. This initiative was presumably a joint venture by Spalding and Swarbreck when they may have still shared half-interests in the tract. The surviving ruins attest to great activity on the site.[66]

Some of what is known about Chocolate's tabby comes from John Livingston Hopkins, son of Francis Hopkins. John Hopkins resided in the former Montalet house at High Point, then owned by the senior Hopkins, prior to his involvement in the shooting death of McQueen McIntosh in 1819.[67] The incident compelled the younger Hopkins to flee McIntosh County, and while away he wrote a paper describing Chocolate's tabby slave houses:

> The negro houses are built of lime (prepared by burning oyster-shells and mixing the calcination with sand) plastered over wattles. The length of a house is from fifteen to twenty feet, and the breadth from twelve to fifteen; the wall is high enough for a very tall man to walk with convenience between the ground to the upper floor; they are shingled with cypress or pine, and have a chimney. The division is into two apartments, in one of which there are stools, slabs for cooking utensils, and a three-cornered shelf in a corner, with a water pail on it . . . there is also a fish net hanging to the walls of one house in three or four [and] there are blankets and chests in which the negroes keep their clothes. . . . The houses are built in a group, or village, and with a regard to health, and a contiguity to the fields of labor. . . . I asked Mr. Swarbreck his motive for building in this way. He replied, "It makes my negroes more comfortable, and I desire to leave my estate as valuable as possible to those who may inherit it."[68]

Site archaeology has revealed the remnants of nine slave dwellings, most of them constructed as duplexes with central chimneys and tabby floors, with each duplex being about twenty feet by fourteen. The conclusion is that eighteen families occupied the nine buildings, which would translate to eighty to ninety slaves. The layout of the two rows of dwellings each facing a central "street" is indicative of a well conceived plan emphasizing structure and permanence, reflecting Spalding's organizational sensibilities. Several outbuildings were constructed, one a large tabby structure with slotted exterior walls to provide ventilation for drying cotton. Because of their proximity, Spalding and Swarbreck likely obtained their oyster shell from the ceremonial ring at Spanish Fort and from Indian middens at Long Row Field.

The provenance of Chocolate's plantation house is less clear. The two-story frame house built upon a tabby basement overlooked Mud River near the slave settlement. While Swarbreck certainly had a dwelling at Chocolate, Ella Barrow Spalding noted in her 1914 memoir that the main house in which her husband T. B. Spalding was born was built in the early 1830s by Charles Rogers who then owned the tract. Rogers built

Tabby ruins of cotton house at Chocolate. The barn is in the background.

The tabby ruins at Chocolate are some of the most extensive on the Georgia coast.

the tabby barn near the house in 1831, thus he may have constructed the house about the same time. Tabby ruins of the house remain on the site, but whether they can be attributed to Swarbreck or Rogers remains to be seen.

Two cotton fields at Chocolate extended north and south in a long strip between the High Point road and the Mud River marsh, with the plantation complex near the center. Long Row Field, the southern tract covering about eighty acres, extended nearly a mile to a tidal slough called Draw Bark. The northern field, about one hundred acres, extended a little over a mile to the Spanish Fort (shell ring). The two fields could produce about twenty-five thousand pounds of long-staple and short-staple cotton annually.

Wylly's memoir provides anecdotal information, not always substantiated, about Chocolate and the North End. Neither Wylly's unpublished account nor the subsequent version of it contained in Caroline Couper Lovell's *The Golden Isles of Georgia* (1932) gives sources. Some of his material is conjectural and conflicts with known facts. Nonetheless, there is an element of truth in the writings. For example, Wylly references "Mr. Wambazee" of Bruro Neck (Sutherland's Bluff and Shellman) as "heir and executor" to Montalet. He notes that "Wambazee" was formerly the Belgian consul at Savannah and a business associate of Swarbreck, the latter "a man with a face that told of long exposure to the sun, sea and wind . . . retired master and shipowner [who] had spent nearly fifty years in trading and voyaging dealing in palm oil, mahogany, ebony, and gold dust."

"Mr. Wambazee" was actually Emanuel Wambursie of McIntosh County, a man of some influence locally, being associated with Swarbreck and Montalet during the first two decades of the nineteenth century. Montalet lived at High Point until his death in 1814, cultivating cotton at Mackays Old Fields (Dumoussay Field).[69] As an executor of Montalet's estate, Wambursie sold Dumoussay Field to Swarbreck in 1820, "with an option on Bourbon and Cabretta attached."[70] Another of Montalet's executors, Francis Hopkins, purchased High Point, which he owned until his death in 1821.[71]

In 1827, Swarbreck sold Chocolate to Charles W. Rogers of Liberty County who cultivated cotton there for fifteen years. Rogers (1780–1849) initially bought just the Chocolate tract but later acquired High Point, Dumoussay Field, and Bourbon from Swarbreck. Rogers possessed ninety-three slaves and twenty-nine hundred upland acres on Sapelo, according to the 1837 tax digest. The 1840 census shows an increase in the slave force to one hundred. Rogers made improvements to Chocolate, including construction of a large tabby barn in 1831 and possibly construction of the main house.

Remains of slave dwellings at Chocolate, circa 1925. (Courtesy of Bill Jones III)

The barn measured forty feet by forty-six feet, with separate lower stalls and a two-level loft that indicate that livestock and hay storage were important components of Rogers's operations.

In 1836, Rogers purchased plantations in lower Bryan County. Seven years later, in 1843, he sold Chocolate and the rest of his North End land to Spalding.[72] This acquisition gave Spalding ownership of all of Sapelo except for Raccoon Bluff. Spalding awarded Chocolate to his youngest son Randolph Spalding (1822–62), who with his wife, Mary Dorothy Bass Spalding (1823–98) of Columbus, Georgia, resided at the plantation. After Thomas Spalding's death in 1851, Randolph inherited his father's lands and slaves on both the North and South Ends of Sapelo, a substantial acquisition by any measure.

The younger Spalding had a profitable plantation at Chocolate until the onset of the Civil War. In 1850 he was cultivating cotton and provision crops on twelve hundred acres of improved land, with a yield of twenty-one bales of ginned cotton at about four hundred pounds each, twenty-five hundred bushels of corn, and twelve tons of hay. His assets included eighty-seven slaves and livestock valued at $1,250. In 1860, Randolph Spalding possessed 2,170 improved acres on the North and South Ends of Sapelo and 252 slaves, including those inherited from his father. He reported the production of two hundred bales of cotton that year from his two island plantations.[73] Spalding likely had part of his labor force working seasonally at Bourbon and Dumoussay Fields, as the Coast Survey maps of the late 1850s show those areas under cultivation.

One of the maps, DuVal's 1857 *Topographical Reconnaissance of Sapelo Island*, is useful in confirming features relating to North End tracts. The map delineates "Chocolate Plantation" and cleared fields extending along Mud River north of the plantation complex to near "Old Fort" (Shell Ring), and at Long Row Field, extending a mile to the south. The barn and other outbuildings are shown, as are the two rows of slave quarters, one east of the barn and the other just to its south. The complex appears to be surrounded by a fence. The map shows the High Point road and fields under cultivation at High Point, Dumoussay Field, and Bourbon Field.

The 1859 finished navigational chart of Sapelo Sound, based on the 1857 survey, reveals more precisely the location of fields on the North End. This map defines Dumoussay Field as a neck bordered on the north and both sides by marsh, and it shows a constructed causeway linking its upper tip to the southeast section of High

Point, possibly to facilitate the movement of cotton to the High Point landing. The chart also delineates a road or trail passing through the high marsh and savanna amid what is now the Reynolds Duck Pond.[74]

The Chocolate main house burned in 1853, leaving only the chimneys and lower tabby walls standing. The Spaldings moved to South End, unoccupied since Thomas Spalding's death two years earlier, and lived there for several years before relocating to the mainland.

Randolph Spalding had an active social life at Chocolate, South End, and Savannah, where he spent considerable time with friends and relatives. Wylly notes that during the 1850s South End "became the scene of constant entertainment to the young and old . . . an atmosphere of gladness permeated room, hall and chamber with the very spirit of hospitality and the graciousness of an unequalled host." Spalding was apparently a heavy drinker, based on letters of the Jones family of Liberty County. A July 27, 1850, letter from Charles Colcock Jones Jr., to his parents, Rev. and Mrs. C. C. Jones, describes a stagecoach trip to Savannah. Noted the younger Jones: "One of the passengers, Mr. [Randolph] Spalding, appeared quite fond of the regular 'brown stuff' and made no bones about indulging his propensities on every occasion, so that by the time we reached Savannah, he was, to use a familiar expression, 'pretty well corned.' A decade later, a Jones letter of November 9, 1861, notes, "Colonel Randolph Spalding is represented to have been so drunk that he could not take command of his regiment when ordered to the relief of Port Royal batteries."[75] After the Civil War Randolph Spalding's widow sold the North End to John N. A. Griswold, a northern land speculator. Griswold appeared on Sapelo only sporadically during the short time he owned Chocolate, instead leasing the land to freedmen. Griswold lost his holdings to creditors, and in 1873 most of the North End was purchased by James Cassin, who also held the tract only briefly.[76]

The title specifics for North End properties from 1793 to 1873 are often unclear due to the loss of McIntosh County records in courthouse fires in 1863 and 1873. However, a brief description of the North End is revealed in the deed of sale upon Cassin's acquisition. It notes the land as "formerly the residence of Randolph Spalding, deceased . . . bounded on the East by Streets place or Raccoon Bluff and Caberita [sic] creek; on the North and West by Mud River; and on the South by lands of Mrs. [Catherine Spalding] Kenan, said Plantation or tract containing Seven thousand acres, more or less, marshes included."[77]

The fifteen-hundred-acre Kenan Field tract, including Hanging Bull, was part of Thomas Spalding's South End holdings. It is south of Chocolate, fronts on the Duplin River, and runs eastward across Sapelo. In 1832, Spalding's daughter, Catherine Spalding (1810–81), married Michael J. Kenan (1807–75) of Milledgeville. Three years later Spalding awarded Catherine the tract and eighty-six slaves.

A plantation house was built overlooking the Duplin shortly after Kenan began cultivating cotton, and in 1854 the Kenan family established full-time residence. The house site was a short distance south of the present state-owned timber barge dock. The 1857 topographical map delineates a prominent single structure by the sandy road along the marsh fronting the river, with an exposure toward the mainland. The structure presumably represents the main house; evidence for this from the map comes from the site being labeled "Mr. Kenan." The 1868 survey has the house in the same location, this time labeled simply as "Kenyon." The plantation house tract is now marked by the remnants of landscaping, including large pecan trees and palms. Nearby is a small burial plot containing the unmarked antebellum graves of six Kenan children aged from infancy to seven years.

"All the best memories I have of Sapelo Island are connected with the home at Duplin," recalled Wylly, "for in it were found the rarest examples of character, sweetness of temper and cultivation of the very highest order." By 1860, the plantation had grown to the extent that it was worked by 118 slaves living in sixteen dwellings.[78] A description of the plantation from Baldwin County deed records (1842) provides context, noting the property as

> containing from 1,400 to 1,500 acres, and bounded on the north and east by Dr. Rogers' lands and Anson Kimberly's land that was on the east [bounded] by Black Beard and Cabaretta Marsh; on the south, and divided from Thomas Spalding's land in the manner following: A line traced from the western Marshes between Sapelo and Little Sapelo until it reaches Thomas Spalding's Savannah Cotton and Corn field (containing about 120 acres), running the Canal of that field all round it again until it comes to the great Canal running into Cabaretta Creek.[79]

Kenan planted cotton through 1861 and then moved his family and slaves to Baldwin County, farming on leased land near Milledgeville. After the war the Kenan family retained the original tract and the Duplin River house until Howard Coffin's acquisition of Sapelo in 1912.

Bourbon Field, site of nineteenth-century cotton cultivation

There are remnants of structures from the Kenan plantation. At Hanging Bull overlooking the upper end of Barn Creek are the ruins of two tabby buildings aligned side-by-side on the west side of the High Point road. These are presumably the remnants of plantation outbuildings, perhaps utilized for cotton processing and warehousing. They were used by freed people as a church after the Civil War, the antecedent of the First African Baptist Church at Raccoon Bluff. The 1857 DuVal map shows conspicuous evidence of a sizeable slave settlement at Hanging Bull opposite the tabbies, on the other side of the High Point road, accommodating more than one hundred slaves to work the nearby cotton fields. The map shows a cluster of sixteen dwellings, not counting the tabbies. DuVal labels the settlement "Mr. Kenan's Plantation" rather than "Hanging Bull" and places it about a mile southeast of the Kenan house.[80]

The "Bourbon" place name apparently was not much used in the plantation era, if at all, for its appearance in a primary source document has not been found until 1871 in the Sapelo journal of A. C. McKinley. Edward Swarbreck purchased the tract shortly after 1817 from the heirs of its former French owner, Picot de Boisfeillet. Swarbreck

The waterfront at Raccoon Bluff, with the south end of Blackbeard Island in the distance

may have built structures at Bourbon for slave housing or crop storage. He sold Bourbon to C. W. Rogers after the latter's 1827 purchase of Chocolate, followed by Thomas Spalding's acquisition in 1843.

The degree to which Swarbreck, Rogers, and Spalding utilized Bourbon Field is uncertain. Some writings suggest that Rogers leased Bourbon to Thomas King, a planter from the South Newport River section of McIntosh County, for cotton cultivation in the 1830s. In her memoir Ella Spalding incorrectly notes that King owned Bourbon. However, King could have leased land there for a time before the tract came into Spalding's possession.[81] If so, King did not long use the tract: by 1840 he had moved to Bibb County. King's possible involvement with Bourbon also raises the possibility that King Savannah, a tract of grassland and pinewoods contiguous to Bourbon and Raccoon Bluff, is named for him.

The Coast Survey's 1859 navigational chart, *Sapelo Sound, Georgia*, and its 1868 topographic map, *Doboy Sound and Vicinity*, both note three structures at Bourbon near the creek leading to lower Dumoussay Field. The provenance of these buildings is unknown—they may have been placed by Swarbreck, Rogers, or Randolph Spalding. Their purpose was likely for slave housing and cotton storage. A 1961 Sapelo map showing points of historical interest, possibly prepared for R. J. Reynolds or the Marine Institute, incorrectly notes "Traces of Home of Picot de Boisfeillet" on the upper part of Bourbon near the creek, but it shows no other structures.

Immediately south of Bourbon is Raccoon Bluff, known as Street Place before and after the Civil War and the only section of Sapelo never owned by Thomas Spalding or his heirs. The tract was part of the French holdings apportioned to Boisfeillet, being farmed sporadically by the investors until the breakup of the partnership.

Between 1820 and 1824, Edward H. Sams (d. 1845) acquired 911 acres at Raccoon Bluff from the Boisfeillet heirs. The 1825 McIntosh tax digest listed Sams as possessing sixty-eight slaves and 1,410 acres in the county, two-thirds of his acreage being at Raccoon Bluff. Sams owned the tract only a short time and probably never cultivated cotton or other crops there. The tax digest suggests that Sams had his plantation (and slaves) on the mainland. His residency is shown in 1825 as being in the twenty-first Georgia Militia District of McIntosh County, a mainland section south of the Sapelo River. By virtue of his having acquired such a large parcel of land, Sams likely had future plans for the tract. Ascertaining the degree of Sams's involvement with Sapelo is complicated by the loss of county records.

By 1830, Sams had relocated to Duval County, Florida Territory. Around 1827, Sams sold Raccoon Bluff to Darien merchant and Spalding friend George Street (1777–1831). Street's widow, Sarah Ann Street, subsequently married George Anson Kimberly (1775–1836), also a Darien merchant, a political rival of Spalding. Kimberly owned Raccoon Bluff until his death in 1836, after which the land was held by the Street heirs until shortly after the Civil War.

There is no indication that Kimberly or the Streets ever lived or planted at Raccoon Bluff. They likely leased part of the tract for farming instead. Most of the tract's interior is now pine land, indicating agricultural use, validated in this case by farming at Raccoon Bluff by the Sapelo freed slaves in the postbellum period. The acreage total remained consistent as records indicate the tract covered slightly less than one thousand acres at the time of its sale by the Street heirs to the freed slaves of the William Hillery Company after the Civil War.[82]

This clearing at Raccoon Bluff may have been an agricultural site.

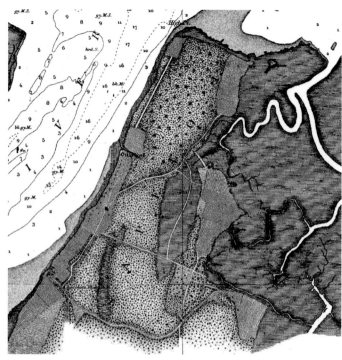

Extract from the 1859 U.S. Coast Survey chart of Sapelo Sound depicting Sapelo Island's North End. High Point is at the top, Chocolate at lower left, Dumoussay Field at center, and Bourbon at lower center. (Author's collection)

A story relating to Spalding, Kimberly, and Raccoon Bluff may explain why Spalding never acquired that part of Sapelo. In December 1818, the Bank of Darien was chartered by the Georgia legislature with an initial stock capitalized at near $1 million. The state appointed Spalding and other locals to open subscriptions for the sale of bank stock, and Spalding was elected first president of the bank. The bank's early years were marked by political infighting, resulting, according to news accounts, in Spalding's "unjust removal" as president in 1826, with Kimberly appointed his successor.[83] Spalding and Kimberly had an unpleasant personal relationship thereafter, never resolving their differences.[84] The reluctance to sell Raccoon Bluff to Spalding by his widow or the Street heirs was probably associated with the Spalding-Kimberly feud.

Looking east on the marsh causeway
from High Point toward the upper end of
Dumoussay Field

Another individual connected with antebellum Sapelo merits mention. James Shearwood (ca. 1774–1819), a Pennsylvania native, was in Georgia by 1794, for in that year he witnessed the sale of French-owned cattle on Sapelo. Shearwood later resided at St. Simons Island and then moved to McIntosh County around 1808. His acquisition or lease of Sapelo land is confirmed in 1816 when he received payment from the navy agent in Savannah for live oak timber from Sapelo. He also had interaction with ship fitters who were cutting oak on neighboring Blackbeard Island in 1817–18.

In February 1819, the *Darien Gazette* noted that Shearwood would "be prepared to receive genteel persons at his residence on Sapelo Island during the summer and fall months. His house is large, and the apartments well-furnished and numerous, all open to the ocean. . . . Carriages, chairs and horses to run on the beach he will likewise supply." Precisely where Shearwood's house was is conjectural. It was likely either at or near Cabretta or further south at Nannygoat, these being Sapelo's beach areas.

Before these plans materialized, however, Shearwood fell ill, and he died March 15, 1819, at the age of forty-five. Administering his estate were his widow, Martha,

Cabretta Island, looking across Cabretta Inlet toward Blackbeard

and Rotheus Drinkwater, a sea captain and husband of Shearwood's daughter, Mary Shearwood. Drinkwater was master of the vessel *Union* when it transported live oak from Blackbeard Island to Philadelphia in April 1818, further validation of Shearwood's involvement in the live oak timber business.[85]

In his memoir, C. S. Wylly briefly alludes to the presence of some of these smaller landowners when he notes, "Mr. Spalding is at the South End. All of the owners of the small tracts, the Shearwoods, the Sams, Millers, and others, have been eliminated by the purchase of both land and stock [except Raccoon Bluff]."

Thomas Spalding's final years were made lonelier by the loss of his wife Sarah, who died in May 1843 at sixty-five. The couple had endured an inordinate amount of grief during their forty-eight years of marriage through the premature loss of many of their children. "By all accounts," notes Ronald Ridgley, "[Spalding] was a gracious man, fond of his family. It was a family that knew deep sorrow because only five of the sixteen children outlived their parents."[86]

Seven children died in childbirth. The first Spalding son, James (1797–1820), barely reached manhood before his life ended. In 1818, the young Spalding won election as McIntosh County state representative. In November 1820, during the legislative session at Milledgeville, he died of influenza. A Spalding daughter, Hester Margery, died in her early twenties in 1824. Margaret died in 1800, aged three weeks; Margery in 1806 at the age of two; Thomas in 1819 at six; Emily Screven in 1824 just before her seventh birthday; and Mary Ann Elizabeth in 1818 just before turning fifteen. The latter death was particularly sad for the Spaldings; they buried Mary Ann at Ashantilly, the first of her family to be interred in the family plot.

Professor Coulter, in a passage of lapidary elegance, places the child there "to sleep the long sleep beneath the giant old live oaks draped with funereal moss—and there to be followed by other Spaldings until there should grow up a veritable Spalding City of the Dead."[87] The longest lived of the children were Charles Harris Spalding, who died in 1887 at the age of seventy-nine; Catherine Spalding Kenan, who died in 1881 at seventy-one; Elizabeth Sarah Wylly, who died in 1876 at seventy; and Jane Martin Leake Spalding Brailsford, who died in 1861 at sixty-five. The youngest child, Randolph, died in 1862 at thirty-nine.

Thomas Spalding made his will in 1848 with provisions to satisfy debts and support and educate several of his grandchildren. The remainder of his property he left in trust for his namesake grandson, Thomas Spalding, son of Randolph and Mary Spalding.

The Spalding family burial plot contains the earliest gravesites in St. Andrews Cemetery near Darien. Here are interred Thomas and Sarah Spalding, many of their descendants, and members of allied families.

At the time he died, Spalding owed $10,000 to the State Bank of Georgia, $5,000 to his friend Edmund Molyneau (British consul at Savannah), and $1,850 on a note guaranteed for his son Charles. At the time the will was made there were 250 slaves in Spalding's estate. Twenty families of slaves were to go to his grandson, William Brailsford of Sutherland's Bluff. Additional obligations compelled Spalding to add a codicil: "I am again unfortunate and must sell forty-nine Negroes and three old nurses in order to pay my debts to the State Bank. This will reduce one thousand dollars to five hundred dollars to my daughter Elizabeth Wylly to educate her two oldest sons."[88]

The final act of Spalding's public life was notable. At the Democratic Party state convention at Milledgeville in December 1850, Spalding argued for the preservation of the Union during a time of national debate over slavery and states' rights. His convention speech was stirring, and it was evident that he sensed that his life was nearing an end as he called the occasion "an appropriate [and] a graceful termination of my long life." He asserted, "From a small people we have become a great nation under our Constitution, and rather than that Constitution shall perish I would wish that myself and every human that has a drop of my blood in his veins should perish. To use the words of Homer: 'Before that dreadful day, may me and mine lay pressed beneath our monumental clay.'"[89]

At nearly seventy-seven, in feeble health and mentally exhausted by his efforts at the convention, Spalding returned home from Milledgeville in wet, chilly weather. He fell ill and died quietly at Ashantilly on January 4, 1851, then was buried beside his wife and mother in the nearby family plot. A local account commented, "If there was nothing in his life to dazzle by its brilliancy, it was one of usefulness and honor—unblemished by none of the vices

into which poor human erring humanity often falls. [He was] exemplary in all the virtues which most adorn the human character."[90] A century later Coulter penned an epitaph that rightfully placed Spalding among the pantheon of outstanding Georgians:

"A high-minded man feels no enmity," Spalding wrote shortly before his death. . . . [His] fundamental good sense, broad patriotism properly integrated with his love of locality and region, his venturesome spirit for economic progress—all were evident to his contemporaries. He had no sense of humor, yet he was fond of paradoxes and was the author of many singular expressions. He abominated music, and he would not tolerate dancing, and card-playing . . . [but] Spalding's life was not a failure; he did not live in vain. He got much out of his seventy-seven years and he gave more.[91]

CHAPTER V   Tabby

A Panegyric to Permanence

THE PROFOUNDEST EXPRESSION of Thomas Spalding's advocacy of permanence and place lies in his use of tabby as a natural building material for his plantation structures. His philosophy of permanence, with a concomitant perception of his environmental circumstances, is demonstrated through a desire for his buildings to last for more than one generation. Spalding's structures were intended to embrace permanence through strength and solidity, differing from the provisionally used wooden buildings, which tended to decay quickly in the humid coastal climate. This is the intrinsic concept behind Spalding's use of tabby and is tactile certification of his passion for order and stability. The remains of tabbies on Sapelo Island and the mainland are Spalding's most observable legacy.

While cotton was the most consistently profitable of Sapelo's market crops, it was Spalding's experimentation with sugarcane and his refinement of tabby in which he made his greatest contribution. His adoption of cane as a rotation crop was a catalyst for his use of tabby. It is important to understand that his experiments with cane and tabby were symbiotic—one went hand-in-hand with the other. Spalding's resourcefulness, along with his characteristic analytical approach, organization, and economy of resources, impelled the parallel development of sugar and tabby, and both succeeded beyond expectations.

Spalding initially planted sugarcane originating in the Pacific islands. Soon thereafter, John McQueen Jr. of Savannah introduced the faster-growing ribbon variety of cane from Jamaica, so-named for its striped stalks. McQueen distributed the cane to his friends, including Spalding, and it quickly replaced the Otaheite variety previously grown on the Georgia coast. In 1829 Spalding described his initial venture with cane at Sapelo as beginning "in the year 1805 [when] I began the cultivation of Sugar Cane with 100 plants. I had long before been impressed with the opinion that it would answer as well in Georgia as in Louisiana, for one of my early friends, the late Mr. John McQueen of Savannah, had spent the winter of '96 and '97 in Louisiana [and had observed how well Jamaican cane flourished there]." Spalding added, quite properly, that he was the first Georgian to plant sugarcane for "sugar as a [commercial] crop."[1]

Merton Coulter rightly refers to Spalding as the "father of the Georgia sugar industry."[2] The progress he made is reflected in his reported earnings: "My sugar works were very costly, though of a very common character; in the year of '14 however, my crop of sugar amounted to $12,500, from the labor of fifty slaves; the next year brought peace with it, and my neighbors, Major Butler, Major Wood, and others, became cultivators of Sugar."[3]

Because of nonimportation and embargo acts placed on sugar in the War of 1812, other coastal planters were led to experiment with cane cultivation. But they and Spalding never dedicated themselves to it exclusively. While he devoted great energy to the staple on Sapelo, Spalding's primary cash crop was always cotton.

Another secondary staple was rice produced by his son Charles at Cambers Island in the Altamaha delta. Rice seed was planted in March and April, with harvest in September and October. Sea island cotton was planted between mid-March and early April, with picking occurring from late August into December. Meanwhile, cane was grown on a different cycle, often on a two- or three-year rotation, with planting between November and February after the majority of the harvesting, ginning, and threshing of the cotton and rice crops had been completed. Cane cutting was usually done in the fall of the following year, after the rice had been harvested and cotton picking was well along.[4] Depending on when the seed was planted, harvesting began in late October or early November, typically when the first frost set the sap. The processes of grinding cane and boiling the expressed juice were facilitated in the winter.

Both the drier soils of the islands and the moist bottomlands of the river plantations were conducive to cane culture. "The best lands for Cane are strong provision land, or river swamp," Roswell King Jr. at Butler's Island averred. "If possible, the plants should be put in the ground in November, about three inches deep; they will be safe against frosts. Strong lands will afford such a growth that very little can be done after the 15th of June until September. . . . I have known Cane to lay all winter in a canal and be perfect. About the 1st of November we commence grinding and boiling."[5] By adopting his planting and grinding techniques, Spalding reported that Roswell King Sr. produced 140,000 pounds of sugar from about 110 acres planted at Butler's Island, an impressive achievement under any circumstances.[6]

Experimentation with cane provided Spalding with the empirical basis for his advocacy of crop rotation and diversification. Confirmation of this prescience is seen in remarks made several years after he began producing the staple: "As the cane grows, it requires to be worked in the same manner and about as often as cotton; so much so, that for three years last past, my Overseer has given each year eight hoeings to my cane as well as to my cotton. The limits to be put then to the culture of Sugar, does not arise in this country from the difficulty of either planting or attending it, but arises from the limited period which we have for manufacturing sugar."[7]

The Milledgeville *Georgia Republican* reported on April 11, 1815, that the Savannah market was offering "ninety-five hogsheads of Georgia Sugar, made by Thomas Spalding, Esq., of Sapelo Island equal, if not superior in quality to any imported from the West Indies." Some optimistic observers predicted that sugarcane would surpass cotton in profitability. Though this never occurred, cane nonetheless remained an important rotation staple for Spalding. "On my plantation, since the War of 1812," Spalding wrote in the *Southern Agriculturist*, "there never has been one Kettle of juice which has failed making Sugar; and the hurricane year [1824] excepted, of making Sugar of a fine quality."[8]

Spalding did not confine his cane planting to Sapelo. In 1825, a Savannah newspaper noted "with much pleasure that Thomas Spalding, Esq. has been thus far successful in the cultivation of Sugar cane on his plantation on Hutchinson's Island, opposite this city. He has sixty acres of Cane, denominated by the Ribbon Cane, which has in Louisiana been considered vastly superior to the white cane. . . . His Sugar Works are now in operation, and he is involved in grinding, boiling and granulating."[9]

While far from ephemeral, coastal sugar production still lacked the sustainability of cotton and rice. Spalding had his best success with sugar in his early years of manufacturing, largely due to tariffs placed on raw sugar during the War of 1812 and

Tabby remains of the cane press of Thomas Spalding's sugar mill on Sapelo Island's South End

the cessation of British imports. The sugar tariff was reduced in 1816 from five cents to three cents per pound, but prices remained high, and the industry continued to prosper until about 1835. The peak years for coastal sugar production were 1828–32. Reduced tariff protection after 1832 led to declining profits, and Georgia cane assumed increasing irrelevance as a market staple.

In 1816, Spalding composed the most instructive of his many treatises, a detailed description of sugar production, including itemized cost estimates and specifications for his animal-powered sugar works, elaborately titled *Observations on the Method of Planting and Cultivating the Sugar-Cane of Georgia and South Carolina, Together with the Process of Boiling and Granulating; and a Description of the Fixtures Requisite for Grinding and Boiling*.[10] The pamphlet was essentially an amalgamation of Spalding's fundamental concepts, codifying the need for crop diversification and the desirability of using tabby for buildings. The paper solidified Spalding's reputation as an authority on Atlantic coast cane cultivation and sugar production.

Tabby is the outstanding example of Spalding's localized ecological enlightenment and his scientific approach to agriculture and architecture in conformity with local conditions. His thoughts about tabby probably issued from its use in the buildings at colonial Frederica. In his younger years at St. Simons he would have observed the ruins of the abandoned town with more than casual interest. Spalding assiduously refined his tabby-making techniques, predicated on optimization of natural materials, in developing his formula that called for equal proportions of sand, oyster shell, lime, and freshwater. The lime was procured from the ash residue of burned shell taken from the Indian mounds conveniently scattered about the islands and shell banks along the creeks.

"Tabby is a mixture," Spalding wrote in a letter to N. C. Whiting of New Haven, Connecticut,

> of shells, lime and sand in equal proportions by measure and not weight, and makes the best and cheapest buildings, where the materials are at hand, I have ever seen; and when rough cast, equals in beauty stone. . . . [T]he drift shells, after the oyster is dead, thrown up along the shores of our rivers, are also used; but the salt should be washed out. . . . In my immediate neighborhood, from following my example, there are more tabby buildings than all of Georgia besides. . . . I generally made my people mix the materials one day and put it into [wooden] boxes the two following, very soft, as the better to amalgamate. 10 Bushels of lime, 10 Bushels of Sand, ten bushels of shells and ten bushels of water make 16 cubic feet of wall. I have made my walls 14 inches thick; below the lower floor 2 feet; for the second story 10 inches—beyond that I would not erect Tabby buildings.[11]

Spalding's letter included detailed sketches of his method of making wooden boxes for pouring tabby, and a separate drawing of a completed rectangular structure. Ideally tabby should be built between March and July, Spalding noted, and roofs should be made flat and covered with tar and sand.[12]

Writing not long after he began experimenting with tabby, Spalding noted:

> As tabby is very strong, the walls need not be any thicker than a brick house. Care must be taken that they are not run up too fast lest heavy rains, high winds, or their own weight, while green, will bring them down. When dry they become like a heap of living rock, and grow stronger with time. They are the cheapest buildings I know of, the easiest in construction, and may be made very beautiful and very permanent. They are the buildings of Spain, the boast of Barbary where some of them have stood for many centuries. All the success is in the making of the boxes carefully, carefully mixing the material, and a thorough dry season.[13]

Spalding's proclivity for tabby is simple to understand. There were no natural stone formations on Sapelo, and he did not wish to build his structures of wood, which was

Barn Creek at Long Tabby was the shipping point for Sapelo's sugar and
molasses. This section of the waterway was later renamed Post Office Creek.
The view is looking south toward Doboy Sound.

prone to decay in the coastal environment. He also saw tabby as superior to brick in durability. Although many adopted his methods, Spalding was surprised that more of his contemporaries did not utilize tabby. He attributed this to "the reluctance that is felt by men in adopting anything that is new."[14]

Much of the current understanding of antebellum tabby emerged from the 1930s investigations of Savannah architect Marmaduke H. Floyd. In a seminal essay, "Certain Tabby Ruins on the Georgia Coast," in *Georgia's Disputed Ruins*, Floyd analyzed coastal tabby ruins, including those at Sapelo Island and the nearby Thicket plantation on the mainland. He concluded that Georgia's tabby was indisputably that of antebellum plantation structures, not the vestiges of seventeenth-century Spanish missions as had been incorrectly claimed by several scholars.[15]

The writings of professors Herbert E. Bolton of the University of California and John Tate Lanning of Duke University and Brunswick, Georgia, historians Mary Ross and Margaret Cate in the 1920s and early 1930s had insisted that the ruins were of Spanish origin. Of particular note were the Spalding sugar mill remains at Sapelo and similar structures at the Thicket, the latter being attributed to the Tolomato mission. Probably as a means of generating tourism interest during the Depression, romantic stories of Franciscan friars and their tabby churches and *conventos* began appearing in major publications such as the *New York Times*, *Atlanta Constitution*, and *National Geographic*.[16] A scholarly volume, *The Debatable Land*, written collaboratively by Bolton and Ross (1925), was universally accepted as proof that the tabbies were Spanish missions. An equally authoritative book, Lanning's *The Spanish Missions of Georgia* (1935), also averred that the tabbies were mission remains.

By 1935, amid the flurry of "Spanish publicity" and spurred by the disputatious feedback from local observers, Marmaduke Floyd and James A. Ford, an archaeologist from the Smithsonian Institution, began putting their investigations into print under the coordination of Coulter and the sponsorship of the Savannah chapter of the Colonial Dames of America. They interviewed knowledgeable residents of Camden, Glynn, and McIntosh Counties, finding unanimity among them challenging the Spanish mission origin of coastal tabby. The locals insisted the tabbies were in every instance the ruins of nineteenth-century plantation structures and that the majority of them evolved from Spalding's revival of tabby construction beginning in 1806. Tabby had been little used since the colonial period at Frederica and Wormsloe.

Based on interviews, manuscript research, and archaeological fieldwork, Floyd and Ford correctly concluded that no tabby could be attributed to the Spanish period. In writing "Certain Tabby Ruins," the largest segment of *Georgia's Disputed Ruins*, Floyd used Spalding's letter to N. C. Whiting and its drawings as evidence "that disproves the present contentions that the large ruins near St Marys, those at Elizafield, at the Thickets, and on Sapelo, were in existence before Spalding's time."[17]

The publication of their findings in 1937 "created a rift in academic circles and generated bold headlines. . . . The scholarship of Bolton and Ross was particularly targeted and harshly criticized."[18] The aggregation of findings consolidated by Floyd with his evidentiary documentation in "Certain Tabby Ruins" dictated that some of the history of coastal Georgia had to be rewritten. Floyd's summation noted:

> The *National Geographic Magazine* in the issue of February 1934 again spread over the nation the myth that tabby ruins in Georgia were those of Spanish missions. An illustrated article by W. Robert Moore carried a number of statements and photographs referring to tabby ruins as missions. . . . Moore described the ruins of Thomas Spalding's sugar works on Sapelo Island as follows: "On the west shore, commanding the approach to the Florida Passage [inland waterway], stand the tabby ruins of the octagonal fort built by the Spaniards in 1680. . . . Spalding built a sugar mill on the foundation, and within recent years the 'long tabby' has been converted into a guesthouse."[19] This statement is obviously based on the 1930 edition of *Our Todays and Yesterdays* which maintained that the nineteenth century planters converted the Spanish mission ruins into sugar houses.[20]

The Sapelo tabby is further addressed in an October 1932 letter from Kate McKinley Treanor of Athens to I. F. Arnow of St. Marys, Georgia. When scholars learned of this communication it must have caused additional discomfiture among those who insisted the tabby remains were Spanish. Treanor wrote:

> During my childhood and youth, I lived on Sapelo Island, in the home of my uncle by marriage. Thomas Spaulding [*sic*].[21] I have the perfectly vivid recollection of my Uncle explaining the uses of the two or three buildings where his grandfather, the first Thomas Spaulding, built of tabby made by his slaves. The octagon was the cane mill; he showed me the tabby walk by which the oxen were taken up to the main story for grinding the cane. The long tabby house which, at that time, he had fitted up as a dwelling had always been known as the "Sugar house." If the Spaniards ever had anything to do with these buildings my Uncle did not know it. He was positive the work was all done by his grandfather. . . . All this is now called the "San Jose Mission." Later on I bought this property, lived in the "Sugar house" for several years and finally sold it to Mr. [Howard] Coffin.[22]

Spalding's Sapelo Island sugar mill, with the octagonal cane press at right and the boiling house (the "Long Tabby") at left. Spalding's highly functional mill designs were emulated by many of his coastal contemporaries. (Courtesy of Bill Jones III)

The appearance in 1940 of Coulter's scholarly study *Thomas Spalding of Sapelo*, three years after publication of *Georgia's Disputed Ruins*, provided additional validation that Spalding's antebellum tabby sugar mills had been mistaken for remnants of the mission period.

Spalding constructed his Sapelo sugar works, the Long Tabby, on the banks of Barn Creek in 1808–9, with the mill probably in operation by 1810 or 1811. Assuming Spalding harvested his first cane crop in late 1806, two or three more years would have been sufficient for him to refine his growing techniques preceding the mill construction. Roswell King and his black workmen were making tabby for the construction of South End House about this same time (1807–10); thus it is reasonable to assume that the mansion and sugar mill, three miles apart, were simultaneous projects.

Spalding's writings are an indicator of when he began manufacturing sugar. Discussing thermometers and his methods of measuring temperature in boiling sugar in the *American Agriculturist* in 1844, he notes, "I am aware that Detrone, a French chemist, had instruments upon one plantation in St. Domingo . . . and had [his] plans published in America, by Porter, Philadelphia, in 1831, ten years after I was using the thermometer, and *20 years after I was using the hydrometer, which guides you as to liming the juice* [emphasis added]." Based on this statement Spalding's mill was in operation by 1811.[23]

The mill had two structures: an octagonal cane press and a rectangular boiling and curing house built to Spalding's specifications, the latter the prototype for similar establishments on the lower Georgia coast built by Robert Grant at the Elizafield plantation on the Altamaha River, Jacob Wood at Potosi near Darien, James Hamilton Couper at Hopeton, and Spalding's cousin, John Houstoun McIntosh, in Camden County near Kings Bay. The novelty of Spalding's design was in its simplicity, hence its enthusiastic adoption by contemporaries.

"The mill house I have erected," Spalding wrote,

is forty-one feet in diameter, of tabby, and octagonal in its form. . . . the danger of fire, the superior durability, and the better appearance of the buildings, should make us prefer either tabby or brick . . . the outer walls of this building are sixteen feet. . . . Within about seven feet distance from the outer wall, is a circular inner wall, which rises ten feet; and from this wall to the outer one is a strong joint work, which is covered with two-inch Planks for a *Tread* for the Mules, Horses, or Oxen, that work the Mill. . . . [T]here are two doors, at opposite sides of the Mill-House in the lower story; the one for bringing cane to the Mill, and the other for carrying out the expressed cane . . . there is also a door in the upper story with an inclined plane leading to it, to carry up the Mules, Horses, or Oxen that work the Mill.[24]

The adjacent boiling house was twenty-two by one hundred feet, constructed on one level. Near the sugar works, Spalding built at least one other tabby structure, a barn or warehouse, contiguous to the creek for the convenience of vessels calling at Sapelo to load sugar and cotton. Cotton was likely brought there to be moted, ginned, and bagged preparatory to shipment.

The cane press was a vertical type, the machinery elevated from the ground's surface on a "strong foundation of masonry, eight feet high, so as to be within two feet of a level with the Horse-way."[25] Slaves fed the cane through iron rollers on the lower level propelled by animals on the upper. Spalding often used mules or horses to power his grinding mill, although he preferred the patient ox. He observed that the "ox appears to be the best companion of man. He is the most docile and obedient in the mill."[26] While using animal power to operate his mill in the early years, Spalding later

A mixture of oyster shell, sand, lime from burned shell, and freshwater made up Thomas Spalding's recipe for tabby.

converted to tidal power from Barn Creek, as noted by *Southern Agriculturist* editor J. D. Legare during his 1832 Sapelo visit. The expressed juice ran through gutters into receivers in the boiling house where it was clarified by adding lime. After boiling, the hot sugar and molasses mixture was poured into coolers and set aside for curing. Molasses drained from the cooled mixture and left a residue of raw sugar in the cooling barrels. Proper boiling left raw sugar of good quality if the grains were lightly colored. Refinement to pure white sugar in that era was rarely practiced, being excessively expensive; processing usually ended with the raw product.[27]

Floyd's essay was the first serious analysis of Spalding's concepts. He also used archaeology to further validate his findings, with some singularly useful observations pertinent to the Sapelo mill. Floyd noted that the cane press foundation comprised "granite-like cobblestones laid in some of the streets of the old parts of Savannah, and the great piles of ballast to be seen on Doboy Island, a short distance from Sapelo Island. Similar ballast stones are to be found at the north end of Creighton Island, on Sapelo Sound, where the timber-loading docks were."[28]

Floyd speculated that the boiling house had been converted to use as a cotton barn after Spalding discontinued making sugar around 1840, "when sugar planting was no longer profitable for him."[29] During Reconstruction, the boiling house was used as a residence by Spalding descendants. Archibald McKinley, who married a Spalding granddaughter and moved to Sapelo in 1869, often wrote of the island's tabby. "We all went down to the Plantation, the Barn Creek sugar mill, where we intend building & I tried my hand at sawing tabby—We sawed twenty blocks & blistered our hands," McKinley observed in 1870.[30] The foundations of the press remain; the boiling house was restored with the addition of a second floor in the 1920s by Howard Coffin. Remains of other Sapelo tabby structures are at Hanging Bull, Little Sapelo Island, South End House, and Chocolate.

Besides Sapelo, the best example of Spalding's tabby techniques is the mill at the Thicket five miles north of Darien. In concert with Spalding, William Carnochan (1775–1825) of Savannah constructed a tabby sugar mill and rum distillery in 1816 that, according to the Savannah *Columbian Museum* in February 1817, would produce "4th proof Georgia Rum equal in flavor and quality to Jamaica" for marketing from Carnochan's warehouse in Darien.[31] The counsel of Spalding, and likely a financial investment as well, enabled Carnochan to construct his buildings on the banks of Carnochan Creek overlooking Doboy Sound and Sapelo. The Thicket manufactory was constructed to specifications almost identical to those of the Sapelo mill. The base of the octagonal tabby cane press was about forty-five feet in diameter; and the boiling and curing house roughly corresponded in size and design to the Sapelo works.[32]

Floyd surveyed the Thicket ruins in 1935–36, finding inside the tabby walls a series of cross walls, likely the foundation for the vertical roller grinding machinery. The octagonal press was made of oyster shells from nearby Indian middens. The boiling and curing house was north of the press, and was actually two buildings set together in the shape of a T—further evidence of Spalding's role in the design. Spalding's writings attest to his involvement with the Carnochan mill as he recommended a "mill-house of about forty feet in diameter, a Boiling and Curing House connected together, of about eighty to one hundred feet in length, and from twenty-five to thirty feet wide," adding that "this house should certainly be of brick or tabby."[33]

North of the boiling house are the tabby ruins of Georgia's first rum distillery, the main portion of the structure being seventy-four feet long and nearly thirty feet wide at one end, with walls at the base two feet thick. In the vicinity of the boiling house and distillery Floyd observed scattered remains of porous, dark brown bricks commonly used around Savannah in the nineteenth century. Darien merchant Theodore P. Pease, owner of the Thicket property from around 1840 until his death in 1878, gave away or sold brick to the freedmen who were building homes and farm structures at the nearby Carnigan settlement (its name a corruption of "Carnochan").

Part of the sugar mill and distillery have fallen into Carnochan (Crum) Creek due to tidal erosion of the bank over the past two centuries. Floyd posited that Carnochan Creek was perhaps more than fifty yards east of its present banks when Carnochan and Spalding built the structures. Cisterns, tabby blocks, and scattered shell are visible at low tide amid the salt marsh and mud flats of the creek. Some of the shell is known to have been brought in by lighter in the mid-nineteenth century by T. P. Pease to help retard erosion of the bluff, a fact substantiated by the recollections of Pompey Grant, born a slave at the Thicket in 1855 and interviewed by Floyd. Grant confirmed that the creek was once much farther away from the mill structures.[34] He noted that the octagonal press was used for various domestic purposes after the Civil War, including as a residence and farm building. Because of continuing erosion of the creek bank, the cane press ruin was in danger of being lost by 2015.

There are ruins of four double-occupancy tabby slave dwellings based on the Spalding method about 250 yards northwest of the mill. These were constructed after 1825 when Spalding acquired the property in his own name following Carnochan's death. He cultivated cotton at the Thicket in operations managed by his son Charles. The paucity of surviving records makes it difficult to assess with certitude the full extent of these activities.

Much of Carnochan's operation was destroyed on September 14–15, 1824, when a hurricane of exceeding ferocity swept the lower Georgia coast. "Mr. W. Carnochan, at the Thicket, lost all his buildings, crops, &c., and one Negro drowned," one account noted. The mill and distillery were never rebuilt, as Carnochan died unexpectedly in 1825.[35] Another tabby sugar works from the same period, built by Robert Grant at the Elizafield plantation, was once thought to be the remains of the Spanish mission San Domingo de Talaje but were later proven by the investigations of Floyd and Ford to be the remnants of a Spalding-type octagonal press and rectangular sugarhouse.[36]

With Spalding's involvement, Carnochan constructed a two-story tabby warehouse on the Darien waterfront in 1819. This structure, the ruins of which are just east of the present Darien River bridge, was built to facilitate the shipment of Thicket sugar, molasses, and rum to Savannah. Carnochan warehoused these commodities until September 1824. There was considerable commercial activity associated with waterfront tabby structures during the antebellum period, and fires in 1812 and 1824 and the 1824 hurricane proved to be only temporary setbacks to Darien's commercial prosperity. Archaeological investigations amid the ruins of Carnochan's warehouse have yielded evidence of barrels and barrel-making consistent with the types of commercial activity known to have occurred on the site: Carnochan shipped his sugar, molasses, and rum in wooden tierces containing about forty-two gallons.[37]

South End House and Ashantilly

Spalding designed and built two tabby residences, one at Sapelo, the other at Ashantilly on the mainland near Darien. Beginning construction in 1807, Sapelo's South End House was completed in 1810–11, with Ashantilly being built a decade later. Spalding envisioned South End as the seat of the Spalding family for generations to come. It is the most palpable legacy to his abiding sense of place and permanence, and it must be considered the capstone of his architectural initiatives.

He designed South End on the Greek-Italianate, Palladian architectural concept. One unsubstantiated story is that Spalding, through his acquaintance with President Thomas Jefferson, visited the Jeffersonian home, Monticello, under construction during Spalding's 1806 term in the U.S. House of Representatives. Monticello was built in the Palladian manner, and several of the concepts embodied in the Virginia residence were incorporated into Spalding's Sapelo house.

Despite the dearth of surviving papers, it is not difficult to apprehend Spalding's approach. Coulter notes, "It was to be more than a house, or even a

South End House was Thomas Spalding's greatest testimony to his philosophy of permanence on Sapelo Island.

home; it was to be part of Spalding himself—an expression, and a useful one, of his idea of permanence on Sapelo . . . it would be strong enough to resist the most furious of hurricanes that were given to sweeping in from the sea; it would be a house cool in summer and warm in winter."[38]

The formal educational curricula of the time made Spalding familiar with Greek and Roman architectural styles, largely through the works of Vitruvius and Palladio, whose classical concepts are concretized in the design of the island home. When Thomas and Sarah Spalding visited Great Britain in 1800, a variation on the classical approach, English Regency, was then in vogue, having become the preferred design for the town and country homes of gentlemen there as in America. This exposure undoubtedly influenced Spalding in the design of both South End and Ashantilly.

With Spalding's fertile mind and organizational bent, the generic became specific: a sophisticated fusion of classical (Palladian) and contemporary (Regency). The Sapelo and Ashantilly houses were both characterized by Italian-style villas and loggias. A central loggia was the governing component of the main, single-story block of the Sapelo house, set between two corresponding dependencies on either side, both with loggias of their own. At Ashantilly two smaller loggias were recessed into the flanking wings on either side of a central two-story block.[39]

Spalding contracted Roswell King Sr. to oversee construction of the island house, with slaves providing the labor, including making tabby. King was both a skilled building contractor and a plantation overseer then in the employ of Major Pierce Butler, being engaged by Spalding under an arrangement with Butler. King (1765–1844) had expertise in tabby, probably the rationale for Spalding contracting him to build South End. King used tabby at Butler's Point at St. Simons and later at his own tabby residence at Blue and Hall near Darien. The Sapelo work may have been King's first experience with using Spalding's tabby method.

A native of Connecticut, King migrated to Darien in 1787, and later managed the Butler plantations from 1802 to 1819. While representing the Bank of Darien, King would travel to northern Georgia during the bank's financing of the Lumpkin County gold rush in the early 1830s, and in 1836 he would found the town of Roswell, north of the later site of Atlanta.

An April 1810 letter by Robert Mackay of Savannah describes the near-completion of the Sapelo house: "[W]as storm bound two days at Spaldings—he was from home, but Mrs. S[palding] really did the honors of the house to admiration . . . we rode the

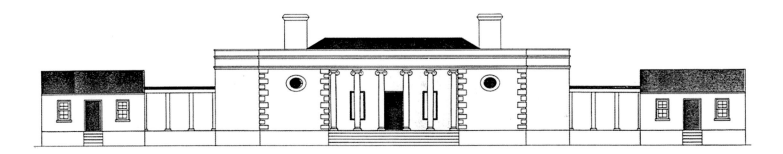

South End House was of Palladian design, featuring Ionic columns on a central block and flanking wings, with loggias linking the wings to the main house. (Author's collection)

length of the Island & met the boat at Montalets [High Point], where I was delighted with the situation & a most elegant Garden—Spalding is building an immense large house on the South End of Sapelo, 74 by 50 feet [*sic*]—with three large Bow windows."[40]

Spalding described his house as being built of tabby "made by my people . . . very soft[,] the better to amalgamate. . . . My house is one story, 4 feet from the Ground, and Sixteen feet in the ceiling, 20 feet in Wall. It is 90 feet by 65 feet in depth, besides the Wings. . . . [T]he house is of the Ionic order . . . and was built by six Men, two Boys, and two Mules, with one white man superintending in two years."[41]

Spalding probably contracted King to begin work in 1807. The structure must have been nearly complete by mid-1810, based upon Robert Mackay's letter above and further validated by Spalding's comment in 1830 that "the first house of any magnitude I erected was twenty years old." Additionally, a letter of January 1810 indicated that Hugh Littell, a plasterer from New Jersey, had been employed by Spalding to finish the interior.[42] In his 1844 letter to N. C. Whiting, Spalding noted that he had lived in South End House for thirty-two years, which indicates that the house was probably ready for occupancy by late 1811 or early 1812.[43]

South End was not typical of the southern plantation "big house." Rather than featuring a high-columned front portico, it was built on one level, low to the ground to better resist hurricanes. The central block had a recessed portico highlighted by six Ionic columns, with smaller columns between the dependencies and the central block. The tabby walls were finished with stucco and decorated with quoins, a water table, bull's-eye windows, and a parapet. The exterior walls were thick, reflective of Spalding's insistence on durability. The central hall featured a fireplace with a parlor in the rear of the central block and Spalding's library on the south. There were four corner bedrooms.

It was an impressive dwelling. As architectural historian Mills B. Lane notes, upon approaching the house, the visitor "ascended front steps to the portico, entered a large central hall, with a corner fireplace, leading to three large rooms: a parlor, a dining room and library, each with a semicircular bay." Outside, colonnaded loggias connected the two wings, the kitchen as the north wing and the farm office on the south.

There are conflicting accounts on Spalding's library. Charles Spalding Wylly, from whom Coulter got most of his material about South End, placed the library on the south side of the central block, with the parlor on the rear (west) side. Lane put the library on the west side in the area of the house where Howard Coffin later built his indoor swimming pool. Coffin, building on Spalding's foundations and using a similar floor plan, built his library in the same part of the house where Wylly and Coulter aver that Spalding had his. I am inclined to accept the Wylly version, since he often visited South End during his childhood and adolescence in the 1840s and 1850s and would likely have recalled where his grandfather had his library.

In early 1810, Spalding instructed Hugh Littell to obtain "stuff and finishing ornaments to the house" from New York.[44] Spalding was not given to artistic excess, and South End lacked much decorative embellishment. His major concessions, according to Wylly, were a bust of Napoleon Bonaparte and LeBrun's *The Crossing of the Granicus*. "There is a dearth of art," notes Wylly. "No pictures adorn the walls except in the central hall . . . no evidences of any sense or feeling toward art. No illustrated books, no bronze or bric-a-brac." But Spalding, with his intellectual inclinations, did assemble an impressive collection of books. He "gathered together in his Sapelo home one of the largest and most intelligently selected libraries in the southern states," notes Coulter. "Many of these books he had brought back from Europe, and as long as he lived he added to his collection, agricultural works and journals, histories, scientific writings, the classics of Greece and Rome, and the best produced by English authors."[45]

As validation of its strength, the house withstood the 1824 hurricane, Wylly noting: "In the darkened room [of South End] was left Mrs. Sarah Spalding, with an infant and three daughters, a nurse for the child, and fear and trembling for their guests. . . . They could be confident that the largest part of the island had overflowed. Few words were spoken. But so solid was the house that they believed no harm could come to it

Sarah (Sallie) Spalding, grand-daughter of Thomas and Sarah Spalding, rendered this sketch of the Sapelo house in 1858. (Courtesy of Bill Jones III)

or to them. . . . Low, massive, thick-walled and flat-roofed, it offered no hold to the wind and bid defiance to the storm and gale."

An 1858 sketch by Spalding's granddaughter, Sarah (Sallie) Spalding (later McKinley) conveys the appearance of the house. The drawing has detail and depth, depicting large oaks on the front lawn, the front portico of the central block with its six recessed columns, oval windows on either side of the portico, and a covered loggia on each side of the central block linking the wings. It is fortunate that this image has survived as no other contemporary drawings of the house are known.

The provenance of Ashantilly is somewhat cloudier, with occasional disagreement over its year of construction. Spalding inherited the Ashantilly tract about 1795, it originally being a bequest to his mother, Margery McIntosh Spalding, from his late father and named for the family's ancestral Scottish home. Spalding completed the house in 1819–20, but some posit an earlier date. No records survive on the original Ashantilly; thus the structure's exact building date is not known. The best estimate places the construction between 1816 and 1820, consistent with the period that nearby Darien, and Spalding's business interests therein, began making great inroads. Archaeologists conducting field investigations at Ashantilly placed the house construction from 1795 to 1801 based on the dating of recovered artifacts.[46] This is conjectural, however, and does not hold up to scrutiny when considering data from available records.

Ashantilly was built of tabby, and Spalding did not use tabby until about 1806–7. Furthermore, Spalding was only twenty-one in 1795, and was just completing requirements for the Georgia bar. From 1795 to 1800 he managed the legal affairs of his late father as well as the St. Simons plantation. This is supported by a communication from his father-in-law, Richard Leake, written to Spalding at St. Simons, lamenting that the Spaldings were not visiting him in McIntosh County with more frequency. Taken together, one can conclude that the time required to coordinate these activities, conducted some distance away in a neighboring county, would have commanded a disproportionate amount of Spalding's attention. It is doubtful that building a house at Ashantilly would have been high on his list of priorities between 1795 and 1801. Also, the Spaldings were in Europe for a year and a half in 1800 and 1801.

Useful insights can be gleaned from surviving family papers, including an 1878 biographical sketch of Spalding by his son Charles Harris Spalding. The younger Spalding references his parents' trip to Europe. While there the Spaldings purchased furnishings for their "jointure house," this being a legal bequest by which Spalding provided property for his wife upon his death.[47] The location of the jointure house is unclear, but it was likely at Ashantilly, probably the first of two houses there. The Spaldings' jointure house, wood frame and smaller than the later tabby-stucco dwelling, was perhaps built in late 1801 or shortly after, with the second, larger house begun about 1816, and completed by 1819–20. Meanwhile, some of the furnishings the Spaldings purchased in Europe may have been moved from the mainland to the new Sapelo residence upon its completion in 1810–11.

Important clues lie in the Spalding genealogy. Two deaths and the birth dates and places of the Spalding children establish with more certitude Ashantilly's construction date. Extracts from the family Bible show that a daughter of Thomas and Sarah, Mary Ann, "died February 18, 1818 *near Darien* [emphasis added], aged fourteen years and nine months." Spalding's mother died a month later, in March. She and Mary Ann were the first two family members interred in the Spalding plot near the Ashantilly house. Another clue comes from Margery Spalding's obituary in the *Savannah Republican*, written by Sarah Spalding, that notes: "Mrs. Margery Spalding the Mother of my dear Husband died the 30th of March 1818 aged 64 years, *near Darien* [emphasis

added], McIntosh County, Georgia."[48] Mary Ann and Margery must have died at a house at Ashantilly, possibly the earlier structure predating the larger permanent house likely then under construction, perhaps near completion, in 1818.

The cemetery plot assumes additional significance when placed in the context of information in the Spalding papers. In a twenty-six-year period Thomas and Sarah had sixteen children. The first, Jane Martin Leake, was born at Savannah in 1796; the second, James, was born at St. Simons Island in 1797; a third child, unnamed, was born and died January 13, 1799, at St. Simons. Margaret was born during the Spaldings' trip to England, May 1800. A year later, Hester Margery was also born in England. Mary Ann Elizabeth was born at Belleville in 1803, and a second Margery was also born at Belleville in 1804 (she died at Sapelo two years later). Elizabeth Sarah (1806), Charles Harris (1808), Catherine (1810), and Thomas (1813) were all born at Sapelo. "Two sons born and died between 1813 and 1817" were also apparently born at Sapelo, and finally Emily Screven was "born at Darien February 28th, 1817 . . . a daughter [was] born and died at Darien in 1818 . . . [and] Randolph,[was] born at Darien, December 23rd, 1822."[49]

All the Spalding children up to 1817 were born at places other than Ashantilly. After Thomas and Sarah's marriage in 1795, the birth dates of the children enable one to track the residency of the Spaldings at various stages over the next quarter century. They lived briefly at Savannah, where their first child was born, then at St. Simons Island, where the next two children were born. There they remained until 1800 when they departed for England, where two children were born. Following the return, two children were born at Belleville in 1803 and 1804, and from 1806 through 1816 six children were born at Sapelo Island. The first of the three children to be born "at Darien" is in 1817. "At Darien" clearly indicates Ashantilly, only a mile northeast of town.

Based on the scrupulous recording of birth dates and places, the argument can be made both for the main Ashantilly house not being under construction before 1816 or 1817, with a completion date of 1819 or 1820, and for the family's use of an earlier house on the site built before Spalding's refinement of tabby. The latter assumption is supported by late eighteenth-century artifacts found on the site, possibly from an earlier dwelling built prior to 1816–17. That dwelling, presumably dating from around 1801 and built as a jointure house for Sarah, also serving as a mainland home for Margery Spalding, was likely a cottage, transitory and less substantial than the later Ashantilly house.

Ashantilly

Residence of Col. C. Spalding near Darien Georgia
The Old "Building"

Ashantilly around 1860, by an unknown artist. The main house is shown in the lower panel. At top is the frame house on the premises, occupied then by Charles and Evelyn Kell Spalding because the main house was in disrepair. (Author's collection)

A sketch by an unknown artist of "Residence of Col. C. Spalding" apparently dating from the 1860s depicts Ashantilly in its original construction—two-story central block and flat roof, with one-story flanking wings—but rather in need of repair. Of more interest in the sketch is a smaller frame dwelling pictured nearby, used by Charles Spalding and his wife before his sale of Ashantilly after the Civil War. The smaller structure may be the house Thomas Spalding built prior to the more ambitious tabby house later.

To this discussion another fact must be appended: Sarah Spalding's mother, Jane Martin Leake, lived at Belleville for several years after her husband's death in 1802. As his father-in-law's administrator, Spalding sold Belleville in 1808. The question arises as to where Jane Leake resided until her death in 1821.[50] Possibly it was at Sapelo, but

perhaps it was at a jointure house near Darien. If the latter case, it adds to the probability that Spalding built a dwelling at Ashantilly before the construction of the larger house.

Finally, it must be emphasized that William G. Haynes Jr. (1908–2001), the last private owner of Ashantilly, who for over fifty years researched the origins of his home in greater depth than anyone, always used the "circa 1820" date for the construction, as frequently seen in his correspondence and publications.

Spalding built Ashantilly for a dual purpose: to serve as a new, larger, jointure house for Sarah and to provide a substantive mainland home when the family was away from Sapelo. Sarah died there in 1843, as did Thomas in 1851. Following their marriage in 1834, Charles Spalding and his wife, Evelyn West (Kell) Spalding, lived at Ashantilly until his sale of the property in 1870.

One thing is certain: the existing house bears little resemblance to the Spalding structure. The original tabby incorporated a five-part concept. Like South End, Ashantilly's central block was connected by covered loggias to flanking wings. The floor plan was symmetrical, with neoclassical details featuring a piazza in the front central core with terra-cotta Ionic columns, and marble columns on the loggias. Much of the original house interior was lost in a 1937 fire, followed by ongoing restoration by the Haynes family over the next fifty years.

The Ashantilly house after repairs and refurbishing following a 1937 fire. Thomas Spalding's original outer tabby walls remain intact, as does his architectural concept, excepting for the roof (no longer flat).

Civil War Sapelo

In the late 1850s and early 1860s, during the secession crisis, there were differences of opinion between the two surviving Spalding sons. Randolph, like his father, was a strong Union man in the years leading up to the war, but he came to support Georgia secession as war clouds loomed. Charles, however, remained opposed to secession. Randolph, who had inherited his father's island plantation, moved from Sapelo to the Ridge in 1857, although South End House continued to be used as a family retreat. The 1858 sketch by Randolph's daughter Sarah shows that the mansion was in good condition up to the outbreak of war in April 1861.

Randolph Spalding received a commission from the state of Georgia as a colonel in the Twenty-Ninth Regiment, Georgia Volunteer Infantry, at the start of the war and was stationed at Darien, Sapelo, and later at Savannah. He died of pneumonia in camp at Savannah on March 17, 1862, at the age of thirty-nine, and was buried in the family plot at Ashantilly.

From the fall of 1861 until the spring of 1862, three companies of the Twenty-Ninth Regiment, Georgia Volunteers, were stationed on the South End of Sapelo. In October 1861, Confederate soldiers of the regiment built Battery Sapelo near the lighthouse, an earthwork and artillery emplacement for five heavy guns to defend the entrance to Doboy Sound. A letter from Pvt. John W. Hagan, on duty at Sapelo Island, to his wife in Berrien County, Georgia, described the earthworks and noted that one of the guns fired a shell weighing 160 pounds. Another letter, dated October 24, 1861, from "Sapelo Battery, Ga." certified the acceptance by Capt. John C. Lamb to the command of Company B of the Twenty-Ninth Regiment stationed at Sapelo.

In February 1862, Gen. Robert E. Lee, appointed to organize coastal forces, ordered the military evacuation of the islands. All troops were transferred to the defense of Savannah, a development that left the rest of the coast largely unprotected. Confederate forces evacuated Sapelo in March 1862 and removed the Fresnel lens from the lighthouse to deny its use to the Union navy.

When the blockade was implemented in the spring of 1862, many island planters, fearing attack from the sea, sought refuge on the mainland. With the departure of protective troops in 1862, Randolph Spalding and Michael J. Kenan began the removal of most of their slaves from Sapelo to Baldwin County, where plans were made to resume farming operations on a rented plantation.

Randolph Spalding died before these plans were completed. Charles Spalding, aided by Allen G. Bass, Randolph's plantation overseer at Sapelo in the first year of the war, completed the transfer of Sapelo slaves to Baldwin County and relocated forty-four additional slaves to a 480-acre plantation purchased in Brooks County in southern Georgia. Randolph Spalding and Michael Kenan had 252 and 118 slaves, respectively, on Sapelo Island, while Charles Spalding had 140, including ninety-six at Creighton Island and Shellman, plantations bequeathed to him by his late brother-in-law, William Cooke.

The great Sapelo mansion, the apotheosis of Thomas Spalding's lifelong commitment to place and permanency, did not survive the ravages of war. The abandonment of Sapelo left South End House exposed to looting and vandalism, often by Union naval forces from blockading vessels patrolling Doboy Sound. Using Sapelo as a source for supplies, water, and firewood, the northerners, abetted by vagrant slaves remaining

on the island, systematically looted furnishings, books, family papers, and other materials from the house. Nocturnal predators from the mainland did the rest until very little of substance remained. The mansion became a virtual ruin. The words of Spalding's biographer, Merton Coulter, are poignant in describing the denouement of both Spalding and his domicile: "Even

his mansion on Sapelo Island did not survive the destruction of a war that fell upon the country a decade after his death. Gone is everything, or nearly everything, to which Spalding's name is attached. . . . And what happened to his doctrine of permanency? He lived almost long enough to learn what wise ones today know, that there is nothing permanent."

CHAPTER VI Geechee Sapelo

From Freedom to Self-Sufficiency

THE LONG WALK HOME to freedom for many of Sapelo Island's former slaves occurred during and after William T. Sherman's march through central Georgia in late 1864. Not all of Sapelo's freed slaves returned home; some remained in Thomas County, others in Baldwin. But many, carrying everything they owned on their backs, did begin walking in the wake of Sherman's army, southeast toward the coast over 150 miles from Milledgeville.

As the March to the Sea neared Savannah, the number of freed people trailing the Union force had swelled to more than twenty-five thousand. The refugees, cold, hungry, and weary, were a heavy burden, and Union general Jefferson C. Davis wanted to separate his army from the multitude. An opportunity presented itself, but it would have tragic consequences. At Ebenezer Creek, a small, muddy tributary of the Savannah River, Union troops hurrying to engage Confederate forces rumored to be nearby removed their pontoon bridges, leaving the stunned freed people behind. As a Union chaplain reported, "There went up from that multitude a cry of agony." The threat of Rebel attack precipitated a rush of hundreds of refugees into the frigid waters of the creek. Struggling to get across, many were swept downstream and drowned, including several women with infants in their arms.[1]

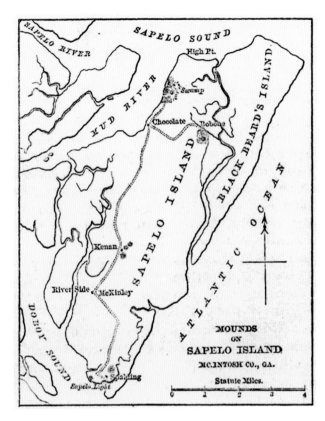

An 1872 map of Sapelo Island. (Author's collection)

Despite the horror at Ebenezer Creek, many of Sapelo's people reached Fort McAllister or Savannah and eventually made their way home to the island. General Sherman's January 1865 issuance of Field Order No. 15 from his headquarters in occupied Savannah awarded the coastal islands from Charleston to the St. Johns River to the emancipated slaves, a decree that received congressional sanction in March 1865 whereby "every male citizen whether refugee or freedman . . . there shall be assigned not more than forty acres of such land."[2]

Later that year Gen. Rufus Saxton at Hilton Head appointed Tunis G. Campbell, an African American agent for the Bureau of Refugees, Freedmen, and Abandoned Lands, to administer this program on "certain of the sea islands of Georgia, including St. Catherines, Ossabaw and [Sapelo]." Soon thereafter Campbell began overseeing the resettlement of freed slaves on the three islands.

The provisions of Sherman's field order enabled the Freedmen's Bureau to begin the redistribution of land in the spring of 1865. In May the bureau divided 390 acres on Sapelo's South End among the freedmen, land that Thomas Spalding had bequeathed to his namesake grandson, the eighteen-year-old son of Mary Bass Spalding. The distribution was measured in plots of fifteen to forty acres. Fergus Wilson was one of the former Sapelo slaves who was an early beneficiary of the military directive. Wilson selected forty acres at Hanging Bull, land he had worked as a teenaged slave before the war.

Also at Hanging Bull were descendants of Minto, Margaret, and Hester, three of Muhammad Bilali's daughters. They included Hester's son, Bilally Smith, and his wife Hagar, and Minto's four sons, Liberty, Bilally, Fortune, and Abram. All had been Kenan plantation slaves. Freedmen's Bureau records show that John Williams was also awarded land at Hanging Bull and that Jack Hillery received twenty acres on "R. Spaulding [sic] P'n, South End." Other freedmen were given plots all over the island.

By June 16, 1865, Campbell was able to report that he had settled 317 former slaves at St. Catherines Island and 312 at Sapelo.[3] Some of

Sapelo's slaves who had remained on the island during the war were already working their own farm plots in response to Sherman's directive. In the late summer of 1865, Freedmen's Bureau agent W. F. Eaton reported that of the 352 freed people on Sapelo, well over half were either self-sustaining or nearly so by farming on their granted land. Over one hundred new arrivals needed assistance. They were gradually adjusting to their first taste of freedom and self-sufficiency.

The land redistribution was not to last, however. President Andrew Johnson issued an amnesty proclamation in late May 1865, with updated provisions throughout the summer that stipulated that Confederate pardons included the return of abandoned and redistributed lands. In March 1866 Sherman's directive was rescinded by U.S. military authorities, enabling the restoration of the sea islands to their prewar owners.[4] Sapelo's freed blacks were, unsurprisingly, reluctant to relinquish any of the island to its prewar owners, even refusing McIntosh County Freedmen's Bureau agent Allen G. Bass admittance to Sapelo—Bass being the wartime plantation overseer and the brother of Randolph Spalding's widow, Mary B. Spalding.

The population distribution of slaves before the war and freed slaves after the war was fairly consistent. The 1860 census listed 370 slaves on Sapelo Island. The 352 freed people in 1865 were enumerated in sections that corresponded to the prewar settlements: 130 in twenty-four dwellings at South End (Thomas Spalding, grandson of Thomas Spalding), 100 at Kenan Place (Michael J. Kenan), and 122 at Chocolate and Bourbon (Randolph Spalding estate). Before, during, and immediately after the war there were settlements at South End, including Shell Hammock, New Barn Creek (Bush Camp Field), Behavior, Hog Hammock, Drink Water and Riverside, Kenan or Middle Place (including Hanging Bull and Lumber Landing), and at North End, including Chocolate, Bourbon, and later Moses Hammock, Belle Marsh, and Raccoon Bluff.

Eaton's September 1865 report to the Freedmen's Bureau documented sixty acres under cultivation on the South End, with "2 dwellings, 22 Miserable Cabins, 130 Freedmen self-sustaining on Spalding's Place. They have raised good crops of corn & cotton."

On the former Kenan plantation one hundred acres were under cultivation, with another seventy-five acres being planted on Randolph Spalding's North End, primarily at Chocolate and Bourbon. The report noted that of the nine hundred acres of Samuel Street (Raccoon Bluff), five hundred acres were cleared but none were under cultivation, and that one hundred acres of Randolph Spalding high land on Little Sapelo Island were cleared.[5] By December, Eaton reported that most of the freed

Boys on oxcart at Long Tabby, 1920s.
(Courtesy of Bill Jones III)

people were self-reliant, having "raised enough produce to supply themselves almost wholly."

When Sapelo was restored to its prewar owners by the federal government, a large number of the black settlers elected to relocate to the mainland. Unprincipled opportunists began to make their appearance about this time, often with unpleasant results for the freed people. In early 1866, two white speculators, S. D. Dickson and his partner, a man named McBride, leased Sapelo Island's South End from the Randolph Spalding estate for $2,500 a year. Dickson offered Sapelo's freed people liberal terms (two-thirds of the crop) to return to the cotton fields, but most were justifiably reluctant to work for whites. Those who did sign contracts were grossly short-changed to the point of abuse, as Dickson and McBride reneged on the original agreement and "did not fulfill the generous terms they had originally offered."[6]

When Dickson and McBride opened a "company store" on Sapelo whereby the freed people could obtain supplies and tools on credit, additional fraud and speculation occurred. Dickson and McBride continued to take advantage of the sharecroppers, cheating them of their earnings from their crops. Toby Maxwell was a Sapelo freedman who contracted to sell his cotton to the speculators' store. He reported

Two Sapelo children, 1920s.
(Courtesy of Bill Jones III)

that Dickson and McBride "stole everything the col[ored] men made & that this stealing and outrage was done by the direction of Genl [Davis] Tillson." The freed people eventually asserted their independence, refusing further contract labor in the fields. "McBride and Dickson fade from the record . . . the [Freedmen's Bureau] could not persuade black farmers to work for the two."[7]

Meanwhile, Tunis Campbell displayed a propensity for exceeding the limits of his authority and by the end of 1866 was no longer associated with the Freedmen's Bureau. He remained on St. Catherines, however, and continued to make regular trips to neighboring Sapelo to counsel the former slaves.

In late 1866, Davis Tillson, Freedmen's Bureau agent for coastal Georgia who had advocated restoration of the Georgia islands to their prewar owners, issued an order that "the Rev'd Tunis G. Campbell, late agent of this Bureau, having been found guilty of dishonest practices [allegedly granting or opposing contracts and selling timber to steamboats] . . . and there being good reason to believe that he is advising the freed people on Sapelo Island to pursue a course unjust to their employers, and injurious to themselves, is hereby forbidden to visit Sapelo Island on pain of being arrested."[8] Campbell was later evicted from St. Catherines, following which he leased the Belleville plantation in McIntosh County.

During this period there were efforts to provide education for the Sapelo freed people. In June 1865, Campbell reported that sixty children were being taught at a school on the island.[9] Some were descendants of Muhammad Bilali, Sapelo's first educated black. Among the first students was Liberty Bell, Bilali's adult grandson. In 1866, Campbell notified the American Missionary Association of the need for additional schools at Sapelo. Largely supported by New England churches, this organization laid a foundation for educating freed children in the South.

In 1868, the Freedmen's Bureau appointed a thirty-two-year-old black Savannah schoolteacher, Hettie Sabattie, to organize classes in Darien. Correspondence between Sabattie and her supervisor reveals that a school for black children was in session on the South End of Sapelo Island in the winter of 1869 under the aegis of the Missionary Association.[10]

Whether the Sun Shine School, as it was called, was the same school earlier established by Campbell is unclear. A year later the teacher at the Sun Shine School, Anthony Wilson, reported that he had twenty-three students, and some were paying tuition. Four students were white, the children of Thomas and Jane Herow.[11]

The 1870 census listed sixty students among the 334 people, black and white, living on Sapelo Island. Only four of the male heads of household among the island's fifty-nine families were shown as being literate. Families with schoolchildren included those of Fortune and Phoebe Bell, Abram and Nancy Bell, and Sampson and Sally Hogg. There were several adult freedmen taking classes as well, thirty-seven-year-old Peter Maxwell and twenty-six-year-old James Walker, both farmers, and forty-eight-year-old John Lemon.

There was possibly a one-room school at Raccoon Bluff as early as 1875 in response to the gradual transition of Geechee residents into the new community.[12] Whether there were one or two schools in the 1870s, educational progress continued to be made. By 1878 there were 139 Sapelo children being schooled, four of them white. By the early 1880s, the children of Sapelo's first blacks to be educated in the 1860s were themselves in school—for example, Margaret and Thomas Bell, the children of Scipio Bell, who as a teenager had studied on the island just after the war.

The foregoing demonstrates that during the postwar Reconstruction and after, important and substantive changes in the dynamics of settlement, land acquisition, and education were made in relation to the Sapelo freed people. Of greatest significance was the beginning and continued steady growth of black landownership on the island. Few other places in tidewater Georgia during the period saw such a pronounced evolution of black land acquisition and community development as at Sapelo.

These sharply defined patterns of property ownership and settlement on Sapelo occurred partly in response to successive cycles of economic and cultural adaptation. Concomitant with the development of their localized, often collectivistic, subsistence agriculture, the solidification of religious, social, and family-centric activities in tandem with the island's isolation enabled Sapelo's saltwater Geechees to achieve an unusually high sense of community cohesiveness. Later in the period there developed additional avenues of livelihood for Sapelo's people, ones extraneous to farming. For example, in the late nineteenth and early twentieth centuries, work in the local timber industry, cattle raising, and seafood harvesting supplemented (but did not supplant) agriculture.

Until Reconstruction, landownership on Sapelo Island had been associated with only three families. From 1870 on, however, black property acquisition and community

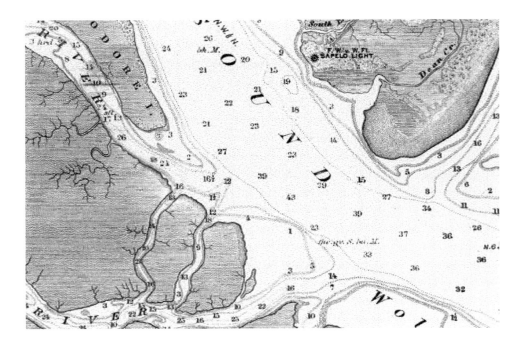

Map of Lower Doboy Sound in 1875, with the southern tip of Sapelo Island at top. (Author's collection)

development in various sections of the island were impelled both by the desire for self-sufficiency by the freed people and the necessity for prewar landowners—primarily the Spaldings and Streets—to divest themselves of their Sapelo land to alleviate financial pressures.

Freed blacks, individually and in groups, built homes, farmed, and established settlements through purchases of small tracts of acreage amid the former Spalding plantations and the Street family's Raccoon Bluff tract. In 1870, there were 130 African American families on Sapelo, many of them farming 502 cleared acres at the South End, Chocolate, and Bourbon. Seventy-three bales of cotton were marketed from Sapelo in the 1869 harvesting season. The residential distribution of families in 1870 was largely at Behavior, Hog Hammock, South End, Hanging Bull, and Chocolate.[13]

During the century after the Civil War, Sapelo's population, mostly African American freed people and their descendants, fluctuated between 250 and a high of over 500 in the early twentieth century. Many were engaged in lumbering, agriculture, and commercial fishing, and they resided in several island settlements, the largest of which were Raccoon Bluff on the North End and Hog Hammock on the South End.

A Sapelo woman with her child, pounding rice at Long Tabby, 1920s. (Courtesy of Bill Jones III)

The 1870 census enumerated the names of the Sapelo freed people, many of whom had been among the island's enslaved people less than a decade earlier. A sampling of these included Bilally Bell, Fortune and Phoebe Bell, Abram and Nancy Bell, Minto Bell, Hester Smith, Bilally and Hagar Smith, Allen and Phoebe Smith, Liberty Bell, Sampson and Sally Hogg, James Lemon, John Lemon, Thomas Bailey, Mack Handy, George Handy, John Grovner, Peter Maxwell, Samuel Roberts, March and Fanny Carter, Prince Carter, John Lemon, Cuffie Wilson, Sampson Bailey, Charles Walker, James Walker, Benjamin Wilson, Sampson and Margaret Hillery, Carolina and Hannah Underwood, Harry Sams, Sylvia Roberts, Flora Barnett, Hercules Bennett, Thomas Mills, Fergus Wilson, Yuamina Johnson, Jack Hillery, John Williams, Toby Maxwell, William Hillery, and March Jackson.

A patchwork of settlements evolved on Sapelo. At times there were as many as fifteen Geechee communities on the island, some with as few as two or three families. In addition to Hog Hammock and Raccoon Bluff, there were Shell Hammock, Behavior/Bush Camp Field, Riverside, Lumber Landing, Belle Marsh, Bourbon, Drink Water, Hanging Bull, Jack's Hammock, Mary's Hammock, Moses Hammock, King Savannah, and Chocolate.[14]

Sapelo's population patterns after 1865 may be deduced by tracking federal census and local records. In 1873, church records indicate that there were 141 members of the First African Baptist Church at Hanging Bull. By 1904, there were 196 members of the same church, which had moved to Raccoon Bluff. The same year there were seventy-four congregants of the St. Luke's African Baptist Church at Hog Hammock. This would suggest a Geechee population on Sapelo of over four hundred residents around the turn of the century, mostly at Raccoon Bluff and Hog Hammock.[15]

The abuse of the freed people by speculators and other outsiders in the first three years of Reconstruction had mostly ended when the Spalding heirs returned to reclaim Sapelo's South End and Kenan Field.

The Spalding Family

A significant development was the sale in 1866 of sixty-nine hundred acres on the North End for $56,000 by Mary Bass Spalding to John N. A. Griswold of New York City and Newport, Rhode Island. Griswold (1821–1909) also purchased the Couper plantation at Cannon's Point on St. Simons Island. Although rarely visiting Sapelo during his brief ownership, Griswold built a house at High Point, possibly using as foundations tabby brought from Chocolate.[16]

In 1873, Griswold sold the North End to one of his creditors, James E. Cassin of New York, for $65,000. The transaction included "all those three small islands or Hammocks attached to Little Sapelo Island, called respectively Jacks Hammock, Mary's Hammock and Pumpkin Hammock formerly of the Plantation of the late Randolph Spalding."[17]

Cassin lost the North End in an 1879 foreclosure to Henry P. Townsend. In 1881, Townsend, a lawyer from New York City, sold the property to Amos Sawyer (1830–1913), a prominent manufacturer of bath and laundry soap from Northampton, Massachusetts. The sale by Townsend was apparently speculative in nature: he seems to have acquired the North End with notions of a profitable resale of the seven-thousand-acre tract. Amos Sawyer's interest in Sapelo, however, stemmed from a familial connection to the island. Sawyer's sister, Priscilla Flint Sawyer (1828–1910), was the second wife of David Crenshaw Barrow Sr. (1815–99) of Athens. She came to Georgia from Boston, and was music teacher and governess to the Barrow children prior to her marriage to the widower Barrow, whose first wife, Sarah Pope Barrow, had died in 1855. Priscilla Sawyer was a graduate of the Boston Academy of Music, founded in 1833 by Lowell Mason, who early in his career was composer and musician of the Independent Presbyterian Church of Savannah. The Barrow family was allied to the Spalding family through marriage: D. C. Barrow's daughter by his first marriage was Ella Patience Barrow Spalding, wife of Thomas Bourke Spalding of Sapelo Island. While he never resided at Sapelo, Amos Sawyer and his family occasionally vacationed on the island, presumably utilizing the High Point house built earlier by Griswold. In 1883, Sawyer hired Arthur A. Loomis (1851–85) of Holyoke, Massachusetts (near Sawyer's home of Northampton), to be the resident caretaker for his holdings on Sapelo's North End. Loomis's wife, Lydia Abbott Loomis, was Sawyer's niece, and she, her husband, and their three children lived on Sapelo for two years until November 1885 when Loomis stepped on a nail and developed lockjaw. He died six weeks later in a Savannah hospital, and his surviving family returned to Massachusetts.[18]

During the restoration of lands to their prewar owners, Thomas Spalding's son Charles H. Spalding, uncle of Thomas Spalding II (eldest son of Randolph and Mary Spalding), successfully negotiated for the return of the South End land that had been willed to his nephew by the latter's grandfather. This order came on December 6,

1867, shortly before the younger Spalding (1847–85) attained his legal majority age of twenty-one.[19] In early 1868 Thomas Spalding II took possession of the reclaimed South End and moved to the island to live, and his brother, Thomas Bourke Spalding (1851–84), known as Bourke, received title to Little Sapelo Island from his mother. In 1874, Bourke Spalding married Ella Barrow (1849–1929), daughter of David C. Barrow Sr. and a cousin of the McKinleys of Baldwin County. The two brothers and their sister, Sarah (Sallie) McKinley, eventually settled on different tracts on the South End, Thomas near South End Creek, Bourke at Marsh Landing, and Sallie at Riverside (Long Tabby).

In 1866, Sallie Spalding (1844–1916) had married Archibald C. McKinley (1842–1917) of Milledgeville, and then in 1871 McKinley's sister, Sarah Barrow McKinley (1847–97), married Thomas Spalding II. Thomas initially restored his grandfather's sugarhouse at Long Tabby as a residence before moving in 1877 to his new cottage built at South End Creek near the abandoned mansion. After the death of her husband, Sarah McKinley Spalding, who later married William C. Wylly, continued to live in that residence until her death in 1897. Bourke and Ella Spalding lived at Riverside (York Landing) near the Long Tabby on Barn Creek, from 1874 to 1882, after which they bought the Marsh Landing tract from Thomas Spalding II and built a home there overlooking the Duplin River. Bourke Spalding's Riverside property was later acquired by his in-laws, the Barrows.

Also at Riverside was a friend of the Spaldings and McKinleys, William Nightingale, who acquired the Long Tabby after Thomas Spalding moved to South End in 1877. The Long Tabby tract was later acquired by the Treanor family, related to the Spaldings by marriage. A. C. and Sallie McKinley built a home overlooking Barn Creek a short distance south of the Long Tabby. This aggregation of intermarried families in the southwestern section of Sapelo became known as the Barn Creek Colony.

Further north at Kenan Field was Spalding Kenan (1836–1907), son of Michael and Catherine Spalding Kenan. Kenan came to Sapelo in 1871, purchasing his parents' tract a year later. A doctor and surgeon, Kenan moved around 1880 to Darien where he practiced medicine and served several terms as mayor. Also at the Duplin River house in the early 1870s were the caretakers, Lewis and Elizabeth Bass Livingston of Columbus, Georgia, and their son, Charles Lewis Livingston. Elizabeth Livingston was the sister of Mary Bass Spalding, widow of Randolph. The Livingstons' daughter, Evelyn Elizabeth Livingston (1836–94), married Spalding Kenan. The Kenans and the Livingstons frequently interacted with their Sapelo relatives at Barn Creek.

The 1870 census listed only a few white residents on Sapelo Island, including Thomas and Bourke Spalding, their sister and brother-in-law (the McKinleys), their mother, Mary Bass Spalding (1823–98), and her brother Allen G. Bass (1814–84) and his son, Charles L. Bass (1853–1919). The census listed Thomas Spalding as holding Sapelo land valued at $33,000. Other whites on the island were James Thompson, a farmer leasing Spalding land, and his wife; and George W. Kinsbury, who lived in the Thompson household. Also on the South End were Thomas Herow, a ship's carpenter; John Smith, a bar pilot; and James C. Clarke and Montgomery Styles, the lighthouse keepers.[20]

During Reconstruction, the Spalding brothers and their brother-in-law A. C. McKinley used Sapelo's resources to engage in several profitable ventures. In late 1870, Griswold rented sections of the North End to McKinley, who planted cotton and subleased land to black tenant farmers. The latter paid rent that year in shares equal to over sixty-four hundred pounds of harvested cotton at Bourbon, Dumoussay Field, and Drism Point near Raccoon Bluff. McKinley and his brothers-in-law later stocked the island in cattle and made contracts for supplying fresh beef to the sailing vessels frequenting Doboy Sound to load pine timber and processed lumber brought out from the Darien sawmills. In September 1874 the men invested in a small steamboat to transport their beef from Sapelo to Doboy Island.[21]

The Sapelo Journal of A. C. McKinley

From 1869 to 1876, Archibald McKinley kept a daily journal during his residence on Sapelo Island. Following are some of the most interesting entries as they pertain to life on the island during Reconstruction. The entries reflect the activities of McKinley and his brothers-in-law, Thomas and Bourke Spalding, pursuant to the leasing of cotton lands to Sapelo's freedmen and the stocking of cattle on the island for the sale of fresh beef to shipping in the local harbor. There are also some references to interaction between the Spalding descendants and Sapelo's freed people.

September 21, 1869. Met Tom & Bourke in Savannah & left with them on the Steamboat *Nick King* for Sapelo. Went outside where the sea was rather rough, making a good many passengers sea-sick. Arrived at the North end of Sapelo Island about 4 o'clock, where we left the boat & went to Mrs. M. J. Kenan's place. [NOTE—"Mrs. M. J. Kenan" was Catherine Spalding Kenan (1810–81), paternal aunt of Tom, Bourke, and Sallie Spalding McKinley].

September 29, 1869. We all went out to the Beach. Surf very rough with N.E. wind. Afterwards went to the South End to see Baba & to see the live oak grove there which is truly grand. [NOTE—"Baba" was a nickname for Betsy Beagle (1796–1890), former Spalding slave and nursemaid to two generations of Spalding children.]

June 21, 1870. Jno. Frazier, a Scotch boy aged 17 and in Tom's employ, shot a negro man today on Sapelo with 12 buckshot. He is not dead yet. Negroes excited.

June 22, 1870. Jno. Frazier was arrested last night & taken to jail in Darien.

July 26, 1870. This morning Dr. Holmes lanced my finger—making an incision about 1 inch long diagonally across the inside of my finger—cutting to the bone. The pain was the most

Archibald C. McKinley.
(Author's collection)

intense I have ever suffered in my life. The doctor thinks the swelling is caused by a spider bite. [NOTE—Dr. James Holmes (1804–83) was a Darien physician for over fifty years.]

November 2, 1870. Hired a negro girl named Sarah Hillery at $2 for the first month, $3 afterward.

November 3, 1870. Sallie, Bourke & I rode up to the extreme north end of Sapelo to look at the house which Mr. [John] Griswold offers to rent me. Very much pleased with it. This view is truly magnificent overlooking Sapelo Sound. While there the steamer *Eliza Hancox* passed with Mrs. Spalding & Tom aboard returning from Savannah.

March 22, 1871. We got today from Creighton Island a boatload of sugar cane which Col. [Charles] Spalding gave us for seed.

November 6, 1871. Went with Bourke to Bourbon, McCloy [Dumoussay Field] & Drisden Point [Raccoon Bluff] to get the amount of land planted there. The rent on these fields amounts to 3213 lbs of seed cotton.

November 25, 1871. Hauled 1284 lbs. cotton from Moses Hammock—this making 6444 lbs rent cotton received thus far from the North end.

January 5, 1872. Bourke & I went to Darien in the sailboat—got becalmed and didn't get there for seven hours. Brought Mr. R. L. Morris, who was drunk, as far as Myhall Mill on our way back. [NOTE—Richard L. Morris (1818–85) was a Darien rice planter at Cathead Creek. "Myhall Mill" refers to a sawmill on Mayhall Island on the Darien River, three miles east of Darien.]

February 12, 1872. Started splitting rails to make a calf-pen in Oakdale. Caesar Sams paid his last year's rent (fifty dollars) for Jack's Hammock today.

February 26, 1872. At work again on our pasture fence. We dug 135 post holes, that putting us within 70 feet of New Orleans creek. Hauled 30 posts.

March 1, 1872. We started for the Ridge shortly after daylight. We had a pleasant sail but on our way back a wind & rain squall struck us off Heard's Island and we stopped there all night with Capt. Aiken. [NOTE—Isaac Means Aiken (1830–1907) was a native South Carolinian and proprietor of the Hird Island sawmill near the Ridge.]

March 5, 1872. Rode up to Moses Hammock this morning to get a bag of shot left there. Sampson Hillery, an old Negro man aged 96 years, died to-day.

March 13, 1872. Spalding Kenan came back & went to Doboy to take the *Lizzie Baker*. I have been busy building a fence across Hog Hammock marsh where I killed two rattle-snakes.

March 21, 1872. We hauled two loads of lumber from the house to the new fence. Bourke & Charlie [Bass] have gone to Doboy to meet Tom who is expected on the *Lizzie Baker*. Yesterday we put six of our hogs on Little Sapelo.

May 16, 1873. This evening we all three went to Doboy to try to raise a loan to enable us to carry on the cattle business, but were unsuccessful.

June 8, 1873. Last night old Carolina's house caught fire & came very near burning the old negros (himself & wife) up as neither one could walk. The house burnt down, though they were saved, being burnt very serious however. [NOTE—Carolina Underwood (ca. 1780–1873) and his wife Hannah, both former Spalding slaves, lived at New Barn Creek, near Behavior. They both died soon after the fire.]

December 19, 1873. We at last got our flat afloat & off for Darien alongside the tug. Driving and flatting the cattle to the Island has been altogether the most exhausting & tiresome work I ever did in my life.

June 30, 1874. I took beef to High Point. Hear to-day that the steamer *Clyde* was capsized & wrecked in Sapelo Sound by the heavy blow on the 27th inst. [NOTE—On June 27, 1874, the *Clyde* was struck by a sudden squall while crossing the exposed waters of the sound between St. Catherines and Sapelo Islands. Despite the capsizing of the vessel, the crew and passengers were saved, with no loss of life.]

August 15, 1874. On getting up this morning I saw out on the quarantine ground a full-rigged ship which I afterward heard was a ship bound from Havana to New Brunswick & put in here last night in distress with yellow fever aboard. Capt. & first mate dead and others sick. [NOTE—The ship *William Wilcox* bound in ballast from Havana to Boston entered Doboy Sound on August 15, 1874, with yellow fever aboard, and was immediately confined to quarantine off Queen's Island near the sound's entrance. The port physician, Dr. J. B. L. Baker, treated the sick; the vessel, with its surviving crew, resumed its voyage several weeks later.]

March 26, 1875. Had to go to King Savannah for beef. Killed two of them.

April 30, 1875. Old T. G. Campbell, a notorious negro, was again indicted for false imprisonment to-day. When the Sheriff attempted to carry him to jail, he was prevented from doing so by a mob of furious negroes who fired into the posse. Several on both sides were shot, but none seriously. Altogether however there is an ugly state of affairs in this County. [NOTE— Tunis G. Campbell (1812–91) was a New Jersey–born African American, former Freedmen's Bureau agent, and state senator from McIntosh County during Reconstruction. His political dynasty from 1868 to 1876 was supported by a large black coalition in Darien. He was indicted for corruption, sentenced to a year in the state penitentiary, and released in January 1877.]

February 10, 1877. Find our steamer sunk half-way to her smokestack at high water. I sold my interest in her tonight to Bourke Spalding for 15 dry cows payable 1st January 1879.

February 12, 1877. Wind blowing tremendously high. Bourke carried the beef on shortened sail. After getting to Doboy though, it was blowing too hard for him to beat back. A tug towed him to the Lighthouse and he rowed up South End Creek.

April 1, 1877. Sister Sarah's 30th birthday. All hands rode down to the South end this afternoon to look at her new home in the Grove. [NOTE—The reference is to Sarah McKinley Spalding, wife of Thomas Spalding II. The Spaldings' new house was near the abandoned mansion of Thomas's grandfather.]

SOURCES: A. C. McKinley journal (copy), Buddy Sullivan Papers, Collection 2433, Georgia Historical Society, Savannah; *Darien Timber Gazette*, various issues, 1874–75.

Doboy Sound was quite active in the 1860s and 1870s. The Hilton Lumber Company had a sawmill, store, and housing for black stevedores at Doboy, and the small island was a regular stop on the inland waterway for steamboats transporting passengers, mail, and freight. McKinley and the Spaldings formed friendships with the masters and crew of ships from the British Isles, Germany, Scandinavia, and the U.S. Northeast, all converging to load timber. The Sapelo men also became associated with the bar pilots, who had a dock for their fast-sailing pilot boats near the lighthouse on South End Creek, from which they met the ships offshore to guide them into the harbor.[22]

McKinley's 1869–76 journal (see box, p. 188) related the vicissitudes of Reconstruction life at Sapelo from the perspective of one of the few white residents but offered little about white interactions with the several hundred freed people then developing their settlements on the island. Nonetheless, a unique picture of postbellum tidewater life emerges from the pages of the journal, in which one reads of McKinley frequently rowing an open boat from Sapelo to Darien as he employed the flooding tide to impel his progress on the twelve-mile route. Colorful descriptions are recounted of shipwrecks and storms at sea, and a yellow fever outbreak in Doboy Sound in the summer of 1874 is described. The white families regularly attended funerals, often for people who had died of illnesses that would later be considered relatively minor and curable. In postscripts, McKinley described the unsettling sensations

The Darien waterfront in an 1874 photograph. The town was burned by Union forces in 1863 but quickly rebuilt after the war to become the leading pine timber exporter on the south Atlantic coast. (Author's collection)

Timber ships in Doboy Sound, circa 1885. Sapelo Island is in the distance. (Author's collection)

felt at Sapelo during the Charleston-centered earthquake in September 1886 and the October 1898 hurricane.

In September 1884, Bourke Spalding, thirty-three, was killed by the accidental discharge of his shotgun while hunting deer on Sapelo. A few months later, in January 1885, his thirty-seven-year-old brother Thomas died in Macon in a railroad accident, being crushed between cars at the station as he was about to return to the coast. Thomas left no children.[23]

After the death of her husband, Ella Barrow Spalding and their only child, Randolph (a second child, Clara Lucy, born on Sapelo in 1881, died at the age of six months, left Marsh Landing to live in Athens with her father, David Barrow Sr. In 1891, Ella and Randolph returned to Marsh Landing with her father and stepmother, living there until 1897. Years later, Randolph Spalding (1879–1954) of Savannah donated Spalding family memorabilia to the Georgia Historical Society, including the family Bible and the only known portrait of Thomas Spalding, his great-grandfather. He never married and was the last of the line of Georgia Spaldings descended from James Spalding.

Lighthouse keepers Clarke and Styles are mentioned above. The circular, brick, fourth-order lighthouse built in 1819–20, was inactive in the Civil War, being used as an observation tower by Union naval personnel scouting for Confederate blockade runners. ("Fourth-order" denotes the degree of illumination, or candlepower, of the light, the largest being a first-order light, such as Cape Hatteras or Tybee Island.) In 1868 the light was reactivated by the federal Lighthouse Service in response to increasing amounts of shipping in Doboy Sound. The lighthouse tract was originally a small island separated from Sapelo itself by marsh and South End Creek. The 1868 U.S. Coast Survey topographic map *Doboy Sound and Vicinity* shows a straight-line plank walk or causeway paralleling the creek through the marsh, linking the South End with the lighthouse island. No trace of this causeway remains today.[24]

In January 1873, a native Irishman, James Cromley, was appointed keeper of the light at an annual salary of $600, becoming the first of three generations of his family to serve in that capacity at Sapelo. James Cromley served as head keeper until 1889, with his son William serving from 1890 to 1900, followed by James (Jimmy) Cromley Jr., who was appointed keeper in 1900. Robert H. Cromley became assistant keeper in 1912 and later served as the last keeper of the light up to its 1933 deactivation.

Ship loading timber through its bow, at Hazzard's Island near Sapelo Sound, circa 1890. (Author's collection)

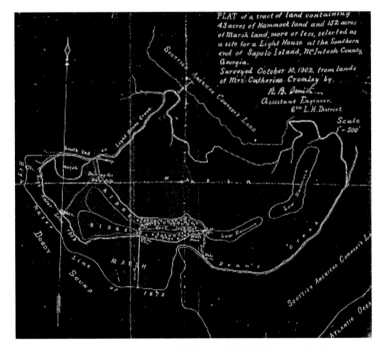

Federal government survey plat of the Sapelo lighthouse island, 1902, pursuant to the building of a new tower three years later. (Author's collection)

About six hundred feet east of the tower, a cast-iron range beacon was constructed in 1877 to implement navigational triangulation with the main light and the Wolf Island beacon across the sound.[25] In 1875, Thomas Spalding II deeded several acres of land on the lighthouse island to Catherine Cromley (for her husband, James Sr.) for $200.[26] The same year, Spalding sold four acres along Dean's Creek adjacent to the lighthouse tract to James Dean for $100.[27] Dean (1829–1903) was a registered bar pilot who lived at the Ridge near Darien and operated his pilot boat *Young America* from South End Creek near the lighthouse.

Erosion of the lighthouse foundation caused by the October 1898 hurricane compelled the Lighthouse Service to survey the tract in 1902 pursuant to the construction of a new tower farther away from the waters of Doboy Sound. The survey determined that the lighthouse island comprised "43 acres of Hammock land, and 152 acres of Marsh . . . bordered on the West by South End, or Light House Creek" and on the east by Dean's Creek. Shown on the plat are the brick tower, a "Boring for New Site" north of the existing tower, and "Dean's house" eastward on the adjoining hammock.[28] The Cromleys sold the lighthouse island to the federal government in 1904. A third-order hundred-foot steel pyramidal lighthouse, with two attached keepers' houses, was completed in September 1905 several hundred feet north of the deactivated brick tower.

As a sideline to supplement their government income, the Cromley men hunted rattlesnakes on Sapelo for profit, as noted in this account published in the *Atlanta Constitution*:

It is a dangerous and exciting sport to accompany the Cromleys on one of their rattlesnake hunts. They find a monster rattlesnake of seven feet long and as large as a man's thigh and by means of a long stick, they drop the looped end of a stout cord over the coiling serpent's head. The other end of the cord is thrown over a tree limb and the men pull the snake up from the ground and let him hang by the neck till dead. By catching these snakes in this way the men are enabled to obtain their skins, unbroken by shot, and unspoiled by the deadly discoloring poison which they will inject from their fangs into their own bodies when maddened by desperation. These snake hunters claim that rattlers are the only venomous species of reptile on the coast. I have seen them pick up other kinds of live snakes from out of the grass with their hands.[29]

A romanticized picture of life for the white residents of Sapelo in the late nineteenth century emerges from an August 1914 letter from Ella Barrow Spalding to Charles Spalding Wylly. It depicts a tidewater life that, while occasionally fraught with uncertainties, also had its idyllic aspects:

My first acquaintance with the dear and beautiful place was in 1870 . . . we went on a maroon to Sapelo, a very delightful experience for a girl from the up-country. Mr. Alex C. Wylly and Thomas Spalding were living at the Kenan place and were our hosts. . . . In January 1871, Thomas Spalding was married to Miss Sarah McKinley . . . and all the family moved to the Cassin house [at High Point] and lived there until the winter of 1871–72, in the meantime making the Long Tabby into a most comfortable dwelling. . . . In November 1874, I was married to Thomas Bourke Spalding . . . we lived about as far on the west [north] side of the Long Tabby as the McKinleys lived on the east [south]. . . . At that time, the three families lived almost in sight of each other on the shores of Barn Creek, a beautiful salt water tributary to the Duplin River. . . . And the view! One could sit on the piazza and there in front ran the creek, beyond for miles the ever-beautiful marsh, over there lay Little Sapelo, and beyond the marsh was Doboy Sound, ever changing, ever beautiful. Across it one could see Doboy Island, Cain Creek, and then afar, the dim coast line, a long low reach of palm and pine. It was very lovely, most of the time calm and peaceful. . . . At that time Doboy was a great shipping port for yellow pine. I have seen ships lying in Doboy Sound four deep at the wharves . . . not coastwise schooners, but big square-riggers of every nationality. . . . There was a big sawmill on Doboy and one on Cain Creek where the logs were "squared" before loading. . . . My husband, seeing the opportunity, bought cattle to raise beef for the shipping. At first he was alone in the enterprise but later his brother and brother-in-law desired to join, forming a company. They bought a little steamboat for delivering the beef, and to carry the captains to Darien for business or pleasure. But the forests were cut away, the bar filled up and the end had come for Doboy . . . the Long Tabby changed hands several times. Mr. William Nightingale bought the place and lived there a year or two but gave it up, and afterward, Mr. William Wylly rented it. His sister lived with him. Mrs. Kate Treanor, a niece of Mrs. Thomas Spalding [II] and of Mr. McKinley, bought and made the

Long Tabby her home for several years. . . . All our friends loved Sapelo . . . The most exciting adventure upon which we sallied was to watch the Cromleys catch rattlesnakes. This horribly fascinating pursuit was followed only in winter when the snakes were torpid and lay in their dens. . . . We grew older presently . . . Mrs. Spalding and I left the island—my son and I in the fall of 1884, she in the spring of 1885.[30]

Raccoon Bluff and the North End

The most prominent land acquisitions by the Sapelo freed people occurred on the North End in the 1870s and 1880s. Starting in 1871, several North End tracts were sold by their white owners to those who had been in bondage a decade earlier. In November 1885, Amos Sawyer sold a fifty-acre parcel on the west side of the island south of Chocolate to Joseph Jones, whose descendants were the Walker family. This became the Belle Marsh settlement. Sawyer sold two other tracts that year, one to Caesar Sams near Kenan Field and the other to James Green north of Raccoon Bluff. The latter tract reverted back to Sawyer in 1890.[31]

In the early Reconstruction period, Raccoon Bluff (Street Place) was owned by the heirs of George Street, including an undivided half-interest in the tract held by Samuel Street. In 1871, Hugh M. Street of Prentiss County, Mississippi, sold the family's consolidated holdings of almost one thousand acres at Raccoon Bluff to a partnership of freedmen, William Hillery and Company. This tract was the first large aggregation of black-owned property on Sapelo Island.

The investors' intent was to establish organized farming operations as Raccoon Bluff had convenient access for the shipment of agricultural commodities via Blackbeard Creek. Hillery, a former Sapelo slave, formed the company with two other freedmen, John Grovner and Bilally Bell, with whom he bought the land jointly for $2,000, with a $500 down payment and a loan repayment arrangement for the balance. The three partners retained 111 acres each for themselves, and divided the other 666 acres of the tract into twenty lots of approximately thirty-three acres each.[32] The Raccoon Bluff lots were all long and narrow, most leading from the interior near the road down to Blackbeard Creek.[33]

A settlement developed at the Bluff, gradually becoming the largest Geechee community on Sapelo. Some of the earliest settlers on land sold by the Hillery Company were Sampson Hogg and his family, who moved from Hog Hammock, along with the

Little remains of the once-thriving settlement of Raccoon Bluff, begun in the 1870s amid the pine flats and saw palmetto on the east side of Sapelo.

Transit between Raccoon Bluff and Hog Hammock, 1920s. (Courtesy of Bill Jones III)

Baileys, Walkers, Halls, and Grovners. Soon after, the Bells, Spauldings, Greens, and Lemons joined them.[34]

The 1880 federal census indicated the rapid growth of the Hillery Company's venture. By then, sixteen freedmen owned property at Raccoon Bluff, while another twenty-two were leasing farmland.[35] The rental properties were likely based on payments that accrued toward the purchase of the property from the company. After investigating surviving documents, William McFeely noted that he "could find no record of the long-term successful marketing of money crops [at Raccoon Bluff] . . . . It was as if Sapelo, having expelled the money-makers, wouldn't allow what the rest of America thought of as the right kind of entrepreneurship to take hold on its sacred sand . . . As her people somehow understand, you do with her only what she has to offer—her oysters, her trees for lumbering. And her demands for respect."[36]

Across the island at Hanging Bull, Abram and Bilally Bell, sons of Minto Bell and grandsons of Muhammad Bilali, organized the First African Baptist (F.A.B.) Church in May 1866. The church had 141 congregants by 1873. Possibly due to the increasing size of the church, the Second African Baptist Church was organized in 1884 and established at Hog Hammock. Damage from the 1898 hurricane compelled the relocation

A Geechee family on Sapelo Island, 1920s. (Courtesy of Bill Jones III)

to Raccoon Bluff of the F.A.B. Church and the remaining Hanging Bull population, largely completed by 1900. The new church at Raccoon Bluff was constructed in 1899.

Twentieth-century Sapelo residents told the story of the new church being constructed of lumber gathered from the marsh, timber that had been swept over to Sapelo from Blackbeard by the 1898 hurricane. This story has merit. The U.S. Marine Hospital Service's South Atlantic Quarantine Station on the south end of Blackbeard, almost directly across the marsh from Raccoon Bluff, included several wood-frame structures. The quarantine station, which operated from 1880 to 1909, was integral to the shipping then frequenting Sapelo Sound and was developed partly in response to the 1876 yellow fever epidemic that claimed 1,066 lives in Savannah.[37]

By 1910, the Geechee communities of Raccoon Bluff, Hog Hammock, Shell Hammock, Lumber Landing, and Belle Marsh were well established. The largest was Raccoon Bluff, where the census that year enumerated 194 persons residing in forty-three households. The 1910 census enumerated 163 persons in thirty-three homes at Hog Hammock, with 52 people in twelve households at Shell Hammock. Five households with 41 people were at Lumber Landing, and three more households were at Belle Marsh (the Walker and Jones families). There were single Geechee families at Chocolate and King Savannah. Sapelo had an African American population of 539 persons in 109 households in 1910, the peak population for blacks on the island, partly attributable to the active timber trade in Sapelo Sound.[38]

The lumbering activity centered at Darien from 1865 to 1916 saw ships using anchorages in Doboy and Sapelo Sounds to load yellow pine harvested in the Georgia interior and processed by McIntosh County sawmills, chiefly the Hilton-Lachlison-Dodge interests. Northern capital financed much of the activity after the war, and timber rafted down the Altamaha River was the lifeblood of the local economy for two generations.

The mills and the loading of timber and lumber on ships at both ends of Sapelo provided employment for many of Sapelo's Geechee residents. Until the mid-1880s timber loading was mostly in Doboy Sound, with mills at Doboy Island on the North River and nearby Rock Island. From 1889 to 1915 there were loading grounds near Sapelo's North End at Dog Hammock, Hazzard's Island, Front River, and Julianton River to accommodate domestic and international shipping. For fifty years, local African Americans were employed in this activity as stevedores, cutters, and sawmill operators in an industry that made Darien the leading exporter of pine timber on the southeast coast.

Sailing vessels, later steamships, called at local wharves to deposit rock ballast and load lumber at tiny Hazzard's Island (Hunter-Benn Company) at the juncture of Front River and Sapelo Sound and farther down Front River near the west side of Creighton Island at J. K. Clarke Company docks known for a time as "Sapelo, Ga.," for the post office there. There was an African American settlement on the north end of Creighton in the 1890s and early 1900s, housing Sapelo Sound timber loaders.

The 1900 census counted over one hundred persons, almost all African American, living at Creighton. At this time timber operations peaked for the Darien sawmills. It is likely that some of Sapelo Island's people employed in this activity lived there seasonally, October through March. There were a store and loading docks at Hazzard's and another store closer to the sound at Dog Hammock.

These and other sections along Front River, and at the disinfecting wharf on the north end of Blackbeard Island, were rock ballast deposit sites for European ships arriving to load lumber. This activity was heavily hit by the 1898 hurricane and tidal wave but recovered and continued until 1915.[39] A few of Sapelo's Raccoon Bluff residents earned money at the Blackbeard quarantine station. For example, Sophie Bell was employed as a laundress on Blackbeard Island in 1896, and members of the settlement often went by boat to the station to sell eggs, vegetables, and chickens.[40]

The wood frame African
American church built in
1899 at Raccoon Bluff is the
only remaining structure in
the former community.
It was restored in 2000.

Raccoon Bluff was an active agricultural community, engaged in both commercial and subsistence farming, with cotton, rice, and corn the most prominent crops at the turn of the century. The 1910 census listed occupations among Raccoon Bluff residents as farmer, farm laborer, sawmill laborer, longshoreman (timber stevedore), timber cutter, sawmill teamster, sawmill fireman, and oysterman.[41] Family surnames then included Bailey, Bell, Carter, Gardner, Green, Grovner, Hall, Handy, Hillery, Jackson, Johnson, Lotson, Lemon, Maxwell, Mills, Moore, Parker, Roberts, Spaulding, Smith, and Walker.

On the west side of Sapelo, the Kenan family never sold land to the freedmen after the Civil War. However, one community within the Kenan tract did continue until the 1890s, the former slave settlement at Hanging Bull, where there were dwellings built before the war.

Not long after his purchase of much of the North End in 1881, Amos Sawyer sold parcels of land to several African Americans. One of these transactions entailed a sixty-acre tract at Lumber Landing, which abutted the north section of Kenan Field near the Duplin River, sold in November 1881 to Caesar Sams (1844–1907). Over the ensuing three decades a settlement developed there, with a sawmill and timber dock eventually nearby. From a population of forty-one in 1910, Lumber Landing declined to a few families by the late 1920s, and the 1930 census counted only two households—those of Mattie Sams and Janie Sams. Most of the Lumber Landing tract remained in the Sams family until R. J. Reynolds Jr. acquired it in 1956.

Many of Sapelo Island's residents engaged in the commercial timber industry and fishing from the mid-1880s through the first three decades of the 1900s, and upper Kenan Field was a focal point. The sawmill and the oyster beds in the nearby Duplin River provided seasonal income during the winter. William C. Wylly operated an oyster cannery at Kenan Field in the late 1890s and early 1900s, providing employment for Sapelo's Geechee community.

There were other pockets of Geechee residents scattered about Sapelo. Several black families lived at Bourbon Field as sharecroppers in the 1880s and 1890s during the Sawyer era of North End ownership. These included Liberty Handy with his three sons, Manson, Abraham, and Edward, and two daughters, Carrie and Lilla, and the families of James Green and Billy Rankin. These were probably the last full-time residents to ever live on the Bourbon tract.

The 1910 census listed one African American family at Chocolate, possibly descendants of slaves who had worked the plantation there. On a canoe transit of the inland waterway in early 1875, Nathaniel Bishop briefly stopped at Sapelo Island and spent one night with a black family at Chocolate.[42] It may be that Jacob Green, aged sixty-two, who lived on the site with his wife Elisa in 1910, was descended from that family. Green continued to live at Chocolate during Howard Coffin's ownership. He farmed and likely worked for Coffin as a caretaker for the tract on which Coffin had restored the tabby barn and a former slave dwelling for use as a hunting lodge. The 1929 soil map of Sapelo notes two structures at Chocolate, one likely being the hunting lodge and the other possibly the Green residence in a restored slave dwelling.

Hog Hammock and the South End

Sapelo's South End was the most productive antebellum plantation on the island, with crops grown at Long Tabby, Root Patch, New Orleans, and Flora Bottom. Ex-slave settlements attached to these areas were at New Barn Creek (Bush Camp Field), Behavior, Hog Hammock, and near the Spalding house. The largest settlement was Behavior and New Barn Creek, two contiguous tracts east of Long Tabby close to the largest agricultural field on the island (the present air strip). Behavior was abandoned as a settlement by the late 1870s due to the growth of Hog Hammock and Raccoon Bluff. In the mid-1880s, Behavior became the island cemetery (see box, p. 204), with the earliest marked burials on the four-acre plot dated 1889 and 1890.

Considering the size of the Behavior settlement, archaeological investigation might identify the tract or a tract nearby as an antebellum slave burial ground. There was a slave cemetery not far from Behavior, at New Orleans, just southeast of Hog Hammock. It is likely this was the primary burial ground prior to the Civil War, but as of 2015, archaeological investigation has not discovered the location of the New Orleans cemetery. There may have also been a slave cemetery at Hanging Bull.[43]

Another Geechee settlement, not precisely located but thought to be in the southwestern part of Sapelo, was Drink Water. This name originates with a sea captain, Rotheus Drinkwater, who was peripherally associated with Sapelo before the Civil War. In a 1964 interview, Charles Hall Sr. (1874–1967) said that Drink Water was in the South End and Kenan Field area, where Liberty Bell and Sam Grovner lived after the Civil War.[44] Liberty Bell is listed in the McIntosh County censuses of 1870 and 1880, and he is thought to have lived near the white Spalding-McKinley residential section, thus possibly placing the Drink Water settlement somewhere in an area between Hanging Bull and Long Tabby (Riverside).

Praise house on Sapelo Island, circa 1938, photo by Malcolm and Muriel Bell. (Courtesy of Malcolm Bell III)

To offset financial encumbrances, Thomas Spalding II began selling pieces of his South End land to his brother and sister and members of the island's black community. McIntosh County deed records indicate the first sales of Spalding land to the freedmen as being May 10, 1878, in Hog Hammock, and September 19 that year for land in Shell Hammock, near the present Marine Institute. There were black residences and a praise house at Shell Hammock until the settlement was acquired by R. J. Reynolds Jr. in 1960 as part of his land exchanges with the island's residents.[45] Enslaved people lived at Hog Hammock before the Civil War, after which freed people further developed the community. Hall noted that Hog Hammock was named for his paternal grandfather, Sampson, who lived there as a slave and adopted the surname Hogg. Sampson was ostensibly in charge of keeping hogs and other livestock for the Spalding plantation. Later the family surname evolved from Hogg to Hall.[46]

The configuration of Hog Hammock, with identification of those who owned its land, was outlined for the first time in 1891 by McIntosh County surveyor Alexander C. Wylly. His detailed plat of the settlement delineated acreage and ownership and was apportioned to a general survey of Sapelo South End. Wylly made a second South End survey in 1897, mapping lands owned by the widows of Thomas Spalding II and Thomas Bourke Spalding.

Although there are a few similarities, the 1891 Hog Hammock plat is in contrast to the layout and property boundaries of the present community. Wylly defined a series of elongated ten-acre strips of property running west to east on the east side of the road through Hog Hammock. The lots were long and narrow, extending toward the marsh and a tidal creek separating the community from the land of Sarah McKinley Spalding Wylly and Cabretta Island. A group of smaller lots of from two to five acres were on the west side of the road. The sandy road of 1891 followed much the same route that the main road through Hog Hammock does today.

The owners of ten-acre lots, from north to south, were James Walker, Davis Gilbert, Glasco Campbell, A. Sams, D. Sams, March Carter (two lots), B. Wilson (two lots), Charles Jones, Pero Dixon (two lots), Peter Maxwell (two lots), Shurrey Dunham, Stephen Wylly (two lots), Jack Lemon, Phoebe Bell and Sam Gerry, Rachel Underwood, and Tom Bailey. On the lower end of the grid were the lands of March Wilson (born a slave on Sapelo), with two lots totaling twenty-five acres, and Glasco Bailey, with a six-acre lot. The smaller lot owners on the west side of the road were James Lemon (who was born a Sapelo slave, and who saw Union Army service late in the war), B. Smith, S. Wilson, Jack Underwood, and Coffee Wilson.

Behavior Cemetery

Behavior was originally a slave settlement. By the mid-1870s, the freed people there had begun relocating to other developing communities on the island. Later, a section of Behavior became an African American cemetery, and it continues to be used today as the final resting place for Sapelo's Geechee people.

Behavior replaced an earlier slave cemetery at New Orleans, just southeast of Hog Hammock. There were possibly additional cemeteries at the Hanging Bull and Chocolate settlements, although no evidence of these has been found to date. The New Orleans cemetery, near the banks of New Orleans Creek, was the burial ground for many of Sapelo's slaves, perhaps including Muhammad Bilali, the patriarch of Sapelo, and his wife Phoebe.

Bilali died in 1859, apparently in Darien, while the year of Phoebe's death is unknown. According to Sapelo historian Cornelia Walker Bailey, a lifelong Sapelo resident, New Orleans remained an active cemetery even after Behavior became the primary island burial ground in the 1880s. Bailey notes that though partly decimated by the 1898 hurricane, New Orleans may have been used for interments as late as 1918. No remains of this cemetery have been found to date.

An early source for how Behavior got its name came from David C. Barrow Jr. (1852–1929) of Athens, related by marriage to the descendants of Thomas Spalding and later president of the University of Georgia. Barrow noted, "This place [Behavior] received its name . . . from being a quarter where the most orderly and well-behaved people lived to themselves as slaves."

The Behavior gravesites are not arranged in ordered patterns, but rather are informally scattered about amid the live oaks and palmettos. It is difficult to determine the exact number of interments there as early gravesites likely dating from the 1870s and early 1880s that had wooden markers have since vanished.

The three earliest surviving markers all date from 1889, being those of Hilary Carr (1857–89), Isabella Robinson (1858–89), and Hannah Watkins (1847–89). The next two oldest graves are perhaps the most interesting in Behavior. Betsy Beagle (1796–1890) was a household servant for Thomas and Sarah Spalding and a nursemaid to two generations of Spalding children. When she died in 1890 at the age of ninety-four she had outlived her former owners by nearly half a century.

Minto Bell's longevity was even more remarkable. This daughter of Muhammad Bilali was born around 1790 in the Bahamas, came to Sapelo with her parents, and was at least one hundred years old when she died August 25, 1890. Minto was recognized as the matriarch of Sapelo's people when she became a free woman. She lived with her sons—Liberty, Billali, Abram, and Fortune—and their families on the land at Hanging Bull on which she had once been enslaved.

Traditional Geechee (Gullah) beliefs held that burial grounds be placed well away from settled areas. Both New Orleans and Behavior conform to this pattern. The physical body was buried at death, but the spirit of the deceased remained active, often lingering to taunt or tease the living. The spirits, therefore, could not be disturbed. To appease them, personal possessions were often placed on and around the graves.

In the early 1880s, David Barrow wrote of Behavior: "I visited [the] graveyard and was never more curiously affected between amused and serious thoughts. . . . [A] grove of large live oaks furnished by the moss, shades the place, giving it a somberness. . . . The epitaphs are written on ordinary headboards and driven in the ground. . . . [The] families have done what they could to perpetuate the memory and properly honor their departed friends, and those plain boards cost greater effort, and therefore I have no doubt greater honor to the simple negroes who lie under the live oaks of Sapelo than do the marble which beautify our city cemeteries."

Behavior Cemetery

In a 1934 *National Geographic* article about the Georgia islands, W. Robert Moore wrote of Behavior, "Short posts are planted at either end of the grave, and upon the mounds of earth are placed cups and dishes, oil lamps, and alarm clocks. . . . [T]he oil lamps are to furnish light through the unknown paths, the alarms are to sound on Judgment Day, and the dishes . . . are for the personal use of their former owner."

A more contemporary observation comes from Cornelia Bailey: "This is our cemetery here. . . . If you can't afford a headstone, the marker . . . will be your favorite thing that you like on the grave. So years later, if I come up here, I can find, 'This is where you are buried at because this is where I put your favorite cup at.' So it's used as a marker."

There is a distinct aura about Behavior that transcends solemnity. It is the most hallowed and sacred ground on Sapelo Island. A connection is inescapable here among and between all those who share their communal and eternal rest that is very unlike that of burial grounds elsewhere. It is no wonder that the people of Sapelo hold these grounds in such reverence. Sapelo resident Cuffy Wilson said in 1939: "Wen yuh hab a fewnul yuh hab tuh ax leab tuh entuh duh cimiterry gate. Duh spirit ain gonuh let yuh in lessn yuh ax leab ub it."

SOURCES: Author's conversations with Cornelia Walker Bailey of Sapelo Island; Kenneth H. Thomas Jr., principal investigator, National Register of Historic Places application for Hog Hammock and Behavior Cemetery, GDNR, 1996; Georgia Writers' Project, *Drums and Shadows: Survival Studies among the Georgia Coastal Negroes* (Athens: University of Georgia Press, 1940), 165.

On the southern end of Hog Hammock the Wylly plat delineated a tract of twenty-one acres owned by the Johnson family without identifying specific individuals. To Hog Hammock's north was an irrigation canal, possibly associated with rice then being grown in the community, and "Dr. Sherman's Land." To the west were the lands of Ella B. Spalding. The community was bordered to its east and south by marsh and the lands of Sarah Wylly.[47]

There were several public buildings at Hog Hammock during this period and shortly after, including a school, one or two stores, and structures for Masons, including members of the Order of the Eastern Star. Later, about 1929, a hall was built for the Masons and for other community meetings and events. Usually called the Farmers' Alliance Hall, it had meeting rooms on its second floor, while the local chapter of the Colored Farmers' National Alliance and Cooperative Union was said to have met on the lower floor. A mainland chapter of the Colored Farmers' Alliance (formed in 1886) began in Darien in 1892; thus it is possible that a branch was formed shortly after at Sapelo, either at Hog Hammock or Raccoon Bluff.[48]

In 1884, the Second African Baptist Church, later renamed St. Luke's Baptist Church, was established from the First African Baptist Church at Hanging Bull. The new church was built on the March Wilson property, but it was identified on the 1891 survey as having its own lot. In 1904, St. Luke's had seventy-four congregants.

Excepting Raccoon Bluff, Hog Hammock was the most populous settlement on Sapelo Island in the late nineteenth and early twentieth centuries. The 1910 census showed that Hog Hammock, including adjacent Johnson Hammock, had 163 residents in thirty-three households, comprising a diversity of Geechee families: Bailey, Bell, Carter, Dixon, Durham, Gerry (Gary), Underwood, Wilson, Wylly, Gilbert, Jones, Lemon, Maxwell, Sams, Johnson, Hillery, Lewis, and Jackson. Occupations listed for Hog Hammock residents were farmer, oyster harvester, and timber longshoreman.

The End of the Spalding Era

By the first decade of the twentieth century the white influence on Sapelo Island had greatly declined, most particularly in terms of the Spaldings and their allied families. The 1910 census counted only sixteen white persons residing on Sapelo, about the same number living on the island a decade earlier. These included Archibald and Sallie McKinley and Sallie's cousin Charlie Bass, living on the McKinleys' hundred acres at Barn Creek near Long Tabby. North of Long Tabby, at Riverside, were Catherine

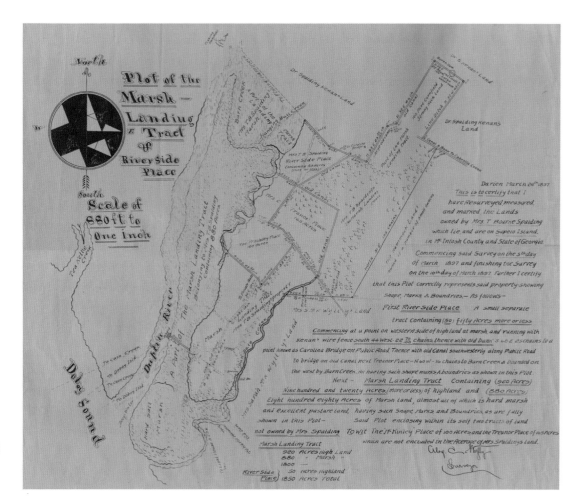

An 1897 survey plat by Alexander C. Wylly delineating Spalding-owned lands on Sapelo's South End, including Marsh Landing and Riverside. The plat shows acreage then held by Ella Barrow Spalding, Sarah McKinley Spalding Wylly, A. C. and Sallie Spalding McKinley, and allied families. (Author's collection)

Malcom and her widowed daughter in one household, and Edward Meadows, a carpenter at the sawmill, and his family living in another.

At the lighthouse island the Cromley families, Jimmy as head keeper and his brother Daniel as assistant, lived in one of the two houses at the base of the light. The other assistant keeper, Robert Cromley, and his wife and two daughters lived in the other house.[49] The two frame dwellings were constructed in 1905 to U.S. Lighthouse Service specifications, being attached to the steel lighthouse erected that year. By then the overseas timber shipping frequenting Darien's harbor was using the deeper Sapelo Sound anchorage rather than the notoriously problematic waters of Doboy Sound off

Sapelo's new one-hundred-foot steel-frame lighthouse overlooking Doboy Sound was built by the U.S. Lighthouse Service in 1905, several hundred feet north of the deactivated brick tower. Also shown are the two attached keepers' dwellings for the Cromley family. (Author's collection)

Sapelo South End. In 1913, the Sapelo lighthouse converted to the incandescent oil-vapor system of lighting, according to plans in the National Archives—the only surviving architectural drawings of either of the Sapelo lighthouses.[50]

The hurricane and tidal wave of October 2, 1898, struck the middle Georgia coast a direct blow and severely impacted Sapelo Island, the worst such storm to affect the area since 1824. The hurricane made landfall at high tide on a full moon and put much of the island under water for several hours before the tide receded. Some Sapelo people took refuge in the brick lighthouse where the water rose up the tower over fifteen feet from the base. The hurricane caused great damage to the coast, particularly to the Darien timber industry and sawmills. Timber was scattered for miles in the Altamaha River estuary, towboats and other vessels were left high and dry in the marsh, and over fifty lives were lost, mostly on Wolf Island south of Sapelo and on the Altamaha rice islands.[51] A firsthand account was provided by A. C. McKinley, who with Sallie rode out the hurricane at Barn Creek:

> We have been exceedingly busy trying to patch up the damage done by the terrible hurricane and tidal wave. . . . For four weary hours we stood waist deep in the water. The waves coming across the island—direct from the ocean, covered the tops of our windows. In the house the water was nearly 3 feet deep. . . . The waves in our yard were fully 12 feet high. [Sallie] was in bed with fever, but when her bed began to float she had to get up & stand waist deep in water for hours. We lost most of our possessions—either outright or from damage by salt water. All our furniture is dropping to pieces.[52]

In 1889, four years after the accidental death of her husband, Sarah McKinley Spalding married William C. Wylly (1842–1923), a Darien rice planter and first cousin of her late husband. For several years, the Wyllys lived in a house built by Thomas Spalding II near the ruined South End mansion. There are no remains of this structure.

In 1890, Sarah Wylly put up Sapelo South End as collateral on a loan of $10,000 from the Scottish American Mortgage Company of Edinburgh, Scotland. She died in 1897, leaving the South End to her husband before the repayment of the debt. As administrator of his wife's estate, William Wylly was unable to satisfy the debt, and in 1900 Scottish American foreclosed on the South End.

It was during the period 1885–1910 that several ventures were explored to produce revenue at Sapelo. Thomas Spalding had been engaged in negotiations for the possible sale of Sapelo South End to Atlanta developers when his untimely death in early

Long Tabby ruins, circa 1920. The former sugar mill would be rebuilt on its original foundations by Howard Coffin several years later. (Courtesy of Bill Jones III)

1885 in Macon ended further discussions. Similar proposals had been explored by the Wyllys, the state of Georgia, and Scottish American. In 1897 there was a scheme to use the island for a state penitentiary or penal farm, one of several proposals studied by state lawmakers in the postbellum period to exile state convicts to Sapelo. The initiative was enthusiastically pursued by Joseph Mansfield, state representative from McIntosh County, who wanted to sell Sapelo South End to the state, noting "that if the state will buy Sapelo Island the convicts can be made self-supporting . . . conditions can be re-established in the growing of sea island cotton."[53]

In the end, it was decided that the island was too isolated and that the logistics of operating such a facility would be too difficult. In 1893 and 1898 there were ideas circulated for the South End to be sold to develop a resort hotel, perhaps fashioned after the new Jekyll Island Club, and in 1905 the idea was floated of using it for a Methodist retreat. Nothing ever came of these proposals, whether for lack of sufficient investment or political support.

Eventually Scottish American Mortgage gained undivided ownership of the South End at a McIntosh County sheriff's sale in August 1900, a transaction consummated for $5,000. The deed described the tract as being five thousand acres "more or less, being the southern portion of Sapelo Island, with Cabretta Island, which is a small island containing about five hundred acres, and separated from the body of Sapelo Island by a marsh and tide water creek."[54]

Scottish American's acquisition did not include the seventy-five acres of the Shell Hammock community. In June 1910, the South End was sold for $10,000 by Scottish American to the Georgia Loan and Trust Company of Macon, acting on behalf of the Sapelo Island Company, a consortium headed by T. H. Boone of Macon. An

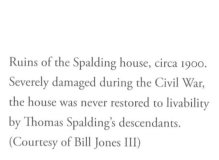

Ruins of the Spalding house, circa 1900.
Severely damaged during the Civil War,
the house was never restored to livability
by Thomas Spalding's descendants.
(Courtesy of Bill Jones III)

agreement was reached by which the Sapelo Island Company would make annual payments of $1,000 at 6 percent interest until the debt was satisfied.[55]

In early 1911, the Sapelo Island Company proceeded with development of the South End as a hunting preserve and began refurbishing the Spalding house to livability. The mansion was a veritable ruin by that time—period photographs show the structure without a roof and with only the exterior tabby walls standing among thick underbrush. The Macon group restored the central block, added a new roof with dormer windows for upstairs bedrooms, and made other improvements pursuant to use of the house as a hunting lodge. The work was nearly complete by the time the Macon group elected to sell the South End to Howard Coffin in the spring of 1912.

When Ella Spalding sold the 1,030 acres of the Marsh Landing tract to Charles O. Fulton of Darien for $10,000 in January 1911, the only remaining Spalding family members still living on Sapelo were the McKinleys. C. O. Fulton (1848–1911) was one of the most prominent citizens of McIntosh County. He and his family lived at a former Spalding property, Black Island, near Darien. Fulton did not get to enjoy his Sapelo property for long—less than six months after his acquisition of the Marsh Landing tract he died suddenly of a stroke.[56]

Sallie Spalding McKinley, the last of her family's blood line on the island, served as island postmaster (her husband Archibald was assistant). A post office designated "Inverness, Ga." was opened on Sapelo in 1891 to serve island residents after the closing of the postal facility at Doboy Island. There was already a "Sapelo" post office at the time at the timber wharfs on Front River for the vessels frequenting Sapelo Sound. The

The Spalding house, circa 1913, as partially restored by the Sapelo Island Company of Macon. The picture was taken shortly after Howard Coffin purchased Sapelo in 1912. (Courtesy of Bill Jones III)

Inverness post office on Sapelo was named after the town in the Scottish Highlands whence the Scots came to Georgia in 1736 to found Darien, originally named New Inverness. In 1914 the post office was redesignated "Sapeloe, Ga."[57]

An era was rushing toward its conclusion. After more than a century, the Spalding family presence on Sapelo Island, three generations, was near an end. Charles Spalding Wylly noted in 1914 that only twice in the previous thirty years had he visited Sapelo, the scene of many pleasant memories of his adolescence:

> My memory has been mostly of men whose names are buried in the oblivion of time. On the visit previous to the last, crumbling walls, threatening soon to pass into dust, were all that met the eye. . . . Since then thirty-odd years have gone, and this century has entered its teens—years of love, of hope, of discouragement, of despondency; and now, in May 1914, I have found the noble house restored; every wall rebuilt, white and spotless, and framed in a garniture of green. Solid and reassuring it stands, to claim a new immunity from time and to bid a new defiance to sea and wind, greeting the eastern sun as it rises in its sumptuous splendor and bidding farewell as it sinks in its glories of color to a bed of solemn repose.[58]

A footnote to Sapelo's Spalding story comes from William McFeely: "The poverty that had set in after the Civil War did not lose its hold on the island's people, black or white. The impecunious McKinleys—she a stooped, white-haired old lady, he a long-white-bearded Confederate veteran—died in 1916 and 1917, fifty years after the birth and death of their only child. There were no more white Spaldings on the island. The land, as property, had been restored to their family, but it had not produced prosperity for them or for any of the white possessors to which they sold it."[59]

CHAPTER VII   Sapelo Regenesis

The Early Twentieth Century

*A*s THE TWENTIETH CENTURY's second decade began, Sapelo Island entered a distinctly new phase in its history and culture, followed by a brief period in the 1920s when the island actually realized a degree of managed development with profits as a goal.

Howard Coffin and Sapelo were in many ways evocative of the era when Thomas Spalding built an island empire with energy, skill, and vision. When comparing the two men who left their mark on the island a century apart there can be very little ambiguity. Coffin surely was to early twentieth-century Sapelo almost exactly what Spalding was to Sapelo of the early nineteenth century. There were commonalities of purpose, intent, and philosophy between the two visionaries, and they were both men of principle, intellect, and wisdom, but the similarities are epitomized by their shared sense of place and permanence regarding Sapelo Island.

Howard Earle Coffin was born in West Milton, Ohio, on September 6, 1873. Upon entering the University of Michigan in 1893, he studied engineering and developed the skills to build a single-cycle, gasoline-fueled internal combustion engine. In 1898–99 he built his first automobile—by hand. Coffin was first employed by Ransom Olds in Detroit as chief engineer in the development of the popular Oldsmobile.

Howard E. Coffin as a young man. (Courtesy of Bill Jones III)

In 1907, Coffin and two friends, Roy D. Chapin and Fred Bezner, also Olds employees, went out on their own and formed their own company. Their firm became the Hudson Motor Car Company in 1909, with Chapin as president, Coffin as chief engineer, designer, and vice president, and Bezner as vice president in charge of purchasing. By the end of 1910, the Hudson Company was experiencing rapid growth and was worth $5 million. Coffin made much of his fortune by developing standardized materials and parts for automobile assembly. He and another of his Detroit colleagues, Henry Ford, played pivotal roles in early automobile design.[1]

To promote their automotive development and outreach, the three partners became proponents of auto racing. It was this interest that first brought Coffin to coastal Georgia. He attended the American Grand Prix road races in Savannah in 1910, after which he was invited to join a fishing trip at a fish camp on nearby Skidaway Island. The visit captured Coffin's fancy, and "Georgia's dreamy coastline ever thereafter would be in his blood."[2]

Coffin's enthusiasm for racing led him again to Savannah in 1911 for the Vanderbilt Cup Race. It was on this visit that he learned through Savannah mayor George Tiedeman and real estate broker Wayne Cunningham that Sapelo Island might be available for purchase. Coffin visited the island later that year as a guest of a Macon hunting group that owned Sapelo's South End, explored Sapelo's beaches, marshes and uplands, and met some of the island's residents. There were only a few white people then living on Sapelo, including the aging McKinleys, Archie and Sallie, and her cousin Charles Bass at Barn Creek, two families at Riverside, and two Cromley families at the lighthouse.

Coffin was intrigued by Sapelo's history and hooked by its beauty and quiet that enabled him to feel blissfully detached from his hectic life in Detroit. With Cunningham as his agent and David C. Barrow Jr. as his attorney, Coffin began negotiations with the various owners of the island. By early 1912 he had successfully concluded the transactions by which he acquired the island that would become the unrelenting passion of the remainder of his life.[3]

For just under $150,000, Coffin acquired approximately twenty thousand acres of Sapelo's upland and surrounding marshes from the Macon group and five families that collectively owned most of the island's acreage. Coffin's acquisitions included five thousand acres on the South End, including Cabretta Island, purchased from the Scottish American Mortgage Company, as lien holder for the Sapelo Island Company; seven thousand upland North End acres, including Chocolate, Bourbon, and High Point,

At the McKinley house on Barn Creek, around 1914. At the top are Sallie and Archibald McKinley; at right are Howard and Matilda Coffin; in front is Charles L. Bass; the woman at left is unidentified but is possibly Kate Treanor. (Courtesy of Bill Jones III)

purchased from the Amos Sawyer family; 1,030 upland acres of the Marsh Landing tract purchased from the C. O. Fulton estate; and 1,400 upland acres purchased from the Kenan family.

Two smaller tracts on Barn Creek were not initially purchased.[4] These were held by the Treanor family (eighty acres at Long Tabby) and the McKinleys (one hundred acres on Barn Creek nearby). Coffin added these tracts to his holdings just after World War I. The McKinleys were by then deceased—Sarah McKinley died in 1916 and was buried at Darien's St. Andrews Cemetery, and A. C. McKinley died a year later and was interred in Milledgeville's Memory Hill Cemetery. Coffin's arrangement with the Treanors and McKinleys when he bought Sapelo was the right of first refusal on their property upon their death or moving from the island. In this manner Coffin acquired the last of the remaining Spalding family land on Sapelo.

In 1920, Coffin bought Little Sapelo Island's two hundred acres of upland and non-cultivable high-phase tidal marsh from Elizabeth Sherman Souther.[5] Coffin did not attempt to purchase African American land in the several communities on Sapelo,

Sapelo's main house, circa 1916, soon after installation of the outdoor swimming pool by the Coffins. (Courtesy of Bill Jones III)

the most prominent being Raccoon Bluff, Hog Hammock, Shell Hammock, Lumber Landing, and Belle Marsh. However, Coffin did purchase several small unoccupied lots at Raccoon Bluff in 1913 and 1914 shortly after he purchased most of the island. This was possibly to facilitate his access to Blackbeard Island, the south end of which was across the marsh from Raccoon Bluff.[6]

Attuned to the island's history, Coffin returned Sapelo's name to its old English spelling, "Sapeloe," soon after his acquisition. For man and island it was an ideal match, as Sapelo became the perfect conduit for Coffin's creative instincts. "The rehabilitation of Sapelo satisfied the urge to construct and develop that was a leading force in Coffin's nature, while the peace, privacy and serenity of the island brought relaxation and escape from the pressures of the outside world. He was the perfect host and delighted in sharing the pleasures of Sapelo with friends and family."[7]

Coffin and his wife Matilda (Teddie) began regular visits to Sapelo from their Grosse Pointe, Michigan, home. For several years they lived in the old Spalding house that had been partially refurbished by the Macon sportsmen in 1911. In 1914–15 the Coffins had an outdoor pool built at the front entrance while making other modifications and improvements.

Much of Coffin's time from 1915 through 1918 was dictated by pressing national events. He was appointed to the Navy Consulting Board by President Woodrow Wilson, and during U.S. involvement in the First World War, in 1917–18, Coffin consulted with the War and Navy Departments regarding military applications of gasoline-powered engines for land vehicles and aircraft. He served on the Council of

National Defense, an unofficial wartime cabinet, and headed the Aircraft Production Board. After the war, Coffin helped organize National Air Transport and encouraged investment in the fledgling aviation business. He served for two years as chairman of the board of the entity that would eventually become the largest privately owned airline in the world, United Air Lines.

Howard Coffin's years at Sapelo Island had important and enduring effects on coastal Georgia. He was rather a late arrival in the cavalcade of wealthy northerners who since the early 1880s had accrued substantial amounts of coastal property, particularly on the sea islands. Coffin continued a trend of the private acquisition of coastal lands that would be held among several prominent families, or groups of families, for three generations until the 1960s and 1970s, when many of the properties came under state or federal management and protection.

It was Sapelo's Coffin, the members of the Jekyll Island Club, the Carnegies and Candlers of Cumberland, the Wanamakers and Torreys of Ossabaw, the Rauers and Nobles of St. Catherines, the Parsons of Wassaw, the Roeblings of Skidaway, and the Berolzheimers of Little St. Simons who were the first true conservationists of Georgia's coast, though perhaps all were unaware of this role during their time on the islands. Coffin, the visionary, had much in common with his corporate, industrial, and financial contemporaries, who energized the development of the United States as the world's leading economic power by the 1890s. These were men eager to project their vision: the "manifest destiny" of the country's role as a global power, with concomitant economic expansion, in the early twentieth century.

Coffin expanded his vision from the Detroit automotive industry directly to Sapelo, then to coastal Georgia and beyond. By the time his efforts at Sapelo reached their apogee in 1930, it had become obvious that Coffin's purpose had an intensely intellectual underpinning. It is no coincidence that his initiatives on Sapelo mirrored those of Spalding a century earlier. Coffin was every bit the dreamer Spalding had been, both for Sapelo and for his adopted state of Georgia. Sapelo—and certainly Sea Island later—represented Coffin's energy, inquisitiveness, and innovation, and the manifestations of his vision there would endure long after his death.

Coffin devoted increasing attention to Sapelo after 1918. He was the first island owner after slave emancipation to develop Sapelo with a mind to economic opportunities for the island's black residents. For the first time the Geechee population found sustained employment available on the island itself. The 1920s saw substantive improvements made to Sapelo—at times, Coffin's initiatives seemed to be endless. Like

Boat landing on South End Creek, early 1920s. The site was later the Coffin-Reynolds farm complex and still later the University of Georgia Marine Institute. (Courtesy of Bill Jones III)

Spalding, Coffin was simultaneously innovator, experimenter, scientist, and amateur architect.

In bringing Sapelo into the twentieth century, he needed a mind as keen as his, with energy and resourcefulness to match, to help him realize his ambitions. Thus it was that in 1923 Coffin brought his young cousin, Alfred W. (Bill) Jones (1902–82) to Sapelo to serve as island manager and to supervise a surfeit of new projects. It was Jones, like a modern-day Bilali, who implemented the day-to-day details of fulfilling Coffin's plans.

Immediately upon arriving, Jones began overseeing the building of a network of shell roads and clearing long-fallow agricultural fields to resurrect large-scale agriculture. He put his engineering skills to good use. Irrigation ditches were blasted out with dynamite to replace Spalding's canals from a century earlier. Culverts were installed to help drain low-lying lands. With characteristic energy, Jones hired Sapelo's black residents to cut the pine timber growing on the former cotton fields of the North End, used other local residents to operate the Duplin River sawmill, and supervised the building of a barn, stables, and other farm structures on the South End near the main house.

The 1929 McIntosh County soil map attests to Sapelo's growth during the twenties by delineating a network of sand and shell roads, irrigation canals, boat docks, and new residential and agricultural structures on the South End.[8] In 1930, Coffin and Jones were employing over two hundred people on Sapelo. Never in anyone's memory had the island been so busy and full of promise for all who lived and worked there:

Duplin River dock at Kenan Field,
near the site of a sawmill operated by
Howard Coffin and later R. J. Reynolds Jr.

It was, as Jones remembers, truly a time of wine and roses, those few years before the crash. Everyone was rich, and enjoying their riches. Coffin, from his investments in automobile stocks, airplane stock, and Detroit real estate, had an income of roughly $800,000 a year. He was spending a quarter of a million dollars a year on Sapelo. Jones soon found himself becoming more and more deeply involved with the management of the plantation. The island needed roads, and he laid out new ones and bossed their construction, curving them around the fine old trees, which he was careful to preserve. . . . All around him things were happening, people were busy clearing the fields and horseback trails, planting pastures for beef and dairy herds, bridging creeks and digging artesian wells.[9]

By the early 1930s, Sapelo had a beef cattle herd of some one thousand head, crossed with pure Aberdeen Angus bulls. Coffin and Jones developed over three thousand acres of open savannas for sustaining the herd, seeded primarily with carpet and Bermuda grasses and lespedeza to enable year-round grazing. There were artesian wells scattered about the island to keep the cattle watered, thirty-six in all, drilled at depths of from three hundred to seven hundred feet.

Another effort was Coffin's drainage of Sapelo's low-lying areas to reduce mosquito infestation. His installation of iron tide gates in a system of dikes is still in evidence today. Freshwater ponds were built, one on the North End in 1927, now the Reynolds Duck Pond, to provide habitat for ducks and other waterfowl.

The lighthouse, circa 1925, as viewed looking south from South End Creek. (Courtesy of Bill Jones III)

The restored Sapelo Island lighthouse as viewed from the waters of Doboy Sound.

Marine railway and boatyard on South End Creek, circa 1924. Though long unused and in ruins, the railway is still in place on the Marine Institute campus. (Courtesy of Bill Jones III)

To expand his timber operations, Coffin acquired seven hundred acres of pineland on the mainland, a transaction facilitated by local attorney Paul Varner, Coffin's land agent. Varner had also supervised the dynamiting of drainage ditches for Coffin on Sapelo. Coffin's purchase of Little Sapelo Island opened further possibilities. The island was utilized as a hunting preserve, which included birds—chachalacas—imported in 1923 from Guatemala. A frame dwelling was built on Little Sapelo to house the caretaker, three artesian wells were drilled, and the tract was developed for the breeding of game birds. This acquisition included the small marsh islands along the Duplin north of Little Sapelo: Mary, Fishing, Pumpkin, and Jack Hammocks.[10]

A greenhouse designed and built in 1925 just east of the Coffin mansion by the William H. Lutton Company of New Jersey exemplified Coffin's enthusiasm for architecture. Here a botanist oversaw a diverse array of plants brought in, and three full-time gardeners were employed.

To maintain his flotilla of twenty-seven boats and barges, Coffin constructed a marine railway on South End Creek. Three boats were built on Sapelo during Jones's tenure as plantation manager, and much of his time was spent coordinating boat operations and repairs. Nearby was the South End farm complex, wooden structures later replaced in 1936–37 by R. J. Reynolds Jr. with the structures that became the Marine Institute in the 1950s. Coffin had adjacent structures to house machine and carpentry shops, with a boathouse on the creek. A power-generating plant was built overlooking South End Creek, later upgraded with new equipment by Reynolds in 1935.[11]

The Sapelo farm complex as developed by Howard Coffin. In 1936–37, R. J. Reynolds Jr. replaced these structures with the buildings now comprising the University of Georgia Marine Institute. (Courtesy of Bill Jones III)

In 1921–22, a two-story Spanish-style administration building was constructed for Sapeloe Plantation between the main house and the South End farm complex. It included first-floor offices for Coffin and the island superintendent, a general office, refrigerator room, kitchen, and dining room. The second floor comprised a central lounge, sunroom, and eight bedrooms, with an open terrace extending across the front.[12]

At the same time, Coffin restored the Long Tabby sugarhouse. Rebuilt on two floors, Long Tabby was designed as a guesthouse and featured a lounge with two fire-places, living room, dining room, butler's pantry, and kitchen, all on the ground floor, with seven bedrooms and two baths on the second floor. In front of Long Tabby, over-looking the Barn Creek marshes and Little Sapelo, Coffin installed an in-ground swim-ming pool for the enjoyment of guests.

Seafood processing had been a part of Sapelo Island's economy since 1900 when William C. Wylly briefly operated an oyster cannery on the Duplin River. Later Coffin and Jones revived seafood operations when they developed a cannery on the upper branch of Barn Creek, a section of that stream that came to be known as Factory Creek. Oysters were harvested from the nearby creeks in the fall and winter, with pro-duction shifting to shrimp in the summer and fall. Managed for a time by Paul Varner, the cannery provided steady employment for the island's Geechee population. By 1922 the cannery was marketing "Sapeloe Plantation Shrimp" and "Sapeloe Plantation

Little Sapelo Island, circa 1927, with the dock and caretaker's frame house overlooking the Duplin River. (Courtesy of Bill Jones III)

Oysters," with labels featuring a picture of South End House. The rusting remains of the cannery's boilers near the creek are testimony to this activity.[13]

Coffin was particularly enthusiastic about his cannery. The venture provided Sapelo's black women with steady employment in the factory and the men with work harvesting the oysters in the nearby creeks. Years later, Bill Jones recalled an amusing anecdote regarding some of the women who worked at the factory. Jones "could never understand why the black oyster shuckers and shrimp peelers would take off their aprons and go next door to the commissary to buy a ten-cent can of Portuguese sardines for lunch." The seafood venture also enabled Coffin to experiment with oyster seeding in the waters around Sapelo, partly in response to scientific surveys relating to production.[14]

Coffin started another canning operation at Darien and purchased all the marshlands with their oyster beds around Altamaha Sound between Sapelo and Little St. Simons Islands. The acquisition included over thirty-five thousand acres of marsh and small tracts of upland on Wolf and Egg Islands. Coffin employed workers with the requisite expertise to implement his scientific oyster-farming project. Seed oysters were planted at carefully chosen depths, and overcrowded beds were broken up where the oysters were too small at maturity to warrant harvesting. The effort was largely successful, and within several years the beds on the lower end of McIntosh County's coast were exceedingly productive. However, Coffin eventually terminated the effort due to the encroachment of poachers who constantly raided the oyster beds.

Irrigation ditches being built by dynamite blasting on Sapelo, 1920s. (Courtesy of Bill Jones III)

Coffin's interest in natural habitats led to his involvement in the protection of federally owned Blackbeard Island. After the South Atlantic Quarantine Station at Blackbeard was deactivated in 1910, the island was largely untended. Coffin wanted Blackbeard to be off-limits to hunters, to enable government-sponsored biological wildlife research to be conducted there. He became something of a self-appointed caretaker for the island and over ten years spent a total of $20,000 to pay security personnel to protect Blackbeard from poachers. Sapelo's game lands were protected in similar fashion.

In 1927, Coffin contracted Luders Marine Construction of Stamford, Connecticut, to build a 124-foot power yacht, *Zapala*, a vessel grossing 159 tons, with a white-painted wood hull, teak and cedar decks, three double and two single staterooms, and a dining salon finished in walnut. A freshwater system supplied fifteen hundred gallons of water in copper tanks. The vessel had a permanent crew of seven and replaced Coffin's earlier pleasure craft, the *Miramar* houseboat. The white frame house at the head of the Marsh Landing causeway, built years earlier by Bourke Spalding, was restored for the use of *Zapala's* captain, engineer, and other personnel.

The Marsh Landing dock was suitably expanded to accommodate the *Zapala* and other vessels arriving at Sapelo Island. In early 1928, Niles F. Schuh, who had succeeded Jones as Coffin's Sapeloe Plantation manager, applied to the U.S. Army Corps of Engineers, Savannah District, for the construction of the new Marsh Landing facility, to be built of cypress decking upon metal-capped palmetto pilings, with a frame of

Nannygoat Beach, 1920s, with Matilda Coffin standing between the horses and riders. One of Howard Coffin's Hudson cars is at left. (Courtesy of Bill Jones III)

creosoted timber. A dock house was built at the end of the pier on the Duplin River and included a waiting room, a storage room, and a telephone connected to the Coffin mansion.[15]

Howard and Teddie Coffin implemented plans in 1918 to begin a complete restoration of the mansion pursuant to their intention to make Sapelo Island their permanent home. Photographs from 1920 depict the mansion completely gutted except for the original exterior tabby walls. Detroit architect Albert Kahn prepared several designs for the rebuilding for Coffin's approval. The construction work was overseen by Arthur Wilson, a Swedish contractor who simultaneously supervised the restoration of the north end residence on nearby St. Catherines Island in which Coffin had a financial interest with Clement M. Keys and James C. Willson. The rebuilt South End House was to be "a palatial estate built on the tabby foundations and walls of Thomas Spalding's original house. . . . The new main house was completed in 1925 with its lavish living room, library, indoor swimming pool, huge upstairs ballroom and nautical recreation room and lounge in the downstairs basement."[16]

Coffin involved himself personally in the reconstruction of the Sapelo house. Using Sallie Spalding's 1858 sketch as a guide, Kahn and Coffin effectively re-created the antebellum exterior as it had originally appeared a century earlier. Sapelo's owner immersed himself into every aspect of the project. Harold Martin, based on his extensive interviews with Bill Jones Sr., noted that "Coffin would come down to Sapelo from Detroit periodically, arriving unexpectedly, to look into every detail of what the house builder,

The Coffin mansion in 1926, shortly after the five-year restoration project had been completed. (Courtesy of Bill Jones III)

Arthur Wilson, had done during his absence. Frequently, he would order what had been built torn down and done over again. As a result, the house was built and rebuilt about three times before Coffin was finally satisfied. . . . Scribbling on the back of an envelope, Coffin would lay out a work schedule for the next two or three months, and Jones and Wilson would have to take it from there."[17]

The restoration was completed by early 1925. A 1930 Savannah press account by Cornelia M. Wilder describes the structure as

a magnificent building, the center part giving the effect of being one-story with extremely high walls and French windows over each of which is a small oval window. At either end are small square buildings, which are connected with the main house by covered passageways. In one of these are the bedrooms, sitting rooms and sun parlor of Mr. and Mrs. Coffin, in the other the kitchen, pantries and servants quarters. Four huge Ionic columns of white stone support the roof which is held over the front piazza, while a very wide and long tiled terrace extends the length of the building. . . . Reflecting the beauties of the house and shaded by magnificent moss-grown live oaks is a sunken pool in the midst of the lawn where flowers

The Coffin-Reynolds mansion today set amid live oaks and
Spanish moss on the site selected for the original mansion built
by Thomas Spalding

bloom and two giant water jars of Spanish pottery and statues of Carrara marble meet the eye. The house faces the ocean which can be seen in the distance, and between it and the house are the extensive gardens and greenhouse. . . . The mansion is very beautiful inside with a huge reception room which opens into the sun parlor the center of which is occupied by a marble swimming pool which is tiled with emerald green and blue, flecked with gold, while at the end of the sun parlor is a fountain which sprays water over a statue of a bathing girl. . . . On the second floor is the suite occupied by President and Mrs. Coolidge on their visit to Mr. and Mrs. Coffin a year or so ago.[18]

Jones recalled that it was a house "centered around a high-ceilinged living room, heavily beamed in the Spanish manner, where Coffin loved to entertain with a lavish hand. . . . Off this room, with its massive stone fireplace, lay the indoor swimming pool where Coffin would take his morning cold-water plunge; the dining room with its long refectory table . . . a billiard room and a library. Off the living room were two master bedrooms, and upstairs was a ballroom, which could also be used as a movie theater. Downstairs, in a vast, stone-floored, rough-beamed basement, was one of Coffin's favorite rooms [the grill room with its specially built fireplace for cooking]."[19]

W. Robert Moore, writing in the *National Geographic* magazine in February 1934, noted, "Nowhere else have I seen such a delightful setting for a great house as that on Sapeloe. In the midst of a cathedral-like bower of oaks, stands the majestic colonial house." Burnette Vanstory said of Coffin, not entirely accurately, "Acting as his own architect and with his Sapelo employees as his builders, he produced a house of unsurpassed beauty and dignity."[20]

Many prominent people visited Sapelo from 1924 to 1934. Two presidents, Calvin Coolidge and Herbert Hoover, came to the island, as did the aviator, Charles A. Lindbergh. President Coolidge and the first lady, Grace Coolidge, were guests of the Coffins as the highlight of a promotional campaign conducted by Coffin's friend Charles Redden for the newly opened Cloister resort at Sea Island. Coolidge's visit occurred in late December 1928 near the end of his administration.

The president's party arrived in Brunswick by special train from Washington, D.C., on December 26, being met there by Mr. and Mrs. Coffin, after which they were conveyed to Sapelo aboard the *Zapala*. The first morning after his arrival Coolidge, an avid sportsman, availed himself of the islands' hunting opportunities. Jones escorted Coolidge to Little Sapelo where the president bagged three pheasants and two wild turkeys in the first of several hunts during his vacation.[21]

President Calvin Coolidge visiting with his host, Howard Coffin, on the terrace of the Sapelo mansion, December 1928. (Courtesy of Bill Jones III)

On Saturday, December 29, the president and first lady were entertained with a "rodeo" at Nannygoat Beach staged by Sapelo's African American residents. The event featured horseback races and terrapin races on the hard beach sand. In 1981 Ronester Johnson of Hog Hammock recalled the events of that day: "We had the horse race on the beach and we had the ox cart race. We had the turtle race. . . . He [Coolidge] was standing on the beach waving with an eleven-gallon hat on. Eleven gallon—largest eleven-gallon hat I ever seen. . . . We killed a deer that morning. . . . He [Coolidge] was in the ox cart. He shoot a deer. . . . He set up in the wagon. He got a gun across his lap."[22]

Also during their Sapelo sojourn the Coolidges enjoyed a trip aboard the *Zapala* to the Cloister at nearby Sea Island Beach. There Coolidge planted a ceremonial live oak sapling that came to be known as the "Constitution Oak." The Coolidges also visited the lodge at Cabin Bluff, Coffin's sixty-thousand-acre hunting preserve in Camden County.

During the Sapelo visit oil portraits of Calvin and Grace Coolidge were rendered by the English artist Frank O. Salisbury (1874–1962) who had accompanied the presidential party from Washington. Salisbury was renowned on both sides of the Atlantic for his work. During his career he painted portraits of Winston Churchill, Andrew Carnegie, Franklin D. Roosevelt, Earl Mountbatten, Richard Burton, and the British general, Bernard Montgomery.

The president and first lady sat for their portraits in the library annex on the main floor of the Coffin mansion. "I painted Mr. Coolidge in a light suit," Salisbury later wrote. "We tried a robe and black suit, but he looked like a parson. He had a great sense of dry humor. I was never able to fathom his silence, whether his mind was solving some abstruse problem or whether it was a mere blank. There were five of us who sat down to meals every day, but he seldom joined in the conversation. . . . After dinner he would sit in the drawing room for coffee, and on one or two occasions entered into lengthy conversations with Mr. Coffin concerning conditions in the motor industry."[23] After the Coolidges returned to Washington, Salisbury remained at Sapelo to paint portraits of Howard and Matilda Coffin. The finished paintings were displayed facing each other on the north and south walls of the mansion's great room.[24]

The Lindbergh visit six weeks later occurred with considerably less fanfare. Almost two years after his historic solo transatlantic flight from New York to Paris in 1927, Lindbergh was flying mail for Pan American between New York, Cuba, and Mexico. On February 12, 1929, the wedding engagement was announced between Lindbergh and Anne Spencer Morrow, daughter of the U.S. ambassador to Mexico, Dwight Morrow. Three days later Lindbergh, en route from Miami to Washington, landed on Sapelo Island where he had a prearranged meeting with Coffin and Clement Keys, the chief officers of the Transcontinental Aviation Corporation, for which Lindbergh was a consultant.

The aviator landed his single-engine Curtiss biplane in a cleared cow pasture on the lower end of Flora Bottom, a short distance from the mansion. After meeting with Coffin and Keys, followed by lunch, Lindbergh flew off Sapelo at 1:48 p.m. The visit had lasted two and a half hours.[25]

Charles A. Lindbergh arriving in his Curtiss aircraft at Sapelo Island, February 1929. (Courtesy of Bill Jones III)

Another aviator associated with Coffin was Paul R. Redfern, a local pilot who, under the sponsorship of Coffin and Paul Varner, undertook to become the first to fly solo from the United States to Rio de Janeiro, Brazil, a distance of forty-six hundred miles. Redfern took off in the *Port of Brunswick* amid great fanfare from Sea Island Beach on August 25, 1927, but the bold venture turned into tragedy. His plane was last observed flying over a town on the coast of Venezuela. It was theorized that Redfern had crashed in the jungles of Dutch Guiana.

Besides Coolidge and Lindbergh, visitors to the island included Coffin's three Detroit friends, Henry Ford, who had established a winter residence near Savannah at Ways Station (later Richmond Hill), H. N. Torrey of Ossabaw Island, and banker and automotive executive Eugene W. Lewis. Other Sapelo visitors included Edsel Ford of Dearborn, Michigan; golfer Bobby Jones of Atlanta; Cason and Fuller Callaway, textile executives from LaGrange, Georgia; Ivan Allen Sr. and Coca-Cola owner Asa G. Candler, both of Atlanta; Clare Booth Brokaw (later Luce of the *Time* magazine fortune); boxing great Gene Tunney; *Atlanta Constitution* editor Clark Howell; and Walter F. George, U.S. senator from Georgia. Tobacco heir R. J. Reynolds Jr. of Winston-Salem, North Carolina, visited Sapelo in 1932 and 1933. The author Ben Ames Williams visited Sapelo during this period, writing portions of his novel *Great*

At Long Tabby, 1932, (*left to right*): Howard Coffin, unidentified Ford brother-in-law, Henry Ford, and Bill Jones Sr. (Courtesy Bill Jones III)

Oaks while on the island. Published in 1930, the book is a fictionalized account of Sapelo's history, based partly on the 1914 Sapelo history prepared for Coffin by Charles Spalding Wylly.

As Coolidge had ended his administration with a visit to Sapelo, so did his successor, Herbert Hoover who, with his wife Lou Henry Hoover, was the guest of Coffin in late 1932. It was an unhappy time for Coffin. He had lost his beloved wife Teddie, who had died of heart failure the previous February, and he was suffering serious financial losses as a result of the Depression. Hoover had been defeated in an electoral landslide by Franklin D. Roosevelt in the 1932 election; thus his one-day visit to Sapelo was a far more somber occasion than the 1928 presidential visit. The Hoovers' signatures in the Coffin house guest register were entered on Christmas Day, 1932.[26]

There continued to be pockets of white settlement on Sapelo's South End from 1920 to 1935. In 1930, there were fifty-two whites living in twelve households on the island. These included members of the Cromley family at the lighthouse, contractors and workmen associated with Coffin's restoration of Long Tabby and the main house, and the Hackels at Riverside. Emanuel Hackel managed the commissary at the oyster and shrimp cannery on Factory Creek, while his wife, Annie, was the Sapelo postmaster in the 1920s. The post office at this time was in the commissary.

The 1930 census noted one white person living at Raccoon Bluff, Katie Campbell, the teacher at the Rosenwald school there. The majority of the occupations identified in the census for both the white and black people of the island were connected with the operations of Coffin's Sapeloe Plantation. Some of these included dragline operator, foreman for road building, machinist, dairyman, stock farm manager, laundress, carpenter, herdsman, gardener, and fisherman. At the South End mansion were a cook, steward, nurse, and four maids.

A number of structures associated with these activities were outlined on the 1929 soil map, including the restored Long Tabby and its accompanying swimming pool, the Factory Creek commissary and cannery, the Coffin mansion, the South End farm complex, and residential structures in the Geechee communities.[27] The 1930 census reflected the peak of Coffin's activities on the island. With the onset of the Depression the white population declined.

In 1933, the federal government deactivated the lighthouse as shipping in Doboy Sound had almost entirely ceased by that time. Light keeper Robert H. Cromley and his family were given the option of retaining occupancy of the lighthouse reservation for five years. A revocable license issued in May 1933 stated: "Whereas, the Sapelo Lighthouse Reservation, containing one hundred and ninety-five acres with two dwellings, out-buildings and Sapelo Lighthouse located thereon under the control of the Secretary of Commerce, will no longer be required exclusively for lighthouse purposes after June 1, 1933." In 1934, the hundred-foot steel tower was dismantled and transported to South Fox Island in Lake Michigan. The two keepers' dwellings were also removed. Nothing remains now at the site of the 1905 tower except for the five concrete foundation pads. After 113 years, lighthouse activity had come to an end on Sapelo Island, and the brick tower built in 1820 stood alone and abandoned, a silent sentinel keeping watch over Doboy Sound.[28]

The automobile had precipitated a transportation revolution in the United States by the mid-1920s, and the Coastal Highway (U.S. 17) was the conveyor for an increasing flow of travelers through coastal Georgia, primarily northerners en route to the warmer climate of southern Florida. Coffin envisioned that the Georgia coastal islands could attract many of these travelers. St. Simons was a potential resort destination, particularly after the construction in 1924 of the causeway and bridges to the island from Brunswick, a project designed and built by local native Fernando J. Torras.

In 1925 Coffin began purchasing former plantation properties on St. Simons, including the Retreat tract, where he laid out the Sea Island Golf Club, followed by his acquisition the following year of a five-mile strip of beach and marsh known locally as Glynn Isle (formerly Long Island), which he renamed Sea Island Beach. There Coffin

Brochure promoting Sea Island and the Cloister Hotel, produced by the Sea Island Company, late 1920s. (Author's collection)

laid plans to develop the Sea Island Company and build a resort hotel. After paving roads and laying lines for electricity, water, and telephones to Sea Island, Coffin and Bill Jones engaged prominent Palm Beach, Florida, architect Addison Mizner to design the new Cloister Hotel, which opened in the fall of 1928. Coffin hoped to attract wealthy northerners to the Cloister as a winter alternative to the developing southern Florida resorts.[29]

The Cloister was an instant success. To facilitate access to Sea Island, Coffin and Jones started a bus line north from Jacksonville, Florida, and one south from Savannah to Brunswick. Another Coffin contribution to the coastal Georgia economy was his support of the growing paper industry, in which southern Georgia pines were industrially converted to pulp and paper products. Coffin's association with George Mead of the Mead Paper Company played a role in the formation of the Brunswick Pulp and Paper Company in 1936 by Mead and Scott Paper Company. This venture evolved into one of the largest pulp-paper manufacturers in the world, now Georgia-Pacific.

Meanwhile, Coffin and Jones brought in skilled people to manage Sea Island and the Cloister, most notably Jones's lifelong friend James D. Compton of Dayton, Ohio. Also on board were Irving A. Harned, Charles F. Redden, T. Miesse Baumgardner, and legal experts Paul Varner and C. M. Tyson. Early support for the venture was provided by Eugene W. Lewis of Detroit, who invested in the Sea Island Company; Cator Woolford, who bought Altama Plantation in Glynn County (later selling it to Bill Jones); and J. W. McSwiney of the Mead Corporation.

The end of the 1920s was a prosperous time for Sapelo and much of coastal Georgia. Economic rehabilitation was well underway, and numerous employment opportunities for the area's poorer and middle classes had been created. A renewed economic and social stability had been achieved in several of the smaller communities between Savannah and Jacksonville, largely on the strength of investments and ideas from men like Coffin, Henry Ford, and Bill Jones.

There were troubling times looming, however. After the October 1929 market crash, by late 1930 a financial burden began to tell on Coffin and Jones, particularly in regard to Sea Island. Coffin was encumbered by debt, having borrowed large sums of money to fund the Cloister, this after having spent huge outlays of cash to build Sapelo Island's new infrastructure during the 1920s.

Jones recalled that in his first five years at Sapelo, "whatever he needed in the way of workmen, materials or money, all he had to do was ask. When the bills came in, he would sit down and dash off a note to Coffin's Realty Investment Company in Detroit, from which, in that booming time, all blessings flowed. Whatever he might ask for, $10,000, $20,000, $50,000, back a check would come, no questions asked." The Sea Island and Sapelo bills mounted, but no one saw the crash coming. When the market imploded, leading to the Great Depression, it was the worst calamity that could have happened, and at the worst possible time, for Coffin.

Despite this, Coffin was still optimistic in the fall of 1930 when he gave an important address to the Georgia Bar Association at Sea Island. He urged the development of more statewide transportation and the promotion of Georgia as an attractive place to

live and do business: "We have a bit of philanthropy, and a good deal of business tied up together in this project [Sea Island]," Coffin noted.

> As a matter of experience, I have had a part in the past in starting at least two semi-philanthropic projects, both of which have paid better than almost anything else I ever went into. . . . In any big project of this kind there is bound to be a lean period, when everything is going out, and very little coming in. . . . It is the people doing things that we want here. It is these people doing things that Georgia needs . . . to the end that we may all take an even greater pride in Georgia as the finest [place] in the whole world in which to live, to work, and to play.[30]

As the Depression worsened in the early 1930s, Sea Island struggled to survive. Coffin turned over the financial management of Sea Island to Jones and the operation of the Cloister to Compton. For legal purposes, Coffin signed over all his assets to Jones in March 1932. Jones and his wife, Katherine Talbott Jones, known as Kit, reduced their own salary to $500 a month, using Kit's own money to pay for groceries at their Sea Island home.[31] Jones was determined to persevere, but cash was immediately needed to redeem outstanding bonds that would keep Sea Island and the Cloister solvent.

The solution was as obvious as it was painful: Coffin's beloved Sapelo would have to be the sacrificial lamb on the altar of financial expediency, to bring desperately needed money into Sea Island. Compton's publicity personnel began cranking out promotional literature about Sapelo in an effort to attract potential buyers.[32] To Jones's vast relief, Richard W. Courts, an Atlanta broker with wide connections in national financial circles, provided the salvation: "Twenty-eight year old Richard J. Reynolds, Jr., tired of wandering the world on his own freighter and beset by family sorrows, was looking for a quiet hideaway. At the invitation of Dick Courts, he was brought down to Sapelo to see the place. . . . Not long after, he agreed to pay Bill Jones $700,000 for Sapelo with another $50,000 added if the yacht *Zapala* was thrown in."[33]

Knowing Coffin and Jones were in financial straits, Reynolds lowballed his offer for the island and mansion. "Sapelo was Coffin's passion and his home. The $50,000 offered for the yacht was a fraction of its commissioning cost. But very few people had as much money as Dick Reynolds. . . . Eventually Jones helped Coffin realize he had little choice; for the Sea Island resort to survive, Sapelo must be sold. Coffin begged Dick to keep the deal secret for a year so that publicity surrounding the transfer would not adversely affect Sea Island's development. Dick agreed. Soon Dick had his seafront residence and one of the world's greatest yachts, obtained at a fire-sale price, perhaps ten per cent of their real value."[34]

The instrument by which Sapelo was sold by Jones (for Coffin) to Reynolds was dated April 14, 1934. The sale did not include the areas of Sapelo that Coffin did not own: the settlements of Raccoon Bluff, Hog Hammock, Belle Marsh, Shell Hammock and Lumber Landing, Behavior Cemetery, and the lighthouse tract.[35]

The complexity of the financial arrangements notwithstanding, the disposal of Sapelo, along with the sale of Detroit Realty bonds, enabled the Sea Island Company to regain its corporate footing and ride out the Depression. The company gradually acquired solvency, and by 1941 it was turning solid profits.

There is a melancholy footnote to the twenty-two-year Coffin experience with Sapelo. Coffin was a lonely man in 1937 when he entered into a disastrous second marriage in New York, to Gladys Baker, a freelance journalist much younger than Coffin. Despondent, Coffin returned to Georgia after only a few months and lived for a time with Bill and Kit Jones at Sea Island. On November 21, 1937, while the Joneses were returning from a trip to New York making arrangements for Coffin's quiet divorce from his second wife, they got the tragic news from Jim Compton that Coffin was dead. "Seeing no way out of his troubles, he had taken his own life with a rifle."[36] Coffin was buried beside Matilda at St. Simons's Christ Church Cemetery, where their plots have been carefully maintained by the Jones family and Sea Island over the years.

Even including Thomas Spalding, no period of Sapelo ownership had seen more dynamism, improvement, and overall benefit to the population of the island than that of Howard Coffin. The significance of his productive impact on Darien, Brunswick, St. Simons, and Sea Island also cannot be overstated. Coffin's ideas, energy, and money helped lift Glynn and McIntosh Counties out of their economic lethargy in the 1920s and early 1930s, possibly creating momentum that made the difficulties of the Depression less oppressive than in other areas. Clark Howell, publisher of the *Atlanta Constitution*, perceptively noted that Coffin "was in some respects a greater Georgian than many of us native sons, for he had the vision to discern and develop what our state possessed when we were perhaps less observant, less audacious, and less willing to gamble on our judgement. His dynamic influence, his creative mind and understanding spirit will be found here so long as a single child remains to play, or a weary soul to seek refreshment."[37] Howell made these remarks in 1939 on the occasion of the dedication of the Howard E. Coffin Recreational Center in Brunswick. Later there was another tribute to Coffin's memory. On January 21, 1944, the World War II Liberty ship *Howard E. Coffin* was launched at the Brunswick shipyard, christened by Kit Jones and Dorothy Torras who broke the traditional bottle of champagne across the vessel's bow. The *Coffin* was the twenty-fourth of ninety-nine Liberty ships built at Brunswick.

Coffin left other legacies to Sapelo. One that is often overlooked stems from his awareness of the importance of historical documentation and its preservation. Many of Sapelo's records, building plans, and other documents are preserved in the Sea Island archives. A large collection of photographs, many taken by Coffin himself, depicts Sapelo's people and places between 1912 and 1934, and has contributed immensely to the historiography of the coast. This collection, in possession of the Jones family, offers rare glimpses of African American life on Sapelo in the early twentieth century and records the progress of Coffin's projects.

Geechee Life at Raccoon Bluff and Hog Hammock, 1920–1940

The 1920 federal census listed 294 black residents in sixty-one households on Sapelo, out of an island population of 299. There were only five white residents on greater Sapelo that year, in two households, headed by Jaives Hart and William Hart. Additionally there were two Cromley families at the lighthouse, and Robert Raiford who farmed and lived alone on Little Sapelo.

Among the residents at Hog Hammock that year were families with the surnames Walker, Gilbert, Campbell, Sams, Hall, Carter, Bell, Jones, Dixon, Bailey, Maxwell, Underwood, Williams, Lemon, and Dunlaw. At Shell Hammock on the South End were families named Dixon, Sams, Hillery, Olane, and Bell, while Andrew and Phoebe Sherman lived at Lumber Landing, and Joseph and Annie Jones were at Belle Marsh.[38] According to the recollections of A. W. Jones Sr., there were "several hundred" black residents living on privately owned lands on Sapelo Island in the 1920s, the majority of whom were at the Raccoon Bluff and Hog Hammock settlements.

The 1930 census showed a population increase to 345 African Americans in seventy-five households, with fifty-two whites in twelve households. Most of the black residents continued to be divided between Raccoon Bluff and Hog Hammock, but the

Sapelo family at Raccoon Bluff or Hog Hammock, circa 1930. (Courtesy of Bill Jones III)

Eddie Hall and his oxcart in a photograph by Malcolm and Muriel Bell on their visit to Sapelo Island, circa 1938, during their work with the Savannah Unit of the Georgia Writers' Project. This and the images of Katie Brown, Shad Hall, and Nero Jones that follow, also taken by the Bells, depict Sapelo's people one or two generations removed from slavery. Photo by Malcolm and Muriel Bell. (Courtesy of Malcolm Bell III)

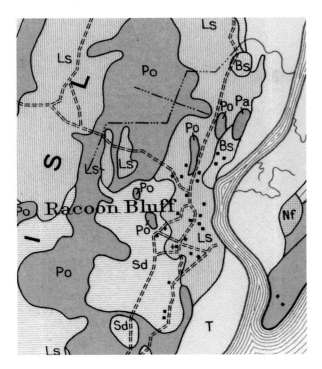

Detail from the 1929 McIntosh County soil survey map delineating the layout of roads and houses at Raccoon Bluff. (Author's collection)

census also listed several households at Shell Hammock and Belle Marsh. The majority of whites in the 1920s and early 1930s were employees of Howard Coffin. The 1920s and 1930s were probably the peak of the Raccoon Bluff community from the standpoint of population and development. Since the late 1890s it had always been the most populous of the Geechee settlements on Sapelo, and the remoteness of the community, not only from the mainland but also from most of Sapelo, enabled Raccoon Bluff to develop its own unique identity.

In 1927, a two-story wooden building was constructed near the First African Baptist Church at Raccoon Bluff to house a "Rosenwald school." Rosenwald schools, at one time numbering almost five thousand in the United States, were built primarily for the education of southern African American children in the early twentieth century. Julius Rosenwald, part owner of Sears, Roebuck, began the Rosenwald Fund to provide seed money for the schools. The school at Raccoon Bluff would be dismantled after the removal of residents to the South End in the 1950s, with only a portion of the brick chimney left remaining. Another Rosenwald school was established at Hog Hammock in an annex building of the St. Luke Church.

There was at least one general store in the community in this period, that being operated by Joseph Walker from his residence as early as 1910, and after his death this continued to be maintained by his widow, Alice. The 1929 McIntosh County soil map delineated twenty-three houses at Raccoon Bluff, among various other structures, including the store, the F.A.B. Church, and the school.[39] The residential dwellings were one-story, wood-frame structures, and there probably were additional houses beyond those shown on the map.

Through the oral histories conducted by Cornelia Bailey and Norma Harris in 1992 and transcribed in *Sapelo Voices*, it has been possible to identify the owners of many of Raccoon Bluff's dwellings in this period. Dan and Rosa Parker were on the west side of the community near the F.A.B. Church, as was Shad Hall. Several Green families were clustered in the center of Raccoon Bluff, including Moses Green and William Green, as were Luke Walker and Joseph and Alice Walker. The homes of James and Ida Green and James Green Sr. were east of the church, near

Katie Brown, photo by Malcolm
and Muriel Bell. (Courtesy of
Malcolm Bell III)

the bluff on Blackbeard Creek. North and east of the church were the households of Alice Smith, Mac Bell, James and Hattie Spaulding, Charles Spaulding, and William Spaulding, with James Bell and Sam Grovner further to the north. Several of these families lived at Drism Point, a section of Raccoon Bluff on its north end, often referred to by Allen Green and other island Geechees.[40]

Southeast of the church were the houses of Sam Roberts and Lucy Roberts near the marsh. On the lower end of Raccoon Bluff, south of the church, were Peter Roberts and the households of Gibb Lemon and Tom and Lula Lemon.

Other families in the community in the 1920s included those named Carter, Handy, Politz, Bryant, Rhodes, Truth, and Braun. *Sapelo Voices* notes that some residents of Raccoon Bluff may not have been counted in the 1920 census. These may have been some who were included in the 1910 census but who had moved away and then returned. It is also important to note that some of the census data in both 1920 and 1930 identified some families only by heads of household or by ownership of houses or property.

Some families apparently departed Raccoon Bluff during the 1920s, as a number of residents in the 1920 census are not shown in that of 1930, including Braun, Politz, Bryant, Rhodes, and Truth.[41] Concomitantly, it is almost impossible to definitively match the census data and information from the oral histories with the dwellings as shown on the 1929 soil map. While useful in establishing the general pattern and layout of structures in Raccoon Bluff, the map probably only roughly represents the houses rather giving than an accurate number of them.

Agriculture was an economic mainstay for many in Raccoon Bluff during this period, both for subsistence and for income. This had been a well-established pattern since the settlement had been founded in the early 1870s. Sizeable portions of Raccoon Bluff and nearby King Savannah were composed of soils especially conducive to crop cultivation. Additionally, part of the Drism Point section of Raccoon Bluff was a low wetland subject to freshwater inundation from natural sources and therefore useful for cultivating rice, as was often carried out by the Bell and Spaulding families that lived there.[42]

Allen Green and his wife Annie Mae Walker Green were born at Raccoon Bluff in 1907 and 1912, respectively, and lived in the settlement up to the time of the Reynolds land swaps in the late 1950s (see chapter 8), with the subsequent relocation of residents to Hog Hammock. When providing their oral histories to Cornelia Bailey in 1992, the

The Geechee Language and Sapelo

The Geechee (Gullah) language is what some linguists have identified as an English-based creole dialect arising amid slavery after the forced resettlement of peoples to the U.S. Southeast Coast from West Africa.

People of diverse backgrounds developed a lingua franca through the blending of languages from a variety of sources. In the case of Geechee, the vocabulary emerged as a mix of the English speech of slave owners and overseers with African "substrate" languages that altered the pronunciation and grammatical usage of most English words. The language, and cultural heritage, of the Geechee people of Sapelo Island is especially linked to this evolution. Because of the relatively isolated nature of Sapelo and other Georgia sea islands, until recent years the preservation of Geechee linguistics has been more pronounced there than in mainland areas.

Lorenzo Turner, an African American scholar who published his analysis in 1949, was the first to study the evolution and intricacies of the Gullah language ("Geechee" in Georgia). His studies showed that it contained a substantial number of words that came directly from African substrate languages, identifying over four thousand words of African origin. Perhaps most significantly for Sapelo and the other coastal islands where Geechee (Gullah) descendants lived, Turner revealed that some men and women could still recall simple texts in various African languages passed down through the generations after emancipation.

Many of the enslaved people from the West African "Rice Coast" were transported directly to South Carolina and Georgia. This enabled the transference and spread of distinctive creole English dialects and speech inflections from Sierra Leone, Gambia, and other areas of West Africa to the rice plantations of the Southeast Coast. These migratory speech patterns eventually

Nero Jones, photo by Malcolm and Muriel Bell.
(Courtesy of Malcolm Bell III)

became a model for other plantation slaves and evolved throughout the eighteenth and early nineteenth centuries.

The term "Gullah" likely came from the African Rice Coast. Turner attributed "Gullah" to Gola, a small tribe in Sierra Leone. Other scholars have argued that the appellative is a derivative of "Angola," itself from the Portuguese colonial name Reino de Angola used in West Africa. Georgia Gullah people came to call themselves "Geechee," which Turner attributed to the Kissi (pronounced "geezee") people of Sierra Leone, and which others attribute to the first settlements of Gullah slaves on the Ogeechee River near Savannah in the 1750s to work the rice plantations there.

Sapelo Island's African American slave descendants are "salt water" Geechees, as opposed to "freshwater" Geechee descendants of the slaves of the mainland river plantations. Examples of the Geechee dialect from Sapelo are contained in the important book *Drums and Shadows*. When interviewed at Hog Hammock in 1939 by the Georgia Writers' Project during research for the book, Shad Hall, one of several descendants of Muhammad Bilali on Sapelo, spoke of the Gullah-Geechee tradition of the beating of drums announcing the gathering time for "set-ups" (wakes) and the association of spirits with this tradition.

"Gran Hestuh tell me bout set-ups," Hall said. "Dey kill a wite chicken wen dey hab set-ups tuh keep duh spirits way. She say a wite chicken is duh only ting dat will keep duh spirits way an she alluz keep wite chickens fuh dat in duh yahd. Lak dis. Hestuh, she hab frien an frien die. Ebry ebenin friens spirit come back and call tuh Hestuh. Hestuh knowd ef she keep it up, she die too. Hestuh den kills wite chicken, tro it out duh doe, and shut doe quick. Wen she tro it out, she say, 'Heah, spirit, moob away—dohn come back no mo.' I dunno wut she do wid duh blood an fedduhs."

Until the scholarship of Turner and more recent revelatory work by Charles Joyner, Emory S. Campbell, Theresa Singleton, Erskine Clarke, Betty Wood, and others, many people stigmatized Gullah-Geechee speakers and regarded their speech as a mark of ignorance. As a consequence—largely to avoid discrimination by outsiders (whites)—Gullah-Geechee people usually spoke their language only within their homes and communities. This made more difficult the task of enumerating speakers and assessing the degrees of de-creolization.

Some speculate that the prejudice of outsiders may have helped maintain the language. Other scholars have suggested that a kind of valorization or prestige remained for many Gullah-Geechee people, and that this complex pride has insulated the language from being completely obliterated. Some examples of how Gullah was spoken in the nineteenth century are: *Uh gwine gone dey tomorruh* (I will go there tomorrow); *'E tell'um say 'e haffuh do 'um* (He told me that he had to do it); *Alltoo dem 'ooman dun fuh smaa't* (Both those women are really smart); *Dem yent yeddy wuh oonuh say* (They did not hear what you said).

SOURCES: Charles Joyner, *Down by the Riverside: A South Carolina Slave Community* (Urbana: University of Illinois Press, 1984); Georgia Writers' Project, *Drums and Shadows: Survival Studies among the Georgia Coastal Negroes* (Athens: University of Georgia Press, 1940).

This house in Hog Hammock reflects Sapelo's African American vernacular architecture of the early to mid-twentieth century.

Greens painted a picture of a quiet, peaceful community, that was different from the rest of Sapelo Island: "When you get to Raccoon Bluff you find more oak trees, and palmetto," they said. "In Hog Hammock there's more pine trees. . . . The soil is different . . . the [Hog Hammock] soil is blacker, a heavier soil. And there's more lighter soil in Raccoon Bluff, and better soil."[43]

According to the Greens the houses at Raccoon Bluff were built "up high and close together, 'cause there was so many people living there." The houses had outdoor privies and wells for their water supply, most furnished with hand pumps. Allen Green noted, "They dig a deep hole . . . and they put a barrel in there. Some people have a top over it, and some had it open. . . . After that they'd get this hand pump. . . . In our yard we had a lot of fruit trees, apple trees. My mother had a lot of apple trees, and a grape arbor . . . and a banana tree." The Greens noted that rice and corn were the chief crops grown in the 1920s and 1930s. "We shell the corn . . . we had a mill, then we ground the corn, and you get three things out of that corn when you grind it. You get grits, and you get the meal, and the husk, 'bout all we have left for the hogs."

Shad Hall, photo by Malcolm and Muriel Bell. (Courtesy of Malcolm Bell III)

A contemporary picture of 1930s Geechee life on Sapelo was provided by relative outsiders as part of the research for the Depression-era Georgia Writers' Project volume, *Drums and Shadows: Survival Studies among the Georgia Coastal Negroes*. A chapter in this compilation of oral histories is devoted to Sapelo. The effort was coordinated by Mary Granger of Savannah and aided by Savannah photographer-historians Malcolm Bell Jr. (1913–2001) and his wife Muriel Barrow Bell (1913–2011).

During their visit to the island in 1939, the Bells photographed Geechee residents in several communities to produce a remarkable set of black-and-white images that forever froze in time the African American faces of Depression-era Sapelo. Granger conducted interviews with Sapelo's people, including Katie Brown (1853–1940), great-granddaughter of black overseer Muhammad Bilali; Julia Grovener (1857–1938); Katie Grovener; George Smith; Shad Hall of Hog Hammock (formerly of Raccoon Bluff); Nero Jones of Belle Marsh; and Cuffy Wilson and Phoebe Gilbert (1891–1947), both of Shell Hammock. In addition to images of Brown, Hall, Wilson, and Jones, there are photos in *Drums and Shadows* of Sapelo's John Bryant (1881–1965) at Raccoon Bluff and Eddie Hall (1908–77) and his oxcart on one of Sapelo's sandy roads.[44]

One passage from the book places the island and its people in a cultural context only one or two generations removed from slavery:

> Small Negro settlements are scattered at the north end of Sapelo and are reached by winding roads cut through the tropical woodlands and brush. The Negroes are descendants of the slaves of the plantation era. Many lead an easy, carefree life which consists chiefly of fishing, crabbing and cultivating a small patch of garden, while others engage in regular employment at the sawmill or in the company offices.
>
> Living an isolated island existence, these Negroes have preserved many customs and beliefs of their ancestors, as well as the dialect of the older coastal Negro. An old oxcart . . . jogging along a tree shaded road is a familiar sight and, under the guidance of a Negro boy named Julius we discovered instances of crude wooden implements in common usage. The many Negroes interviewed gave a graphic picture of survival elements that have persisted since the days when slave ships brought their ancestors to the new country.[45]

Among the occupations listed for Sapelo's Geechees in the 1930 census were farmer, housekeeper, maid, and cook. The census data matched several occupations

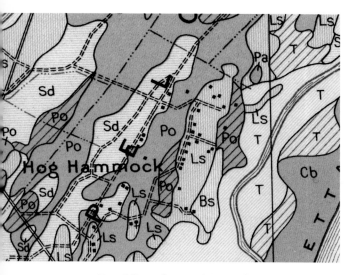

Detail from the 1929 McIntosh County soil survey map showing the layout of roads and houses at Hog Hammock. (Author's collection)

with the people who held them, including Alex Johnson (laundry foreman), Ascilba Kittrell (porter), Grant Johnson (truck driver), Emmett Johnson (carpenter), Joseph Bill (fisherman), Alice Walker (general store owner), Katie Campbell (Raccoon Bluff teacher), and Berdis Palmer (Shell Hammock teacher). The occupations indicate that many residents were employed by Coffin on the South End at the oyster cannery, at the boat yard and marine railway, and on construction projects for shell roads.[46]

The 1930 census identified thirty-seven residential dwellings at Hog Hammock and adjoining Johnson Hammock, consistent with the 1929 soil map. Most of Hog Hammock's population at this time was concentrated in the middle and northern portions of the community, largely comprising families such as Hall, Hillery, Bailey, Wilson, and Williams. Several Johnson families comprised the majority of residents on the south end of Hog Hammock and included Bennie and Theresa Johnson, Emmett and Emma Johnson, and John and Maggie Mills.

The soil map delineated the St. Luke's Baptist Church, the school north of Johnson Hammock, and the Farmers' Alliance building a little further north. Specific households included those of Richard and Eliza Bailey, Cuffy and Hannah Wilson, Katie Underwood, March and Bella Maxwell, Aaron and Sarah Wilson, Gardner and Clara Hillery, March and Nancy Bailey, and Edward Camel, among others. One white resident lived at Hog Hammock in 1930, retired lighthouse keeper Jimmy Cromley, who operated a general store in the settlement.[47]

Samuel Hillery, born at Hog Hammock in 1914, recalls that when he was growing up, the community had "the church [and] a little prayer house. But I ain't never remember going to the prayer house. . . . St. Luke, that's the first church I was going to school at. You didn't have no school house [until later]—then they had a little school coming from the road by Jimmy's house." Hillery recalled three public buildings in Hog Hammock in the 1930s: the school, St. Luke's Church, and the Farmers' Alliance hall. He placed the construction of the last at about 1929 or 1930, with the structure containing a social hall, and a meeting room on the first floor for several organizations, including local farmers and Masons.

Hillery emphasized that Sapelo's communities were largely self-sustaining. "You didn't have to buy all them rice and grits you have to buy now. You beat your own rice and grind your own corn. Most everybody always had they own corn mill. Had they own mortar to beat they own rice. . . . You could do all that, [and also]

Family in cart,
Sapelo Island,
1930s. (Courtesy of
Bill Jones III)

fishing and hunting. No reason for no fish. . . . I used to plant most anything, corn, rice, potatoes, peas, beans, greens, turnips, cabbage." Several Hog Hammock residents planted sugarcane and pressed it to make syrup. Hillery and his family always had an abundance of hogs and chickens and fed them kitchen scraps and residue from crops.

Rosa Jones Mills, born at Hog Hammock in 1914, recalled that a horse or a cow was used to plow for corn planting, adding that livestock were an essential component in the well-being of the community. "Cows and horses and the hogs, you had to feed them corn shucks and rice straw. You don't throw nothin' like that away," Mills recollected. "You had corn, and then you had scrap potatoes and stuff to feed the hogs with. And in the summer you go in the marsh and cut the marsh grass, and you give that to the hog, and he eat that, and you have to keep the trough full of water."[48]

In addition to subsistence crops grown at home there was an abundance of food away from the settlements. For the men, hunting was an integral part of community life, with rabbit, raccoon, opossum, deer, and wild turkey taken in the woods. On the marsh fringe mink and otter were plentiful. Sam Hillery and others made their own cast nets to gather shrimp and fish—mullet, trout, bass—in the tidal creeks around

Lula's Kitchen, Lula Walker's business at Hog Hammock, today provides the public with nourishing home-cooked meals with all the modern conveniences while retaining the island's ambience and the cultural legacies of its past generations of people.

Sapelo. "Try and catch catfish too. Catfish just ties up your net." Cast-netting was often facilitated from skiffs known in the coastal region as bateaux. "Well, most of 'em bateaux. We call 'em a bateau, you know."

Life was quite purposeful in Sapelo's Geechee communities. People were resourceful. They worked hard, little time was wasted, and everything was grown, handmade, or manufactured, incorporating value and utility. These traits extended to the children. "Plenty of children in Hog Hammock then," Hillery recalled. My dad got a little trash, better rake 'em. . . . In them days children will rake you the whole yard if you got a bag for it, the trash too. You give about fifty cents. That was big pay."

In 1930 there were eleven families at Shell Hammock on the South End, including Lee and Bell Sams, Anthony Sams, Peggy Dixon, Herman and Anna Hillery, Gibb and Dianna Hillery, Dan and Nettie Dixon, Phoebe Gilbert, Dan and Rosa Parker, Ascilba and Belle Kittrell, Randolph and Gracie Lewis, and Rayfield and Isabelle Hillery. A short distance north, at Oakdale, was the family of Robert and Mary Olane. There was also a praise house at Shell Hammock.[49]

By the late 1920s, most of Sapelo Island's population was concentrated in the three settlements at Raccoon Bluff, Hog Hammock, and Shell Hammock, the number of families at Lumber Landing having declined to only two. The 1930 census showed that Mattie Sams and three daughters—Jessie, May, and Marie—lived on the north end of Lumber Landing on the High Point road nearest the marsh, while Janie Sams lived on the other side of the road with her two sisters, May and Daisy. An earlier resident, Phoebe Sams Sherman, moved to Hog Hammock before the 1930 census.

Another family, that of Georgia Jones, widow of Charlie Jones, and her six sons and four daughters, also relocated to Hog Hammock just before 1930, The Jones family had lived in the old Kenan house, although the condition of the dwelling was probably poor, it having been built well before the Civil War. There were two families at Belle Marsh in 1930: Nero and Nancy Jones occupied a house with their children Freddie and Anna, and Hicks and Hettie Walker lived in a house with their son Gibb. These two homes were located between Moses Hammock and the High Point road, as shown on the 1929 soil map.[50]

CHAPTER VIII   Sapelo in the 1950s

Autumn of the Old Regime

EXCEPTING THE PRESENT African American community, Sapelo Island's last era of private ownership was that of R. J. Reynolds Jr., the high-flying, free-spirited heir to a North Carolina cigarette fortune. Reynolds brought to Sapelo modernity, mechanics, and science—in addition to four different wives—during a thirty-year span. Reynolds's outlook and lifestyle contrasted with those of his Sapelo predecessors, Thomas Spalding and Howard Coffin. Unlike them, Reynolds never made Sapelo his full-time home, but regularly visited the island for stays of varying length, often simply to escape the vicissitudes of his personal and professional life on the mainland.

Richard Joshua Reynolds Jr. (1906–64) of Winston-Salem, North Carolina, known to family and friends as Dick, was the son of that city's founder of the Reynolds Tobacco Company and like Spalding was twenty-eight when he bought Sapelo in 1934. His life would be one of paradoxes. Reynolds was wealthy, witty, ambitious, highly intelligent, philanthropic, an icon of his times in industrial and financial America. His business and political acumen—and his father's tobacco fortune—made him well-known by the middle of the twentieth century, yet he was tragically flawed. He had a

R. J. Reynolds Jr. as a young man.
(Courtesy of Noah Reynolds)

disastrous and turbulent personal life filled with infidelity, broken relationships, and alcoholism, and he died at the age of fifty-eight under what some have called questionable circumstances.

As a young man Reynolds became a key player nationally in business, politics, and philanthropy. In 1940 he salvaged a failing Delta Airlines with the purchase of a large block of stock that gave the airline financial stability. The same year Reynolds's energetic fund-raising efforts in North Carolina helped secure Franklin D. Roosevelt's unprecedented third presidential term, for which Reynolds was rewarded by being appointed treasurer of the Democratic National Committee. In 1941 he was elected mayor of Winston-Salem with a 90 percent plurality. Yet for all these achievements he remained unsettled in both his personal and public lives—he was as restless as he was successful.

A licensed pilot, Reynolds often traveled the country by air, and he was a leader in the U.S. aviation industry, but his real love was the sea. He was a world-class yachtsman, read extensively on maritime history and the marine sciences, and was a decorated naval officer in the Pacific theater of World War II. Reynolds got much use out of Coffin's yacht *Zapala*, part of his Sapelo purchase package. For several years, Reynolds and his first wife made annual voyages to the Mediterranean in the *Zapala*, as well as to Bermuda.

Pursuant to these nautical interests, and not long after acquiring Sapelo, Reynolds had a workboat designed to fulfill specific logistical requirements. Ronester Johnson of Hog Hammock recalled that Coffin initiated boatbuilding on the South End in the early 1920s, work continued by Reynolds at the boatyard and marine railway on South End Creek. Johnson noted that his father, Emmett Johnson Sr., was a skilled boat carpenter: "He built on the *Kit Jones*, [which] was built right here on Sapelo—every bit, except for the keel—the pine wasn't long enough. It was built of yellow pine. And all the ribs were cut from oak. And there was no nails, all pegs."[1]

The *Kit Jones*, a sixty-one-foot workboat designed to transport freight and passengers, was propelled by a one-hundred-horsepower Atlas diesel engine. Reynolds named the boat for Katherine T. Jones, wife of his Sea Island friend, Alfred W. Jones Sr. The *Kit* was designed to towboat specifications in 1938 by the New York firm of Sparkman & Stephens on contract to Reynolds. Using Sapelo oak and pine, Norwegian boatbuilder Hulga Spar was engaged to construct the vessel at the South End boatyard. The *Kit Jones* was a solid, durable craft used for passenger, mail, and supply delivery

The *Kit Jones* was built on Sapelo Island in 1939–40 for use as a utility vessel for the Reynolds operations. The *Kit* later served as a ferry and research vessel for the Marine Institute for many years. (Courtesy of Noah Reynolds)

between the mainland and Sapelo. When Reynolds later acquired a new ferry, the *Janet*, he awarded the *Kit* to the University of Georgia Marine Institute for use as a research vessel. Later the *Kit* was used in a similar capacity by the Savannah-based Skidaway Institute of Oceanography before it was sold to the State of Mississippi for research purposes. By late 2015 the *Kit* had been deactivated and placed in dry dock at Biloxi, Mississippi, its future undetermined.

In many respects, Reynolds proved as energetic as Coffin, continuing the agricultural and timbering operations initiated by his predecessor. In 1935–37 Reynolds rebuilt the quadrangle farm complex on the South End, constructing office and apartment buildings and a two-story masonry barn with a red clay–tiled roof. These new structures replaced Coffin's earlier frame buildings on the same site. Reynolds also commissioned a German sculptor, Fritz Zimmer, to render the Turkey Fountain statuary in the quadrangle courtyard.

Reynolds employed 180 workers in 1935, most working in road, artesian well, and other building projects supervised by his island manager, Girard Bullen. Cattle grazing was expanded, and dairy facilities were developed in the new barn to process milk for sale to mainland outlets. Reynolds employed a number of Sapelo's Geechee residents in

R. J. Reynolds Jr. in his late thirties, in his U.S. Navy uniform. He served with distinction in the Pacific theater of World War II. (Courtesy of Noah Reynolds)

the dairy, as domestics at the main house, as boat operators, and at the Duplin River sawmill.

As Reynolds was completing his purchase of the island in 1934, the National Park Service conducted a study considering the feasibility of making Sapelo a national seashore. In the end, a report viewed the proposal unfavorably, concluding that public access and federal acquisition of the island were probably insurmountable hurdles. "Access seems inadequate for this project," the study noted, adding that automobile access could be achieved by building a causeway and bridges from the mainland to Creighton Island, then to the west side of Sapelo, "But the cost of such work over the seven-mile stretch of marsh and open water seems prohibitive. . . . The beach area [of Sapelo] does not have sufficient elevation or width for permanent or intensive use. . . . If the problems of providing access, and the cost of acquisition come within the realm of reason, this area should be considered of unusual merit for its scenic beauty and historic interest rather than for its value as a bathing beach for intensive public use." The report noted that Sapelo's new owner was unlikely to be willing to sell to the government, but if he did sell, his price would be at minimum $1.33 million.[2]

Reynolds met his first wife, Elizabeth Dillard (1909–61), in the summer of 1932 at Reynolda, the family estate in Winston-Salem. After a short engagement they were married on New Year's Day 1933. Nicknamed "Blitz" by Reynolds for her assertive, often fiery personality, she bore Reynolds four sons: Josh (1933), John (1936), Zach (1938), and Will (1940).

The United States entered the Second World War in late 1941. In June 1942 Reynolds resigned as mayor of Winston-Salem and met with FDR to submit his resignation as DNC treasurer, following which he began U.S. Navy training in navigation and aviation. Reynolds served with distinction during the war years, attaining the rank of lieutenant commander. In the fall of 1944 he sailed from San Diego to the war front in the South Pacific theater, serving as navigation officer aboard the escort carrier *Makin Island* (CVE 93). Reynolds earned campaign ribbons, including a Bronze Star, by guiding the carrier through several kamikaze attacks by Japanese warplanes in high-intensity operations in the Philippines at Leyte Gulf and Lingayen, and later at Iwo Jima and Okinawa.[3]

The "Turkey Fountain" in the center of the Marine Institute quadrangle. It was sculpted by Fritz Zimmer in the mid-1930s as part of the development of R. J. Reynolds's farm complex on Sapelo's South End.

While its owner was half a world away in the Pacific, the global conflict had its effects on Sapelo Island. Two Coast Guard submarine watch stations were maintained, one at High Point and the other at the abandoned lighthouse tract. German U-boats prowling the U.S. East Coast often attacked American cargo ships and tankers in 1942 and 1943 (two tankers were sunk off St. Simons Island), and personnel at coastal watch stations played an important role as spotters for the submarines that occasionally surfaced in nearshore waters to charge batteries and seek supplies.

Reynolds and Blitz divorced in 1946, and in August that year he married his second wife, movie actress Marianne O'Brien (1917–85). Reynolds had met O'Brien in the fall of 1944 just before his departure for the Philippines from San Diego on the *Makin Island*. His marriage with Blitz had grown stale, and the redheaded actress was like a breath of fresh air for the returning war hero.

As in his first marriage, Reynolds often entertained lavishly during his trips to Sapelo, both at the main house and aboard the *Zapala*. Being wealthy, Reynolds was often excessively extravagant in his entertaining. But occasionally "the eating, drinking, and partying wore thin. . . . To get away from the guests, Dick and Marianne fled to a tree house near Cabretta beach, a two-mile stretch of long-dead trees and driftwood. Blackbeard was rumored to have buried his treasure there, Dick told Marianne as they cuddled in the tree house and cooked chili, away from the intruders they'd invited to their paradise."[4]

The main house was undergoing gradual modernization during this period. In 1936, Reynolds hired Atlanta architect Philip T. Shutze (1890–1982), a Georgia Tech graduate, to design and oversee the modification of the house and update it to suit his preferences.[5] Shutze contracted the Greek-born Atlanta artist Athos Menaboni (1896–1990) and his wife, Sara, to paint murals of tropical birds and flora on the walls in the swimming pool area and solarium and the pirate murals in the downstairs game room. In 1939 Menaboni coordinated the redesign of the upstairs ballroom in a motif that appropriately reflected its new name, the Circus Room.

Under contract to Reynolds, R. N. White Jr. conducted a survey of Sapelo Island in 1940, the result of which was a detailed map updating the location of all the island's structures.[6] White consolidated data from aerial photographs and U.S. Geological Survey topographic maps to compile an accurate cartographic picture of Sapelo that showed houses, roads, bridges, fences, culverts, docks, artesian wells, power lines, cultivated fields, abandoned fields, and pastures. Cleared fields were shown south of Long

The commissary at Barn Creek, north of Long Tabby, originally built as a store and post office by Howard Coffin, continued to be used in the Reynolds era. (Courtesy of Noah Reynolds)

Tabby where Reynolds, in 1934, had laid out a grass airstrip and built a metal hangar for his private plane, and at Flora Bottom and Root Patch northwest of the mansion. The Geechee communities were shown, as were natural features, including pine and hardwood forests, grasslands, high and low marshes, ponds, and beaches. The White map also noted the location of the Sears, Roebuck kit homes assembled by Reynolds, one at Chocolate overlooking Mud River, and others on the South End. These structures were transported to Sapelo in parts and assembled on site.

Reynolds upgraded Coffin's power-generating plant near the mansion. He named his small electric company Atlas Utilities, and it generated electric power for the South End, with lines eventually extended to Hog Hammock in the late 1950s. The first power lines from the mainland were run to Sapelo by the Georgia Power Company in the early 1960s. Atlas Utilities also managed the island's telephone service, named the Sapelo Island Telephone Company until its acquisition by Darien Telephone in 1972. At that time the Sapelo Island exchange had forty-five extensions on the South End. The only telephone at Hog Hammock was a pay station at the home of Herman Hillery, whose job it was to answer the phone and hand-deliver messages to residents. This rather primitive system of communication improved when Darien Telephone installed lines in the community in the 1970s.[7]

R. J. Reynolds Jr. undertook ongoing modernization
and upgrades to the South End mansion after his
acquisition of Sapelo in 1934.

Primary access across Doboy Sound from Sapelo to the mainland landing at Meridian dock continued to be by water, first with the *Kit Jones*, then in 1960 with the *Janet*, by which Reynolds established regular ferry service. Hog Hammock cousins Fred Johnson and Benny Johnson were captains of the *Janet*, which was replaced in 1978 by the new Department of Natural Resources state-run ferry, *Sapelo Queen*.

In 1949, so that he might write off some of the great expense associated with maintaining Sapelo, Reynolds embarked on a business enterprise that briefly opened the island to the public. The Sapelo Plantation Inn provided visitors with a unique—and expensive—opportunity to experience the hospitality of Sapelo's owner in a variety of ways. Guests could enjoy movies in the dairy barn's second-floor theater. They could browse the shops on the quadrangle courtyard, savor the amenities of the main house and nearby Azalea Cottage, and sunbathe on Nannygoat Beach a short distance away. A 1949 article by Atlanta journalist Andrew Sparks extolled the virtues of Reynolds's venture:

> One of Georgia's most fabulous spots, Sapelo Island, was recently opened to paying guests. . . . Sapelo is still a private paradise, owned by Richard J. Reynolds of Winston-Salem, N.C., but now its mansion has been turned into the sort of exclusive guest house where luxury-affording visitors can find wilderness seclusion in the midst of every comfort. There are also handsome [quadrangle] apartments; about 40 guests can be accommodated. . . . The island is accessible only by plane and boat. . . . [F]rom Darien to Meridian, a white shell road turns off from the pavement and winds through the marsh down an avenue of stunted cedars to the Sapelo dock. . . . At the dock we were met by Ted Peterson, manager. . . . We boarded a work boat, the *Kit Jones*, and cruised through wide tidal waters into Doughboy [sic] Sound where one has an expansive view of the Atlantic between the abandoned lighthouse on Sapelo and the tip of Wolf Island. On the horizon was a string of tiny rock islands built up where English sailing ships dropped ballast on their trips to the New World. The *Kit Jones* turned into Teakettle River, part of the inland waterway, then into Duplin River to the Island dock.[8]

Dick and Marianne Reynolds's second son, Patrick Cleveland, born in 1948, described the venture in somewhat more acerbic terms in his book about the Reynolds family, *The Gilded Leaf*: "While the paying guests were about, a bathing-suited Marianne would emerge to dip in the outdoor pool or just to take in the sun. Her movie-star figure made the male guests gawk; they'd talk with her and she with them. . . . Benevolence and anger: alcoholics often veer back and forth between these,

1944-1945

Although we are separated by the distances of war, we are united in our thoughts of friends far and near at this Christmas season, and trust that the New Year will bring to all of us many occasions for being thankful.

Reynolds family Christmas card, 1944. Shown at left is R. J. Reynolds Jr. aboard his Pacific escort aircraft carrier. Opposite are his wife Elizabeth Dillard Reynolds (Blitz) and (*left to right*) their sons, Zach, Josh, Will, and John. (Author's collection)

embracing extremes as the tides of inebriation and sobriety come and go. In 1949, Dick didn't stay on the wagon long. How could he have guests staying in his South End mansion without having a polite drink with them? He loved being a good host."[9]

A typewritten booklet about Sapelo's history compiled by Reynolds for his guests provides some insight into his eagerness to share the island's past with his visitors:

Sapelo was known for its princely hospitality and tired city friends like William Scarborough of Savannah, who in 1831 wrote of visiting Thomas Spalding "for a change of air and a sea bath." . . . Following the Civil War Sapelo went into a decline until Howard Coffin fell in love with the island . . . and purchased Sapelo and began [its] reconstruction. . . . Mr. Coffin began the restoration of the mansion with a new roof, floors, bathrooms, and the addition of a swimming pool. During the Twenties, once again Sapelo brought happiness to its guests. . . . After Mrs. Coffin's death, Mr. Coffin did not like to entertain without her, and I bought the island in 1934, having also fallen in love with it when I visited him some years before for a shooting party. With Mr. Coffin's continued interest and valuable advice, I completely air-conditioned the mansion (one of the first big private homes), built a modern power plant, docks and barns. The work was completed by Christmas 1936, when Mr. Coffin visited me and enthusiastically approved the work and the redecoration of the mansion. Some of the furniture and rugs are from my father's old home in North Carolina. The sideboard in the dining room is the original one that Thomas Spalding had in the same place. I obtained it from Randolph Spalding of Savannah.[10]

In 1949–50, Reynolds entered discussions with local and state officials over a proposal to construct a causeway linking the mainland with Sapelo and Blackbeard Islands. Seeking increased profitability, Reynolds wanted to provide automotive access—quick and convenient—for guests visiting the Sapelo Plantation Inn. Meanwhile, the state of Georgia was exploring the idea of acquiring Blackbeard from the U.S. Department of the Interior and developing a state-managed beach resort similar to that envisioned for Jekyll Island, which the state had acquired several years earlier. Engineering studies were conducted, the results of which determined that a causeway was not financially feasible, based on a projected a $3 million price tag, an exorbitant amount of money in 1950. Also, the federal government was unwilling to cede Blackbeard to the state.

The Plantation Inn venture ultimately proved unsuccessful—there simply were not enough high-paying guests to suit the proprietor—and Reynolds ceased the business in 1951. Two years later Reynolds granted the dairy barn and other buildings around the quadrangle to the University of Georgia for a marine biological research station (see chapter 9).

During this period, Reynolds operated a summer camp for underprivileged boys under the direction of his friend, Richard Orme Flinn Jr., pastor of the Carrollton, Georgia, Presbyterian church. From 1948 to 1952, the Long Tabby guesthouse and its swimming pool were used for the boys' camp, and several bunkhouses and a dining hall were built close by. Additional projects evolved during this period. Having long been interested in forest management and its applications both scientific and economic, Reynolds revived Sapelo's timber operations in 1954. North End timber, much of it destined for Cuba and Haiti, was processed at the Duplin River sawmill on the upper end of Kenan Field.

Reynolds developed lasting ties with several members of the Darien community, including his attorney and agent, Paul Varner, and county sheriff Tom Poppell. The local Durant family was also closely associated with Reynolds and Sapelo. Tom Durant

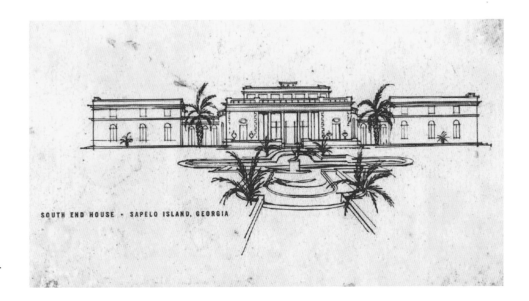

An early 1950s illustration of the Reynolds house on Sapelo Island. (Author's collection)

(1909–61) was Reynolds's secretary and manager of the Plantation Inn during its three years of operation and also served as island manager during the 1950s. Durant was discharged by Reynolds in 1960, allegedly for disloyalty—Reynolds thought Durant was feeding information about his finances and declining health to his third wife, Muriel Reynolds, near the end of their marriage. Reynolds then appointed Durant's brother, Frank E. Durant (1899–1983), as island manager. He would serve in that capacity through the 1960s. Charles Durant, Frank's nephew, was employed on Sapelo by the University of Georgia in the post-Reynolds era and played a role in the growth of the Marine Institute.[11]

Reynolds divorced Marianne in 1952 and later that year married two-time divorcee Muriel Greenough (1915–80) of New York City but a native of Calgary, Alberta. The marriage vows were spoken on the front lawn of the Sapelo mansion.

In the late 1950s, Reynolds's health declined, exacerbated by years of excessive drinking. A heavy smoker, he also began to experience increasingly frequent bouts of emphysema. "Sapelo, an island of fantasy for Dick Reynolds, now became Sapelo, air-conditioned prison. In the latter part of 1958, Dick was confined mostly to the air-conditioned patio [solarium] and bedroom, separated from the moist atmosphere of the indoor pool by a glass wall."[12]

Reynolds's relations with Muriel grew increasingly contentious. Muriel is said to have frequently engaged in odd behavior. "She was outspoken to the point of rudeness not only to Dick and the servants, but also to the occasional guests. Dick suspected that she was paying or had coerced some of the employees to spy on him."[13] Doctors from Atlanta, Savannah, and Winston-Salem attending to Reynolds on Sapelo noted that his declining health typically improved during the periods when Muriel was away from the island.

Matters reached a head, and divorce proceedings began in May 1960. Muriel's lawyers "tried to get the trial shifted away from Darien, arguing that because Reynolds was McIntosh County's most prominent citizen, his wife could not get a fair trial there. . . . Dick had financed Sheriff Tom Poppell's [1960] re-election campaign and paid for an American Legion building in Darien, a gymnasium for the black high school, and a community swimming pool. The local judge, offended, ruled that Dick could get a fair trial in Darien."[14] Thus it came as no surprise that after a two-week trial a local jury awarded Reynolds the settlement he desired.

Less than a year later, in April 1961, the fifty-five-year-old Reynolds began his fourth marriage, wedding Annemarie Schmidt (born 1929) of Germany. Meanwhile, Muriel won an appeal of the 1960 divorce, partly because Reynolds did not testify in person at the first trial. A second trial was held in Darien in May 1962 and amounted to a media circus. Reynolds gave testimony (taking oxygen every few minutes while doing so), defending himself against Muriel's charges of his alcoholism and mental abuse.[15] This time, the local jury ruled even more favorably for Reynolds than it had at the first trial, "stating that he did not have to pay a cent of alimony to Muriel. . . . It was a complete victory for Dick."[16]

Despite the favorable court outcomes, Reynolds felt besieged by Muriel after the divorce as her lawyers promised continuous appeals and press coverage. Dick decided that he had had enough of America, and after meeting with his four oldest sons at Sapelo in the late spring of 1962, he and Annemarie departed for Europe to take up permanent residence in Switzerland.

There is a story that just before departing Sapelo for the last time, the ailing Reynolds took Fred and Cracker Johnson and other trusted blacks from Hog Hammock to help him retrieve bags of gold he had hidden in various parts of the island over the years. He is said to have assured the Johnsons that they would be taken care of in the event of his death and that Ledyard Staples, his accountant and

Sapelo Island Place-Names

Earliest known primary source references and provenance (if known) for selected island place-names:

Barn Creek—Coast Survey topographic map, 1868. Duplin River tributary, South End.

Behavior—McKinley journal, 1872. South End settlement and cemetery.

Belle Marsh—McKinley journal, 1872. North End.

Blackbeard Island—Yonge and DeBrahm survey, 1760.

Bourbon Field—McKinley journal, 1871. North End.

Bush Camp—Confederate outpost on South End, 1861–62. North of Behavior.

Cabretta Island—Yonge and DeBrahm survey, 1760. On seaward side of Sapelo north of Nannygoat Beach.

Chocolate—1797 deed and correspondence. North End.

Dean Creek—1875 deed. South End east of lighthouse tract. Named for James Dean, postbellum bar pilot.

Doboy Island and Sound—late 1500s French map. Named for Jacques Dubois, or DuBoys, French navigator. Earliest English reference: 1760 Yonge and DeBrahm survey.

Duplin River—Kenan family correspondence, 1850s.

Factory Creek—early 1920s. Named for site of commercial oyster and shrimp cannery on upper Barn Creek.

Hammocks—1873 deed. Duplin River. South to north: Mary, Fishing, Pumpkin, Jack.

Hanging Bull—Chappedelaine will, 1794; McKinley journal, 1870. Lower end of Kenan Field.

High Point—Reuben King journal, 1806, and traditional. North End.

Hog Hammock—Coast Survey topographic map, 1857.

Inverness—postal map, 1894. Sapelo post office, 1891–1914. Early name for Darien.

Jack Hammock—McKinley journal, 1872. North End.

Kenan Place—1840s deeds; Coast Survey topographic maps, 1857 and 1868.

King Savannah—McKinley journal, 1875. North End.

Little Sapelo Island—Yonge and DeBrahm survey, 1760.

Marsh Landing—McKinley journal, 1870. South End.

Moses Hammock—McKinley journal, 1871. North End.

Nannygoat Beach—Yonge and DeBrahm survey, 1760.

New Barn Creek—traditional, post–Civil War. Upper part of Behavior, includes Bush Camp Field.

New Orleans—McKinley journal, 1872. South End.

Oakdale—McKinley journal, 1871. South End.

Post Office Creek—traditional (later official), 1891, for post office at McKinley's. Lower Barn Creek.

Raccoon Bluff—French documents, 1792.

Riverside—McKinley journal, 1870. Barn Creek near Long Tabby. Used interchangeably with "Long Tabby"; generally refers to the same section of Sapelo.

Sapelo—1889 deeds. North end of Creighton Island near Sapelo Sound.

Shell Hammock—named for Indian shell deposits nearby. South End Geechee settlement.

"Spanish Fort" (Shell Ring)—1760 Yonge and DeBrahm survey. North End.

Street Place (Raccoon Bluff)—1871 deeds. North End.

Teakettle Creek—Yonge and DeBrahm survey, 1760.

York Landing—Early 1800s. Long Tabby, Barn Creek.

The abandoned Sapelo lighthouse, circa 1960.
(Author's collection)

business manager, would keep the main house open for visitors so that the island's blacks could have continued employment. True or not, Reynolds left Sapelo for the last time, "with his treasure, his oxygen bottles, his fourth wife . . . and his memories."[17]

His health continued to deteriorate, though, and he died suddenly in Lucerne on December 14, 1964, at the age of fifty-eight.[18] Two days later Annemarie gave birth to Reynolds's seventh child, his first daughter, Irene Sabine Reynolds. In the following weeks, Reynolds's family in the United States, including his sons, were stunned to discover that they had been disinherited. Reynolds had left everything, including Sapelo, to Annemarie.

Elizabeth "Blitz" Reynolds died of colon cancer in 1961 at the age of fifty-two. In the late 1960s, two other ex-wives, Marianne and Muriel, became close and often met to discuss their belief that Annemarie had not only convinced Reynolds to change his will but also caused Reynolds's death. There were legal claims to over $50 million of Reynolds's estate, and to Sapelo. (Marianne claimed that Reynolds left her the island with a deed written on a paper napkin during their engagement.) Numerous suits and appeals by the two ex-wives and other family members were to no avail, and none of the suspicions over Reynolds's death, the legitimacy of his will, or the settlement of his estate were ever legally resolved.[19] Muriel Reynolds and Marianne Reynolds died in 1980 and 1985, respectively.

Ledyard Staples continued to have oversight of Sapelo for the Reynolds estate in the 1960s and 1970s during the period when the island was transitioning to state ownership. He played a major role in the business and financial management of Reynolds's Sapelo Island Research Foundation. In 1969, Annemarie Reynolds, as executor of her husband's estate, facilitated the first of two transactions by which Sapelo Island was sold to the state of Georgia.

CHAPTER IX   Scientific Sapelo

Conservation, Community, and Challenge

THE MOST IMPORTANT LEGACY left by R. J. Reynolds to Sapelo was his enabling the establishment of a marine biological laboratory on the island in 1953. The scientific research at the facility that evolved into the University of Georgia Marine Institute played the key role in Sapelo's later acquisition by the state and the consequent provision of educational, research, and conservation programs on the island for academics and the general public.

The seeds for the Marine Institute were planted in the summer of 1948 when two University of Georgia (UGA) biology professors, Eugene P. Odum and Donald C. Scott, and a young Georgia Game and Fish Commission biologist, James Jenkins, visited Sapelo in hopes of spotting a bird species introduced to the island from Central America by Howard Coffin, the chachalaca. While at Sapelo, Odum, Scott, and Jenkins enjoyed an unscheduled visit with Reynolds, who was enthusiastic about the natural history of the coast, though his primary interests lay in agriculture and forestry.[1] Reynolds had also been expanding his interests in animal husbandry with his Sapelo dairy cattle operations. During their visit Odum and Scott broached to Reynolds the idea of Sapelo as site for a marine research laboratory.

The University of Georgia
Marine Institute main lab

Reynolds was not enthusiastic initially, but four years later, by which time his
Plantation Inn had closed, he was receptive. In 1952 he invited UGA president O. C.
Aderhold, Gene Odum, and other UGA scientists to Sapelo to discuss establishing a
foundation for biological and agricultural research. Odum once again saw the opportunity to conduct applied ecological research using Sapelo Island as a remote campus.
Interested in pursuing research related to the Georgia salt marshes, Odum, with Scott's
support, made a proposal to Reynolds for the university to use Sapelo as a biological
station. Field investigations in marsh ecology and other disciplines related to marine
biology would be conducted in tandem with research in forestry and agriculture to satisfy Reynolds's interests.

Reynolds was enthusiastic and finalized a contract with Aderhold and George H.
Boyd, dean of the Graduate School at UGA, in the summer of 1953 to establish the

Birth of the University of Georgia Marine Institute in August 1953: seated are UGA president O. C. Aderhold at left and Richard J. Reynolds Jr. Standing, *left to right*, are the early scientists at the Marine Institute, E. J. Kuenzler, Lawrence R. Pomeroy, and Eugene P. Odum. (Courtesy of University of Georgia Marine Institute)

University of Georgia Marine Biological Laboratory. Reynolds agreed to provide the scientists the South End marshes, to conduct field research, and the buildings on the quadrangle of the former dairy complex, including barn, shops, and apartments. By late August 1953, using an initial grant of $25,000, Odum had in place the first resident director of the Marine Laboratory, Robert A. Ragotzkie, a hydrologist who had recently earned his PhD.[2]

Ragotzkie began converting the dairy barn into a laboratory and added resident research staff. In early 1954, Theodore J. Starr, a microbiologist, became the first recruited scientist. He pursued studies at Sapelo until the fall of 1955. In September 1954, Lawrence R. Pomeroy, an invertebrate zoologist, arrived at the laboratory, followed in June 1955 by John M. Teal, an ecosystem ecologist who had pursued energy flow studies as a graduate student. Ragotzkie, Pomeroy, and Teal worked together on Sapelo as full-time scientists for four years. They resided in the quadrangle apartments, worked in the marshes and uplands of Sapelo, and consolidated their investigations at the barn laboratory. They used the *Kit Jones* to transport supplies and equipment from the mainland.

The work of these early researchers laid the foundation for the scientific achievements for the next fifty years at Sapelo. Teal departed for Nova Scotia in 1959, and after that he went to the Woods Hole Oceanographic Institute. The legacy of his Sapelo research has been perpetuated by two enduring studies that evolved from his experiences on the island—*Portrait of an Island* and *Life and Death of a Salt Marsh*, both cowritten with his wife, Mildred Teal.[3] Ragotzkie and Pomeroy left in 1960 for the University of Wisconsin and the Athens main campus, respectively.

George H. Lauff was the second director of the laboratory, during 1960–62, with Vernon J. Henry serving as director during 1964–70. The laboratory's official name was changed to the University of Georgia Marine Institute (UGAMI) in 1959, with Boyd serving as administrative head from Athens. The name of Reynolds's foundation was changed the same year, from the Sapelo Island Agricultural and Forestry Foundation to the Sapelo Island Research Foundation (SIRF), with annual funding allocated to support research programs at the Marine Institute.

Scientists pose at the entrance to the Marine Institute's main research laboratory housed in the former Reynolds dairy barn. *Left to right*: Lawrence R. Pomeroy, Herbert W. Kale, Eugene P. Odum, and Donald C. Scott. (Courtesy of University of Georgia Marine Institute)

Although Odum conducted research on Sapelo in its early years, he had no administrative role in the facility. Nonetheless, the findings emanating from the Marine Institute in its first two decades influenced his evolving philosophy of ecology and environmentalism:

> We moved up tidal creeks in small outboard motor boats on ebbing tides, we found ourselves in deep canyons of golden mud banks . . . topped by six-foot high stands of marsh grass looking for all the world like a well-fertilized stand of sugar cane. The notion came to us in those early days that we were in the arteries of a remarkable energy-absorbing natural system whose heart was the pumping action of the tides. The entire tideland complex of barrier islands, marshes, creeks, and river mouths was a single operational unit linked together by the tide. If we were right, each part of the system would have to be dependent for its life-sustaining energy not only on the direct rays of the sun, but also on the energy of the tides. . . . Does nature routinely exploit tidal power as men have dreamed of doing for centuries? In the past biologists who studied estuarine and seashore organisms had been preoccupied with how such life adapts to the obvious stresses; that some of the stresses might be converted to subsidies was, and still is, something of a new theory. This germ of an idea, subsequently developed by twenty years of team research on Sapelo, will, we hope, provide the basis for man to design with, rather than against, nature on this remarkable sea coast.[4]

E. J. Kuenzler (*left*) and John M. Teal conducting ecological research at Sapelo, 1950s. (Courtesy of University of Georgia Marine Institute)

The early use of the institute as a site for field research by undergraduate and postgraduate students from the Athens campus was first encouraged by Paul Burkholder, a UGA scientist who conducted microbiological studies at Sapelo. Over time, this off-campus use of the Sapelo laboratory expanded to its use by students from all over the southeastern United States. As papers of the resident scientists began to make their way into prominent scientific journals in the 1950s and 1960s, the reputation of the institute began to grow. There began a momentum impelled by the accumulation and dissemination of significant ecological data.

Important geological investigations at Sapelo were undertaken by John Hoyt and Vernon J. Henry in the early 1960s. The revelations evolving from their work made lasting contributions to an understanding of the relationship between sea level variations and barrier island formation. Hoyt and Henry made the connection between the transport of mud and sand with the formation and movement of the islands. Hoyt and Robert Weimer linked the burrowing habits of ghost shrimp to determine the heights of former sea levels, work expanded upon in the 1970s by Robert Frey and James Howard. Orrin Pilkey's research concluded that Holocene formations, such as Blackbeard and Cabretta Islands and Nannygoat Beach, were not the result of sediments conveyed by the rivers from the interior to the coast—a long held assumption—but rather were the formational sands of areas actually originating from the continental shelf offshore, findings further confirmed by Hoyt and Henry.[5]

In the marshes, the early field research of Odum, Pomeroy, Teal, and C. L. Schelske began making the scientific connections between the degrees of efficiency and conditions by which the tidal ecosystem harnesses and consumes energy, recording important data regarding the natural processes by which the marsh system functions.[6] Pomeroy and Schelske expanded these studies to incorporate the methodology of measuring marsh production through the conversion of light energy (photosynthesis) into usable carbohydrates.

The ecological research at Sapelo Island in the first forty years of the UGA presence there often entailed field studies determining the water flow characteristics of *Spartina alterniflora* (smooth cordgrass) marsh and the chemical and biological processes associated with *Spartina*, in concert with the marine organisms that proliferate the marsh ecosystem or are directly affected by the marsh.[7] Eventually an important connection was made between the dynamics of the natural processes occurring in the salt marshes and the sustainability of marine life in the nearshore and estuarine waters, as Emory Thomas points out:

> This transmittal through tidal action of organic matter is primarily in the form of detritus which is mostly decomposed *Spartina*. The process by which detritus enters the ocean is called "outwelling" and the initial hypothesis among Odum and the other scientists at the University of Georgia Marine Institute was that this outwelling from salt marshes and estuaries lay at the base of the food chain which supported the abundant marine life found off the east coast. Thus there seemed to be an empirical connection between *Spartina* and shrimp cocktail at least.[8]

Not all the early research was conducted in Sapelo's marshes and tidal streams. From 1961 to 1966, for example, Sam Gray was the biological specimen collector for the Marine Institute. Many of the specimens came from an offshore live-bottom formation eighteen miles east of Sapelo. Gray developed the first formalized species list for what later became known as Gray's Reef, in recognition of the important research he conducted there. Gray's Reef was designated a protected National Marine Sanctuary by the National Oceanic and Atmospheric Administration (NOAA) in 1981.

Relative to the evolving research, a symposium of lasting significance was held on Sapelo Island in March 1958. The Salt Marsh Conference was hosted by the University of Georgia and the Marine Institute, with funding support from the National Science Foundation and R. J. Reynolds Jr. The conference attracted fifty-five scientists from the United States, Canada, Europe, and New Zealand. Interdisciplinary workshops included discussions on geology, tidal river hydrology, physiological stresses, marsh production, and the role of salt marshes as historical records. The conference's published proceedings represented a major contribution to the field of coastal research. The conference was important and might be said to have been the Marine Institute's debut on the national scientific scene.[9]

The 1960s and 1970s were dynamic decades for the Marine Institute. The disciplinary approaches to applied research began to have measurable ramifications for the sustainability of coastal marshes and estuaries. The realization began to emerge that the marshes, in tandem with the tides, played a critical role in the natural balance of the southeastern Atlantic coast ecosystem.

John Teal checking marsh monitoring instruments, circa 1959. (Courtesy of University of Georgia Marine Institute)

Expanding on the earlier work by Odum and Pomeroy, Robert Reimold and Jack Gallagher employed conventional high-resolution photography to document vegetation changes, and infrared photography to map water-flow patterns, tide height, and diseased areas of vegetation. Reimold's findings on phosphorous movement in *Spartina* provided useful insights into phosphorous cycling in the marsh.[10] Pomeroy and William Wiebe conducted salt marsh detritus studies, and in the mid-1970s Pomeroy and Richard Wiegert followed a carbon model as a method of quantifying the contribution of identified subsystems to the entire ecosystem. These findings established the connection between *Spartina* and carbon since carbon is a readily monitored variable and is universal since all living matter is carbon based.

Building on the success of the 1958 Salt Marsh Conference, the Marine Institute faculty, in association with scientists at the Athens campus, conducted additional conferences and symposia in the mid- to late 1960s that were to have notable consequences for the preservation of Georgia's marshlands and shoreline. In 1964 the Conference on Estuaries was held at Jekyll Island, with planning underwritten by the SIRF. Emerging from this meeting was a multidisciplinary volume, *Estuaries*, edited by George Lauff and published in 1967. It became a primary text for coastal ecological studies for decades. The declining Georgia oyster industry and proposals for its reinvigoration were the focus of the Oyster Culture Workshop conducted by the Marine Institute in 1967.

Several factors merged in 1968 to produce arguably the most important conference on estuarine preservation ever conducted in coastal Georgia. Biological research at the Marine Institute had theretofore achieved the first real understanding of the interactions that occur in the salt marsh and estuarine environment: the significance of the remnants of *Spartina* decay (detritus) to the marine food web, the excretion of organic and inorganic matter by a variety of marine organisms and plants, and the concomitant use of excreted materials by other organisms in the food web. Thus when a proposal surfaced for large-scale industrial strip mining of the Georgia marshes for phosphate, the institute's demonstration of the fragile stability of marshes and island ecosystems was of critical public importance.

In October 1968, the Conference on the Future of the Marshlands and Sea Islands was held at the Cloister Hotel on Sea Island to address the mining proposal and other factors related to the potential degradation of the coastal ecosystem. The diversity of conference participants, and the range of the topics they addressed, attested to the

Marsh Conference participants, Sapelo Island, March 1958. (Courtesy of University of Georgia Marine Institute)

seriousness with which the scientific community and many in the public sector considered the mining threat.

Among the participants were Hoyt and Henry on barrier island geology, Charles Fairbanks on the archaeological resources of coastal Georgia, Sandy Torrey West of Ossabaw on her Ossabaw Island Project, Reid W. Harris on proposed Georgia coastal wetland conservation legislation, Frederick C. Marland on "The Impending Crisis: Phosphate Mining off the Georgia Coast," Gene Odum on a proposal for protected marshlands and the zoning of coastal estuaries, and John Milton of the Conservation Foundation on the future protection of the state's marshes and islands. The published proceedings of the conference, *The Future of the Marshlands and Sea Islands of Georgia*, were significant and hard-hitting in validating the criticality of coastal conservation.[11]

The papers demonstrated that marsh mining was neither environmentally nor economically sensible for Georgia. Soon thereafter, a special commission from the University System of Georgia provided Governor Lester Maddox and the state General Assembly with the academic input that resulted in the Marshland Protection Act of

1970, a stringent protective device and one of the most consequential pieces of public legislation ever enacted on behalf of the Georgia coast. The Marshland Act, and its companion piece, the Shoreline Protection Act, served as models for similar legislation by other coastal states for the remainder of the twentieth century. The legislation placed Georgia's marshes under state ownership, excepting some deeded to private owners through Crown or state grants. Georgia state representative Reid Harris played a key role in the creation of the 1970 Coastal Marshland Protection Act. Harris was head of the environmental section of Governor Jimmy Carter's Goals for Georgia program and later chairman of the governor's State Environmental Council.

These conspicuous developments were the tangible results of the applied research at Sapelo, work that continued to bear fruit. From 1974 to 1990, Evelyn and Barry Sherr examined microprotozoans with other components of aquatic food webs, salt marsh root rhizomes, and carbon and nitrogen cycling in coastal ecosystems. Terrestrial and salt marsh plants, and the stresses placed on them by their habitats, were the research foci of E. Lloyd Dunn in the 1980s and 1990s.

Steven Y. Newell conducted substantive research during the same period, investigating the relative roles of fungal and bacterial invasion of dead *Spartina*, and its role in the release of nutrients into the marsh environment. Newell studied the dynamics of biomass and productivity in the attached microflora of smooth cordgrass, and he conducted field experiments to determine the extent to which water and nitrogen availability controlled microbial activity within the marsh decomposition system. Part of this work was conducted in tandem with another institute faculty member, Robert D. Fallon.

Donald Kinsey, Marine Institute director in the late 1970s and early 1980s, worked to develop coherence in resolving questions relating to "outwelling," a phenomenon whereby excess plant matter produced by the marshes is assumed to be transported by the tides to the nearshore zone, thereby contributing to the overall estuarine food web.

Ronald T. Kneib focused his early to mid-1980s investigations on the characterization of invertebrate distribution in the marsh. Kneib's findings identified tidal distribution patterns exhibited by marsh fauna, assessed temporal changes in abundance, and tested the relative importance of physical and biological factors underlying the observed patterns gleaned from his monitoring. His other interests included salt marsh food webs and the export of shrimp from the estuarine environment to the nearshore zone. In related research that continued into the 1990s, Kneib examined the effect of

shrimp on benthic invertebrate densities and predator-prey interactions in the marsh, the high-tide use of intertidal marshes by juvenile fish and crustaceans, and the effects of resident species on the growth and survival of juvenile *penaeid* shrimp.

From the mid-1980s into the 1990s, Marine Institute director James J. Alberts examined the chemical processes associated with acids from *Spartina* and the marsh mud and compared these with findings related to the effects of sunlight on the structure and photochemical reactions of compounds in the marsh, including acids, bacteria, and fungi.[12]

Most of the Marine Institute's research was conducted within the Sapelo Island National Estuarine Research Reserve (SINERR), which included the Duplin River watershed. Continuous monitoring stations were established at Flume Dock in the upper Duplin north of Moses Hammock, and on the lower end of the river at Marsh Landing. Marsh and river dynamics were analyzed and cataloged for a suite of parameters—tide heights, water turbidity and salinity, temperature and humidity, rainfall, and solar radiation. Data began to be collected through electronic reading in 1984. The SINERR assumed the collection and collation of water and weather monitoring data from the Marine Institute in 1995 as part of the reserve's monitoring program for a national database in collaboration with the National Estuarine Research Reserve System.[13]

The complexity and scope of UGAMI research evolved in response to technological advances. An example was work begun in 1990 by Alice G. Chalmers, in association with Alberts, Roy Welch, and Marguerite Remillard, to develop a Geographic Information System (GIS) for the Marine Institute and the SINERR. An integrated resource database was developed for Sapelo Island for the period 1953 through 1989 to document topography, land changes (for example, sand accretion on the South End), vegetation, drainage patterns, and land use within the watershed. Digitized topographic data were photogrammetrically produced from large-scale aerial photographs.

In the mid-1990s, the maps and database incorporated a desktop mapping system to project conditions in the physical and biotic environments of the SINERR from 1953 to 1993. GIS methodologies evolved and now address multiple coastal management problems of current and future concern, with the expansion and refinement of the database continuing in the first decade of the 2000s by the SINERR and the University of Georgia, with improved resources and technology.[14]

State Acquisition and the National Estuarine Sanctuary

Three sections of Sapelo Island were purchased from the Reynolds estate with public funds at different times. Each of the funding sources placed stipulations on the use of the relevant properties. It is fortunate that when Reynolds died in 1964 he was married to the only one of his four wives that had an interest in science and the general conservation of Sapelo. It is possible that any one of the three previous wives, or their heirs, would have sold the island to private entities, potentially opening the way to commercial and residential development reflecting that of other areas of the Southeast Coast in the previous decade.

As a widow hoping to extend her late husband's legacy to Sapelo and coastal Georgia, Annemarie Schmidt Reynolds remained involved with the island through the 1970s, particularly with the Sapelo Island Research Foundation (SIRF).[15] In 1969 Mrs. Reynolds made it possible for the state of Georgia to purchase the North End tract of about eighty-two hundred acres (the upper two-thirds of Sapelo), the result of which was the creation of the R. J. Reynolds Wildlife Refuge, later redesignated R. J. Reynolds Wildlife Management Area (WMA).

The state acquisition was facilitated through the Georgia Game and Fish Commission, and achieved through Pittman-Robertson Federal Aid funds, 75 percent, and state funds, 25 percent.[16] (The Game and Fish Commission was redesignated as the Georgia Department of Natural Resources—GDNR—in 1973. The Game and Fish Division of GDNR became the Wildlife Resources Division in 1992.)

The Sapelo Island Research Foundation retained sole control and oversight of the lower third of the island from 1969 through 1976, including the Marine Institute campus, main house, and Marsh Landing.

Since the Reynolds Wildlife Refuge was a federally aided initiative based mostly on funds derived from hunters, the primary use of the North End was to provide wildlife enhancement programs and public hunting opportunities. Much of the active wildlife management continues to involve game species, particularly white-tailed deer. Beginning in 1970, the Game and Fish Division of the Department of Natural Resources began wildlife and forest management activities in the refuge, programs designed to improve habitat diversity and increase populations of game and nongame wildlife. Surveys, inventories, and other studies were conducted to develop professional habitat management. Game and Fish also implemented seasonal public hunting, a popular program that continued to grow, particularly with GDNR's construction of a hunting camp at Moses Hammock.

In 1975 a three-year research initiative was implemented to assess the size and structure of Sapelo's wild turkey population, habitats used for nesting and brood rearing, and the role of predators in nesting areas. In addition to game species, GDNR actively managed and documented the island's nongame and endangered species, such as loggerhead sea turtles and bald eagles. During the 1970s and 1980s GDNR's Coastal Resources Division periodically sampled the Duplin River estuary for the status of fish populations and characterized populations of larger fish species and crustaceans.

State acquisition of the remaining portion of Sapelo, and consequently nearly the entirety of the island's 10,900 upland acres, was completed with two purchases from the SIRF in 1976. The first, the Sapelo Island Natural Area, was acquired with funds from the Land and Water Conservation Fund matched equally with state funds. This area south of Hog Hammock and east of the East Perimeter road was designated for public recreation, education, and scientific research. "Natural area" was somewhat of a misnomer, as that part of Sapelo had been impacted by human activity for over 150 years.

Of greater significance was the state's acquisition in late 1976 of 5,905 acres of upland and marsh on the western and southern sections of Sapelo (nearly a third of the island), designated the Sapelo Island National Estuarine Sanctuary (SINES). The tract entailed about four thousand acres of marsh in the Duplin River estuary and almost two thousand acres of upland south of the Reynolds WMA, including the SIRF's land comprising the Marine Institute leased to the University System of Georgia's Board of Regents. This addition gave the state oversight for all of Sapelo excepting the Hog Hammock community's 427 acres, several small disputed tracts at Raccoon Bluff, and two hundred acres of upland and marsh at the lighthouse.

In 1972 Congress had enacted the Coastal Zone Management Act and authorized the secretary of commerce to establish estuarine field laboratories along the nation's

coastlines, including the Great Lakes, under the implementation and administration of the NOAA. The state of Georgia proposed an estuarine sanctuary for its coast in January 1975. GDNR prepared an environmental impact statement describing its proposal, with Sapelo Island as the recommended site. An executive statement, signed by Governor Jimmy Carter, announced that

> The Duplin Estuary, west of Sapelo Island, is nominated as representative of the Carolinian biogeographic classification of estuaries. A request for funds to purchase research and support facilities currently operating on the southern end of Sapelo Island is included in the proposal. . . . Georgia's coastal islands and marshlands represent some of the last sections of shoreline on the East Coast retained in essentially a natural condition. Georgia's environmental legislation, and particularly protection offered to marshlands through the Coastal Marshlands Protection Agency, provides the basic framework for managing the Duplin Estuary, and other marshlands. In effect, a "research park" already exists in the Duplin Estuary and on Sapelo Island, where cooperative programs between the University of Georgia and the Sapelo Island Research Foundation have, over the last 20 years, established a baseline of data on the area, and gained national and international recognition for research conducted there.[17]

After reviewing alternatives and considering public comment, the Department of Commerce approved the state's proposal. Georgia received funds from the NOAA's National Estuarine Sanctuary Program in June 1975 to purchase from the Reynolds estate (through the SIRF) the tract to be designated the Sapelo Island National Estuarine Sanctuary (SINES), the second program to be established in the new national system. The state provided matching funds and further agreed to match annualized federal grants for the research and public education programs to be implemented by the state. The SINES was officially proclaimed by Georgia governor George Busbee on December 22, 1976.

Concomitant to the sanctuary designation was an agreement by which GDNR leased to the Board of Regents for fifty years the fifteen-hundred-acre Marine Institute tract comprising upland and marsh for the continuation of its scientific estuarine research. Significantly, this tract was entirely within the boundaries of the new sanctuary.[18]

In 1987 the NOAA redesignated the federally administered sanctuaries, and the SINES became the Sapelo Island National Estuarine Research Reserve. As of 2015, there were twenty-eight reserves from twenty-two coastal states in the National Estuarine Research Reserve System established "for purposes of long-term research, environmental monitoring, education, and stewardship."[19] Georgia DNR and the NOAA have administered the SINERR as a state-federal partnership for the implementation of education and outreach programs and a comprehensive scientific research program, including continuous water quality and weather monitoring.

The sanctuary and later reserve included the Long Tabby administrative complex, the Marine Institute, the Reynolds main house, Kenan Field, Nannygoat Beach, the lighthouse, and a mainland visitors' center built in 1995 at the Meridian ferry dock. In 1978, pursuant to the provision of education and recreation opportunities as a condition of receiving federal funds for the WMA and sanctuary, GDNR initiated public access to Sapelo with the new 150-passenger ferry *Sapelo Queen*. The vessel also enabled Hog Hammock and the Marine Institute to have improved, reliable access to the mainland. The *Queen* replaced the *Janet*, the old island ferry that had outlived its days after eighteen years in service. The *Sapelo Queen* operated until 1993 when a new vessel, the *Annemarie*, replaced it, being christened in ceremonies on the island by its namesake, Annemarie Schmidt Reynolds. GDNR operated this vessel until 2007, when it was replaced by the new twin-hulled *Katy Underwood*, built at New Iberia, Louisiana.[20]

In 1950 the federal government sold the 206-acre lighthouse tract, comprising upland and salt marsh, to R. J. Reynolds Jr. Reynolds built a causeway through the marsh, linking the lighthouse to the beach road. The SIRF's sale of the South End to the state in 1976 included its undivided one-half interest in the lighthouse tract, the other half being held by the second wife of Reynolds, Marianne O'Brien Reynolds. Following their divorce in 1952, Marianne Reynolds kept her half-interest; then upon her death in 1985 it devolved to her sister and heir, Dorothy E. (O'Brien) Cook of New York City.

The state purchased the Cook half of the lighthouse tract in 1992 for $500,000, with the assistance of a grant from the NOAA. The tract was incorporated into the SINERR, bringing the reserve's total acreage to 6,110 (marshes and upland).[21] In 1998 the abandoned brick lighthouse was restored by GDNR as a working aid to navigation and opened for public historic interpretation.

Consolidation of Sapelo's Geechee Community

About 250 African Americans lived on Sapelo Island in the early 1950s, mostly at Raccoon Bluff and Hog Hammock. The 1954 U.S. Geological Survey topographic map of Sapelo showed about forty structures in Hog Hammock, mostly dwellings.

In 1963, the Geechee population was down to 211 living almost exclusively at Hog Hammock. Roughly half that number comprised those who had relocated to Hog Hammock from Raccoon Bluff through a series of land exchanges instigated by Reynolds. There was continued population decline as residents moved to the mainland, and by the early 1970s there were only about 150 Geechees still on Sapelo. By 1990 Hog Hammock's population had fallen still further, to about seventy people.

The story is a depressing one in almost every particular. Reynolds wished to acquire the lands contained within Sapelo's black communities, particularly those on the North End. In 1950, his attorneys initiated land exchanges to consolidate the island's Geechees into one community at Hog Hammock.[22] The largest community to be consolidated was Raccoon Bluff, but Reynolds also wanted the land at Belle Marsh, Lumber Landing, and Shell Hammock, plus some scattered private plots in other parts of Sapelo.[23] Reynolds facilitated this with the intention of transforming everything north of Hog Hammock into a limited-access wildlife and hunting preserve.

It was a gradual process: Belle Marsh was closed in 1950, Lumber Landing in 1956, and Shell Hammock in 1960, and by 1964 Raccoon Bluff had been vacated.

Understandably, most of Sapelo's people were not enamored of the arrangement. As an inducement Reynolds ran a line from his South End generator plant to provide electricity to Hog Hammock. Water lines were installed, several houses were built, and a schoolteacher was hired to instruct the community's children. Reynolds also provided a few jobs for residents. "Since nearly all the residents now worked for him, [Reynolds] sometimes held court like a feudal lord, adjusting disputes, meting out small punishments."[24]

Another of Reynolds's motives for consolidation was control. He wanted as much of Sapelo's acreage under his imprimatur as possible, and the way to achieve that was direct acquisition of the Geechee land at Raccoon Bluff and Shell Hammock. During the 1950s he purchased some lots and pressured residents for the exchange of other properties for land at Hog Hammock. Virtually all of Raccoon Bluff had been bought or exchanged by the time Reynolds died, though he failed to obtain clear title to some tracts. By then, the families had relocated to Hog Hammock and rebuilt homes there.

Raccoon Bluff, dating to the 1870s, had been Sapelo's largest community for years. Reynolds changed everything. The loss of traditional lands was traumatic, transformative, and permanent, evolving with little or no negotiation. By mid-1964 Raccoon Bluff was completely vacated, with many houses dismantled and moved, leaving Hog Hammock as Sapelo's only Geechee settlement. At the time he died, Reynolds possessed virtually all the land on Sapelo outside of Hog Hammock, excepting small tracts at Raccoon Bluff. The upper two-thirds of the island had been depopulated to facilitate Reynolds's hunting preserve.

Many of Sapelo's people were unhappy and dispirited with what amounted to their forced removal. Most moved against their wishes, although there were a few incentives: more homes added to the electric power service, a school built, and a modern new sanctuary erected for Raccoon Bluff's First African Baptist congregation. After the church acquired land in Hog Hammock in 1963, services continued to be held at Raccoon Bluff until completion of the new Hog Hammock building in 1968.

Island lore relates that Eddie Hall and Allen Green were the last Raccoon Bluff residents to relocate to Hog Hammock. Green (1907–98), who became known for the craftsmanship of his sweetgrass baskets, was born at Raccoon Bluff and, except for several years as a young man, had lived there his whole life.[25] For a time Green refused to leave his home, but he was eventually forced to do so (see box, p. 286).

Allen Green of Raccoon Bluff

Allen Green, circa 1993, Sapelo Island home.
(Author's collection)

Allen Green and his wife Annie Mae were among the last residents of Raccoon Bluff. When R. J. Reynolds Jr. was consolidating the island communities in the 1950s, Green made it known to anyone who would listen that he had no intention of leaving his home at "the Bluff."

"Allen Green wouldn't move 'til hell freezed over," Matty Carter told interviewer William McFeely in 1992. "Well, hell ain't freezed over, and Allen Green right here in Hog Hammock." With Raccoon Bluff residents relocating to Hog Hammock, Green was steadfast in his refusal to leave. He only relented and moved in 1960 after Reynolds threatened to close the roads to Raccoon Bluff. Over the years up to and after his death in 1998 at the age of ninety-one, Green's strong will to hold on to his ancestral Sapelo home was representative of the resentments felt by older members of Hog Hammock who had been forced to relocate.

Green was born at Raccoon Bluff in 1907, as was his mother. His father, James Green, was born at nearby Bourbon Field and was a descendant of Muhammad Bilali, black overseer of the Sapelo plantation. James's grandfather was Allen Smith, born a slave, then emancipated, who in turn was the son of Bilally Smith, grandson of Bilali.

Green's memories of growing up at Raccoon Bluff included swimming with friends and relatives across the creek over to Blackbeard Island, a place that was mysterious and uninhabited. It was there, William McFeely writes, "when he was eleven, that his grandfather gave him his instruction in basket making. And it was from the foot of the bluff that he and the other boys would swim across to Blackbeard Island and walk round to the ocean side to ride the waves." Green also related to me his occasional adventures on Blackbeard. He recalled the abundant prevalence of the eastern diamondback rattlesnake there, and of seeing the ruins of the abandoned quarantine station, once an important aspect of Blackbeard's late-nineteenth-century history. Those were the days when transportation was limited. Green and other young people frequently walked the sandy roads of Sapelo to get where they were going. Occasional conveyance by cart was not always available as mules and oxen were in use in the fields.

Green, eighteen and curious about the outside world, moved to the mainland and then migrated to Florida. Later he returned to Georgia and lived and worked in Brunswick in the late 1920s. After a first marriage, he married his second wife, Annie Mae Walker (1912–2002), with whom he had grown up on Sapelo, and moved back to Raccoon Bluff. There Green worked as a prawn fisherman, hauled boatloads of oyster shells to the mainland, grew rice, and was employed by the federal government as a caretaker on Blackbeard.

Green's mastery at an early age of traditional Geechee (Gullah) basket-making became his lasting legacy to the people of Sapelo. This was particularly true for those who learned the craft from the master himself, including Sharron Walker Grovner, Yvonne Grovner, her husband Ira Gene, and others who acquired the unique basket-making skills. A basket crafted on Sapelo Island, like those of Charleston and Mt. Pleasant in the South Carolina low country, represents one of the most tangible expressions of traditional Geechee (Gullah) culture. Evolving from similar craftwork originating in West Africa, baskets are made of various combinations of sweetgrass (*Muhlenbergia*), palmetto fronds, longleaf pine needles, and needlerush.

Sweetgrass is a fine-bladed, sweet vanilla-fragranced perennial that grows in moist soil in the inter-dune meadows behind barrier island sand dunes. The technique of weaving palmetto strands and sweetgrass requires skill, dexterity, coordination, and patience. Pine needles are often interwoven with the light-colored sweetgrass to add color and patterns as well as strength. Sweetgrass baskets are more than just decorative—they are useful for carrying or displaying fruits and breads, personal items, and even outgoing mail. Some are so unique, however, that they are only used as art objects to display their beauty and the artist's skill. Large, complex pieces often take months to make, and some are purchased by collectors and museums, such as the Smithsonian Institution Museum of American History.

Several times I was lucky enough to sit under a shade tree with Allen Green at his Hog Hammock home and watch him weave sweetgrass baskets as he carried on conversation in his Geechee dialect. Surrounded by palmetto fronds and sweetgrass, and deftly employing his knife to weave and shape the strands, Green reminisced about his youthful days at Raccoon Bluff and his emergence into adulthood. His resilience demonstrated a sea island life that few except his peers could understand or even relate to. Green was one of a kind, uniquely the best of both old Sapelo and modern Sapelo.

SOURCE: William McFeely, *Sapelo's People: A Long Walk into Freedom* (New York: W. W. Norton, 1994); Buddy Sullivan, conversations with Allen Green, 1993–94.

The story of Green and his unhappy removal from a lifelong home perfectly symbolizes the persistent struggle of Sapelo's Geechee community to preserve its identity. The community has endured the travails of private, then state management of the island, with increasing acquisition of Hog Hammock land by outsiders in the 1990s and 2000s. The consolidation completed in the early 1960s was followed by Hog Hammock's seemingly continuous rearguard war of attrition to stave off development, land sales and exchanges, and the growing encroachment of nontraditional property owners.

Sapelo's people, some with ancestral island roots reaching to the late eighteenth century, came to realize both in a physical and a psychological sense that they were losing that sense of place that had existed for them for generations. The cultural integrity of Hog Hammock, and that of the lost island communities, was in peril of being severely diluted. Lifelong resident Cornelia Bailey (born 1945), descendant of Muhammad Bilali, black overseer of Thomas Spalding, is one who refuses to concede an inch of her precious, hard-won land: "We don't need a sign that says Hog Hammock *was* here," she says. "We want a sign that says Hog Hammock *is* here."

Pulitzer Prize–winning historian William S. McFeely put it best in the evocative and poignant story of his sojourn on Sapelo in the early 1990s learning the lifeways and traditions of the island's people: "The story of these long twentieth century years, years within the memory of Sapelo's people, is not the story I came back to the island to tell. I came not to interrogate, but to visit. I was there not to master the intricate, delicate negotiations attendant to the community's painful efforts to survive, but, instead, to grasp its domestic tranquilities. The pain of loneliness, of uncertainty, of old age, lies beneath its quiet, of course. There are, after all, only sixty-seven people left in Hog Hammock. But what strikes you over and over again is the duration of their story, of their endurance."[26]

With the end of the Reynolds era, and with the Marine Institute providing only minimal employment in the 1970s, many Hog Hammock residents relocated to the mainland, a trend particularly prevalent among the younger people seeking jobs. Community assistance in the form of small grants ($25,000 annually in the 1970s) came from the Sapelo Island Research Foundation. The SIRF aid was far from adequate, and some community residents were nearly destitute during this period. "Fred and Cracker Johnson, and their wives, who had cared for Dick in his time on the island—and especially when he was sick—discovered to their horror that the destruction of Dick Reynolds' records in 1964 had made it next to impossible to prove they had been employed by Dick and therefore ought to be receiving Social Security payments for the years they spent working for him."[27]

State acquisition of Sapelo lands in 1969 and 1976 placed new, unanticipated pressures on the island's future preservation. The Reynolds house provided some employment for residents, being managed in the 1980s and early 1990s by the Marine Institute as a conference facility for scientific and educational groups. However, the house urgently needed repairs and modernization. The mansion was showing visible signs of wear by the time President Jimmy Carter and his family used it during an Easter visit to Sapelo in April 1979. Unfortunately, the necessary funding to undertake improvements was not forthcoming from the Board of Regents, and the historic structure continued to deteriorate.

During the mid-1980s there was a proposal by the state to convert the South End into a convention center, with use of the main house and construction of additional lodging and meeting facilities. The plan was to make Sapelo more attractive to tourists, thus generating funds for repairs to the island's infrastructure. Conversely, such an initiative would clearly jeopardize or disrupt Sapelo's delicate ecological balance, the coherence of ongoing scientific research, and, not least, the Geechee community. The outcry and opposition to the proposal from coastal environmentalists was swift and vehement, and GDNR shelved the plan in 1986. Repairs to the mansion were finally implemented when GDNR assumed management of the house in 1993. The facility continued to be operated by the state as a public lodge.

GDNR's gradual expansion of Sapelo Island's public access and educational opportunities provided employment for Hog Hammock residents as ferry operators, tour guides, mechanics, and maintenance workers, while the Marine Institute also continued to provide jobs. Most significantly, however, the entrepreneurial spirit of some Hog Hammock residents began to manifest itself. Several overnight lodging facilities were started, a store or two opened to serve island residents and visitors, and locals began offering guided tours of the South End with the emphasis on Geechee culture and history.

Church offerings were accumulated and saved, and matching funds from the SIRF enabled the purchase of a small motor vessel for the community—the *Miss St. Luke*—with experienced watermen such as Tracy Walker and George Walker operating the boat to provide services, most importantly as a means of emergency medical transport

to the mainland. In 1996 Hog Hammock's 427 acres and Behavior Cemetery were placed on the National Register of Historic Places. This was a signature recognition facilitated by the Department of Natural Resources and coordinated by state historian Kenneth H. Thomas of GDNR's Historic Preservation Division, who prepared the National Register application.

The physical nature of the community at the turn of the twenty-first century showed it still to be bounded by marsh on the east and southeast, the "Autobahn" to the west, and a northern boundary that was originally an irrigation canal and embankment that separated the 1969 South End division of the island from the North End. There were about fifty houses scattered in an irregular pattern through the community. Among these were several historic structures, including the St. Luke's Baptist Church

(dating from around 1924), the Farmers' Alliance Hall (ca. 1929), First African Baptist Church (1968), and the former Rosenwald school now attached to St. Luke's.

The frame homes are largely simple, vernacular-style structures, one story, most with gabled roofs and front porches. In his survey of Hog Hammock preparatory to its listing on the National Register, Thomas indicated that some of the community's dwellings were built in 1920–40, while others date from after World War II. Other houses, also in the vernacular style, were built 1955–65 in response to the gradual infusion of residents from the other settlements on the island.

A Community's Struggle for Survival

Greater access to Sapelo after 1980 resulted in increasing exposure of its natural and cultural uniqueness, with a consequent rise in public awareness and interest in the island. Not surprisingly, this trend initiated a growing reach for property ownership by outsiders. Hog Hammock, being essentially the only developable private tract on Sapelo due to state ownership of the island, was logically the focus of property acquisition. In the 1980s and 1990s, nonresident heirs of traditional Sapelo landowners gradually sold off Hog Hammock property. By 2000, traditional Geechees' hold on their community was becoming extremely tenuous as outsiders' movement for land acquisition gained momentum. Part-time and seasonal homes were being constructed, some quite elaborate by Sapelo standards, and mostly by nontraditional (white) residents, accompanied by concern and resentment by traditional residents, of whom only about seventy remained by 2010.

"If you're going to keep the culture, it's a black culture," said Charles Hall, former president of the Sapelo Island Cultural and Revitalization Society, a preservation organization started by slave descendants. "It's a black language. So every time you dilute it, you're getting away from it." Cornelia Bailey, slave descendant and Geechee historian of Sapelo, was even more pointed: "On the verge of sounding racist—which I have been accused of, which I don't give a hoot [about]—I would rather my community be all black. I would rather have my community what it was in the '50s. Am I in your mainland community trying to buy your land?" she asked. "Why are you trying to buy mine? Can you sleep in two beds at once? I tell them, 'My land is for my children, my grandchildren, and even for the unborn.'"[28]

In an attempt to allay the growing gentrification and to protect the integrity of Sapelo's culture, the state established the Sapelo Island Heritage Authority to control and theoretically protect 180 acres within Hog Hammock. The legislation said in part:

> There is an urgent public need to preserve important and endangered historical areas in Georgia for the benefit of present and future generations; many historical areas, because of Georgia's rapid progress over the past decade, have been altered and their value as a part of our heritage lost, and the few such remaining areas are in danger of being irreparably altered; black culture is an important component of the history of Georgia; the State of Georgia possesses a rich heritage of black culture in its architectural, historical, and archeological resources associated with the life and culture of black Georgians; there exists on Greater Sapelo Island . . . a black community known as Hog Hammock which is composed primarily of the direct descendants of the slaves . . . this community is the last community of its kind in . . . Georgia; the Hog Hammock community . . . dates back to the mid-nineteenth century; it is important to the citizens of Georgia that this community, which reflects the past culture of this state, be preserved for the benefit of present and future generations; the best and most important use of this area of Greater Sapelo Island is for said community to remain, as it currently exists, a historic community, occupied by the direct descendants of the slaves of Thomas Spalding.[29]

The construction of expensive homes by nontraditional residents led to greatly elevated property taxes for all in Hog Hammock. This had an especially harsh impact on the community's traditional residents, adding an additional threat to the sustainability of Sapelo's traditional culture. After McIntosh County's property revaluation in 2012, many Hog Hammock home owners saw their assessments increased 500 to 800 percent. For Sapelo's traditional residents the tax increases meant the potential extinction of their community.

This unfortunate situation captured national attention in 2012 and 2013, with coverage from the *New York Times* and CNN, among other media. Bailey publicly expressed her shock at seeing the taxes on her property rise from $256 to almost $2,000 in one year. "People are calling and offering sympathy and saying, 'I wish they couldn't do that to you all,'" she said. "We need legal help. We need money to pay legal help. We need good ideas and suggestions. If we don't get these taxes down to a decent level, we don't have a chance in hell to bring back young people to the island."[30] Local tax assessors and judicial officials were inundated with appeals contesting the land appraisals. In 2014 McIntosh County provided a modicum of relief by implementing a 30 percent reduction of Hog Hammock property assessments under appeal for 2012 and 2013 taxes. Most saw it as only a temporary reprieve.

What does the future hold for Sapelo's traditional community? Will Hog Hammock's culture and values be further diluted by the kind of external threats that no one visualized in the 1970s and 1980s, more new construction by nontraditional landowners and more accompanying tax increases? Added to these pressures are the illusory, often specious aims and ambitions of some, even within the community itself, and supposedly with the best interests of the traditional residents at heart. These have served as distractions and fomented disagreement, resentment, and polarization, and have long had the attention of state officials but disappointingly little from McIntosh County officials for the last fifty years.

Legislative action at the state level might ultimately provide an answer, but only unrelenting clamor by community advocates will keep Hog Hammock's precarious situation in the consciousness of politicians and the public. As of 2015, in an era of fiscal austerity and stringent budgets, the situation continues to be problematic and challenging yet not hopeless. But for the passion, persistence, and commitment of Bailey and others like her, the lights in Sapelo's Geechee community might have been extinguished long ago.

Afterword

To describe growing up in the lowcountry, I would have to take you to the marsh on a spring day, flush the great blue heron from its silent occupation, scatter marsh hens as we sink to our knees in mud, open you an oyster with a pocketknife and feed it to you from the shell and say, "There. That taste. That's the taste of my childhood." And I would say, "Breathe deeply" and you would breathe and remember that smell for the rest of your life, the bold, fecund aromas of the tidal salt marsh, exquisite and sensual, the smell of the South in heat . . . a smell all perfumed with seawater. . . . [M]y heart belongs in the marshlands. The boy in me still carries the memories of those days when I lifted crab pots out of the Colleton River before dawn, when I was shaped by life on the river, part child, part sacristan of tides.—Pat Conroy, *The Prince of Tides*

My journey to Sapelo Island began almost with my first conscious awareness of place. Unremarkable though it certainly was to me at the time, my first memory surely was that of the smell of the salt marshes at Cedar Point on the McIntosh County mainland. That distinctive aroma must have indelibly etched itself upon my soul long before I understood the breadth of its import. I cannot express that with nearly the poetic elegance of Pat Conroy, my contemporary in age and upbringing, whose life has in some interesting and unintended ways paralleled that of my own. Like many of my generation whose roots are firmly implanted in the low-country coast, I can easily identify with the associations and near spirituality evoked in Conroy's noble passage that impel my attitudes about the marshes.

In my lifelong love affair with the coast I subconsciously envelop myself within the protective embrace of the place: the oak and palm forest, the fragrant red cedar on a ballast hammock, the restless beach dunes, serpentine creeks impelled by tides and winds, the egrets, herons, pelicans, and dolphins—truly everything about this extraordinary ecosystem. Proportional to the passage of the years, I return to the salt marshes with increasing gratitude and appreciation. As for Conroy, the place for me is spiritual. I am energized by the marshes' sanctity and purity, their vicissitudes, their endless fluidity, their pungency at low tide on a languid summer afternoon. There is nothing in nature comparable to these marvelous, majestic marshes.

Very early in their lives I encouraged my children to breathe deeply and savor the aromas of the coast and home. The last thing I said to my daughter Amanda when she went away to the University of Georgia was, "No matter what you do in life, or where you are on this earth, you will always be drawn back by the smell of the salt marsh and its association with the memories of your childhood." We have all come back home at some point in our lives. All the generations of my family have done this. We are drawn back by the lure of the sea, salt water, *Spartina*, tides, summer trade winds, and the graceful blue heron ever in search of the elusive fiddler crab.

Cedar Point represented place during my childhood in the 1950s and 1960s. It was the tidewater locale where I acquired through family and acquaintances my interest and appreciation for local history, especially its maritime aspects. There were intrinsic, thoroughly understood trappings of low-country life, the variations of which were limited only by one's imagination, that formed the tapestry of my being: messing about in wooden bateaux; navigating around shoals and sandbars at low tide; crabbing with chicken necks, a dip net, and a peach basket; cast-netting for white shrimp in the creeks; water-skiing behind a fast boat over short, choppy waters; camping on ballast hammocks; and working summer jobs on the local shrimp boats.

With emerging maturity, I became more consciously aware of an increasing connectedness to my native landscape and seascape. The little coastal settlements all elicited pleasant associations: Cedar Point, Crescent, and Valona, all with their sandy shell roads that were hot to one's bare feet in the summer, fringed by the local islands— Sapelo, Doboy, Blackbeard, and Creighton. I can see the distant greenish-blue tree line of Creighton even now in my mind's eye, reposing across the broad green-gold expanse of marsh to the east. It was an exposure to which I related countless times sitting on the steps of the "big house" at Cedar Point, Creighton, long, low, and always to my childhood imagination looking like a sleek passenger train racing toward its terminus by the sea. And always the endemic smells associated with my developing years, intoxicating aromas of marshes, burning oak leaves in the early spring, and deer tongue

plants drying in the sun, and odors of shrimp docks, with their mix of fish and crab, diesel fuel, tar and pitch, the briny salt air mixing with the smell of alluvial mudflats at low tide. These were the essence and the substance of my adolescence. They have never left me.

Early on, I was intrigued and captivated by Sapelo. Sapelo, that alluring, unattainable, almost mystical fringe of upland far in the distance beyond the mainland, was unlike anything else in our little section of the coast. In the late 1950s the island seemed to us mysterious, almost forbidding, the private enclave of the very private and very inaccessible R. J. Reynolds, the North Carolina tobacco king. As I grew into adulthood my curiosity about the island developed. What was the history of the place and its people? I read about Thomas Spalding and Howard Coffin, heard the stories of the island's Geechee settlements, and I wanted to go there.

My evolving interest in local history made me ever more curious about Sapelo, but for eighteen years as a professional journalist Sapelo eluded me. In 1985, when I came home to a position as editor of the *Darien News*, my long-awaited union with

Sapelo was at last attainable. From that point on, little could keep me away from the island: day trips on the *Sapelo Queen* to interview researchers at the Marine Institute, hours spent in the institute library researching Sapelo's history under the guidance of Lorene Townsend, pleasant hours sitting under the oak tree at the confectionary in Hog Hammock listening to Benny Johnson tell stories about cooking barbecue for the president of United States, Jimmy Carter, during his 1979 Sapelo visit, learning about Geechee history from Cornelia Bailey, whose inestimable friendship has meant so much to me over the years.

Eventually I would even come to reside on my magical island for a time. For more than two decades I was in the employ of the Georgia Department of Natural Resources, coming full circle to a dream job of supervising the Sapelo Island National Estuarine Research Reserve. By now the island was in my blood. People and place on Sapelo had become thoroughly imbued in my consciousness, both personally and professionally.

I had the benefit of firsthand experience and the people whose island roots ran deep and who cared just as deeply about the future of their island—Cornelia Bailey, Ben Lewis, Carolyn Dowse, Ben Hall, Netty Evans, James and Mattie Banks, Lula and George Walker, Benny and Viola Johnson, Tracy Walker, Allen Green, and others. In the years I have been associated with Sapelo they all told me their stories of the island and its people. I wrote about Sapelo's people and the island's history, conducted tours for the public, gave lectures and informal talks to anyone who would listen, showed off the island to state and federal officials, and advocated for the conservation and protection of Sapelo's natural and human environment. My state mentors—GDNR commissioners Joe Tanner and Lonice Barrett—were consistently supportive, giving me free rein to explore Sapelo's history and culture while on the job. I had the satisfaction of participating in the restoration of the iconic Sapelo lighthouse, consulting with Hog Hammock leaders on historical matters, and assisting the Sapelo Island Cultural and Revitalization Society in the promotion and preservation of Sapelo's Geechee culture.

I am not sure what the future holds for Sapelo. No one can be sure, any more than anyone can claim to be the final arbiter of all that has happened on Sapelo over the last four hundred years. Those who care about this place must be vigilant, remain steadfast, and stay the course, never wavering in their commitment to the preservation of Sapelo's ecological and cultural identity. It will continue to require not only a grassroots but a top-down commitment, for as Bill McFeely puts it, "As long as there are governors and commissioners who respect the unique and truly valuable natural

resource that the island is, real estate and recreational predators are held at bay. But governors and commissioners can change. Some arrangement more solid than that presently existing is needed to hold the line."

It is apparent that despite positive changes that are occurring, pressures and encumbrances have arisen to present new challenges to the preservation of Hog Hammock's cultural integrity and that of greater Sapelo. The demands of outsiders seem never to be satisfied, and their hunger for their own personal sliver of Sapelo oftentimes seems insatiable. And so it goes.

Despite the struggle, visiting Sapelo remains a joy for me—as much now as it did on every one of those morning ferry commutes to work for more than twenty years. The island will forever hold me tightly in its grip. It will entice me across the sound toward the smell of the marshes at Barn Creek. I will feel the hypnotic rush of the tide through the *Katy Underwood*'s cutwater as she slices through the bumpy waters of the sound. I will savor the music of the terns and pelicans wheeling across the vessel's wake—music that is never monotonous. Bill McFeely spoke for me and countless others when he said years ago, "I'm not sure the island will let me go. Not sure I want it to."[1]

Notes

Abbreviations

GDAH   Georgia Department of Archives and History, Morrow

GDNR   Georgia Department of Natural Resources, Atlanta

GHS   Georgia Historical Society, Savannah

NARA   National Archives and Records Administration

RG   Record Group

RMCG   Records of McIntosh County, Georgia

SINERR   Sapelo Island National Estuarine Research Reserve

UGAMI   University of Georgia Marine Institute, Sapelo Island

Chapter I. Ecological Sapelo

1. Albert Sydney Johnson, Hilburn O. Hillestad, Sheryl Fanning Shanholtzer, and G. Frederick Shanholtzer, *An Ecological Survey of the Coastal Region of Georgia*, Monograph Series 3 (Washington, D.C.: National Park Service, 1974), 14–16.

2. J. R. Hails and J. H. Hoyt, "An Appraisal of the Evolution of the Lower Atlantic Coastal Plain of Georgia," *Proceedings of the Institute of British Geographers* 46 (1969): 53–68.

3. Alice G. Chalmers, *The Ecology of the Sapelo Island National Estuarine Research Reserve* (Silver Spring, Md.: National Oceanic and Atmospheric Administration, 1997), 20–21.

4. The most readable account of the natural history of Sapelo, devoid of technical jargon, remains John Teal and Mildred Teal, *Portrait of an Island* (New York: Atheneum, 1964).

5. Albert Sydney Johnson et al., *Ecological Survey*, 35–40.

6. Chalmers, *Ecology of the Sapelo Island National Estuarine Research Reserve*, 21.

7. Ibid., 16; Albert Sydney Johnson et al., *Ecological Survey*, 91.

8. R. G. Wiegert and B. J. Freeman, *Tidal Salt Marshes of the Southeast Atlantic Coast: A Community Profile* (Washington, D.C.: U.S. Department of the Interior, Fish and Wildlife Service, 1990); R. A. Ragotzkie and R. A. Bryson, "Hydrography of the Duplin River, Sapelo Island, Georgia," *Bulletin of Marine Science of the Gulf and Caribbean* 5 (1955): 297–314. The published papers of scientists conducting estuarine research at Sapelo Island are contained in *Collected Reprints of the University of Georgia Marine Institute*, 28 vols., 1962–2004, UGAMI. Chapter 9 of the present study includes an overview of Marine Institute research.

9. E. P. Odum and C. L. Schelske, "Mechanisms Maintaining High Productivity in Georgia Estuaries," *Proceedings of the Gulf and Caribbean Fish Institute* 14 (1961): 75–80.

10. J. R. Wadsworth, "Geomorphic Characteristics of Tidal Drainage Networks in the Duplin River System, Sapelo Island, Georgia," PhD diss., University of Georgia, 1980; R. W. Frey and P. Basan, "Coastal Salt Marshes," in *Coastal Sedimentary Environments*, 2nd ed., ed. R. A. Davis Jr. (New York: Springer-Verlag, 1985), 225–301.

11. Wiegert and Freeman, *Tidal Salt Marshes of the Southeast Atlantic Coast*. For the general reader, the outstanding study of salt marshes and the coastal Georgia ecosystem is Charles Seabrook, *The World of the Salt Marsh: Appreciating and Protecting the Tidal Marshes of the Southeastern Atlantic Coast* (Athens: University of Georgia Press, 2012). See also the many technical papers relating to marsh studies in *Collected Reprints*, UGAMI.

12. Larry R. Pomeroy and R. G. Wiegert, *The Ecology of a Salt Marsh* (New York: Springer-Verlag, 1981).

13. John M. Teal, "Energy Flow in the Salt Marsh Ecosystem of Georgia," *Ecology* 43 (1962): 614–24.

14. L. R. Pomeroy, W. M. Darley, E. L. Dunn, J. L. Gallagher, E. B. Haines, and D. M. Whitney, "Primary Production," in Pomeroy and Wiegert, *Ecology of a Salt Marsh*, 39–67.

15. J. R. Robertson, K. Bancroft, G. Vermeer, and K. Plaiser, "Experimental Studies on the Foraging Behavior of the Sand Fiddler Crab," *Journal of Experimental Marine Biology and Ecology* 52 (1980): 47–64.

16. D. E. Schindler, B. M. Johnson, N. A. MacKay, N. Bouwes, and K. F. Kitchell, "Crab-Snail Size-Structured Interactions and Salt Marsh Predation Gradients," *Oecologia* 97 (1994): 49–61.

17. Wilbur H. Duncan, *Vascular Vegetation of Sapelo Island, Georgia* (Athens: University of Georgia, Department of Botany, 1982).

18. Hubert J. Byrd, D. G. Aydelott, Daniel D. Bacon, and Edward M. Stone et al., *Soil Survey of McIntosh County, Georgia*, Series 1959 (Washington, D.C.: U.S. Department of Agriculture, 1961), 8–9, 18.

19. Duncan, *Vascular Vegetation of Sapelo Island*.

20. Ibid., 13–18; G. L. Fuller, John W. Moon, and B. H. Hendrickson et al., *Soil Survey of McIntosh County, Georgia*, Series 1929 (Washington, D.C.: Bureau of Chemistry and Soils, U.S. Department of Agriculture, 1932), 24.

21. Duncan, *Vascular Vegetation of Sapelo Island*.

Chapter II. Archaeological Sapelo

1. Two excellent interdisciplinary studies relating to the Guale are David Hurst Thomas, *Native American Landscapes of St. Catherines Island, Georgia*, Anthropological Papers of the American Museum of Natural History 88 (New York: American Museum of Natural History, 2008), and Victor D. Thompson and David Hurst Thomas, eds., *Life among the Tides: Recent Archaeology on the Georgia Bight*, Anthropological Papers of the American Museum of Natural History 98 (New York: American Museum of Natural History, 2013).

2. John E. Worth, *The Struggle for the Georgia Coast*, Anthropological Papers of the American Museum of Natural History 75 (New York: American Museum of Natural History, 1995), 9–55.

3. Quoted in Lewis H. Larson, *Aboriginal Subsistence Technology on the Southeast Coastal Plain during the Late Pre-Historic Period* (Gainesville: University of Florida Press, 1980).

4. Morgan R. Crook Jr., *Mississippi Period Archaeology of the Georgia Coastal Zone*, University of Georgia Laboratory of Archaeology Series Report 23 (Athens: University of Georgia, Dept. of Anthropology, 1986), 34–42.

5. Alan E. McMichael, "A Model for Barrier Island Settlement Patterns," in Daniel P. Juengst, ed., *Sapelo Papers: Researches in the History and Prehistory of Sapelo Island, Georgia*, Studies in the Social Sciences (Carrollton: West Georgia College, 1980), 48.

6. Morgan R. Crook, Jr. "Spatial Associations and Distribution of Aggregate Village Sites," in Juengst, ed., *Sapelo Papers*, 82.

7. Crook, *Mississippi Period Archaeology of the Georgia Coastal Zone*, 41–42.

8. William McKinley, "Mounds in Georgia," *Smithsonian Institution, Annual Report* 27 (1873): 422–24. The visit is noted in Robert L. Humphries, ed., *The Journal of Archibald C. McKinley* (Athens: University of Georgia Press, 1991), 69.

9. Clarence B. Moore, *Certain Aboriginal Mounds of the Georgia Coast* (Philadelphia: Journal of the Academy of Natural Sciences, 1897).

10. Charles E. Pearson, C. C. Birchett, and Richard A. Weinstein, "An Aptly Named Steamboat: Clarence B. Moore's Gopher," *Southeastern Archaeology* 19 (2000): 82–87.

11. Moore, *Certain Aboriginal Mounds*, 55. An unnamed tidal stream emptying into Blackbeard Creek a short distance to the east affords access to the northeastern portion of Bourbon Field.

12. Ibid., 55–67.

13. Ibid., 56–57.

14. McKinley, "Mounds in Georgia," 424.

15. Moore, *Certain Aboriginal Mounds*, 67–71.

16. McKinley, "Mounds in Georgia," 423.

17. Morgan R. Crook Jr., "Archaeological Indications of Community Structures at the Kenan Field Site," Juengst, ed., *Sapelo Papers*, 89–100.

18. McKinley, "Mounds in Georgia," 422–23.

19. Moore, *Certain Aboriginal Mounds*, 71–73.

20. A. J. Waring Jr. and Lewis H. Larson Jr., "The Shell Ring on Sapelo Island," in Stephen Williams, ed., *The Waring Papers: The Collected Works of Antonio J. Waring, Jr.* (Cambridge, Mass.: Peabody Museum, 1968), 263–73.

21. Victor D. Thompson, Matthew Reynolds, Brian Haley, Richard Jefferies, Jay Johnson, and Catherine Humphries, "The Sapelo Shell Rings Site: Remote Sensing on a Georgia Sea Island," *Southeastern Archaeology* 23 (2004): 192–201; Richard W. Jefferies and Victor D. Thompson, "Mission Period Native American Settlement and Interaction on Sapelo Island, Georgia," paper presented at the annual meeting of the Southeastern Archaeological Association, 2005; Victor D. Thompson, "Questioning Complexity: The Prehistoric Hunter-Gatherers of Sapelo Island, Georgia," PhD diss., University of Kentucky, 2006.

22. J. Michael Francis and Kathleen M. Kole, *Murder and Martyrdom in Spanish Florida: Don Juan and the Guale Uprising of 1597*, Anthropological Papers of the American Museum of Natural History 95 (New York: American Museum of Natural History, 2011), 39–40. Using Spanish manuscript sources, this monograph provides a reinterpretation of the 1619 history of the Guale revolt by Fr. Luis Geronimo de Ore, long considered the standard account by historians.

23. Francis and Kole, *Murder and Martyrdom*, 11–12.

24. Ibid., 6–8.

25. The definitive account of the discovery of Santa Catalina is David Hurst Thomas, *The Archaeology of Mission Santa Catalina de Guale: 1. Search and Discovery*, Anthropological Papers of the American Museum of Natural History vol. 63, pt. 2 (New York: American Museum of Natural History, 1987). See also David Hurst Thomas, "The Archaeology of Mission Santa Catalina de Guale: Our First Fifteen Years," in B. G. McEwan, ed., *The Spanish Missions of La Florida* (Gainesville: University Press of Florida, 1993), 1–34; Elliot H. Blair, "The Guale Landscape of Mission Santa Catalina de Guale: 30 Years of Geophysics at a Spanish Colonial Mission," in Thompson and Thomas, *Life among the Tides*, 375–94.

26. See especially Richard W. Jefferies and Christopher R. Moore, "Mission San Joseph de Sapala: Mission Period Archaeological Research on Sapelo Island," in Thompson and Thomas,

eds., *Life among the Tides*, 345–74; Worth, *Struggle for the Georgia Coast*; Amy Turner Bushnell, *Situado and Sabana: Spain's Support System for the Presidio and Mission Province of Florida*, Anthropological Papers of the American Museum of Natural History 74 (New York: American Museum of Natural History, 1994).

27. Jefferies and Moore, "Mission San Joseph de Sapala," 348.

28. Worth, *Struggle for the Georgia Coast*, 15–16.

29. Ibid., 93–94.

30. Mark F. Boyd, "Enumeration of Florida Spanish Missions in 1675," *Florida Historical Quarterly* 27 (1948): 181–88.

31. Joseph W. Barnwell, "Fort King George: The Journal of Col. John Barnwell in the Construction of the Fort on the Altamaha in 1721," *South Carolina Historical and Genealogical Magazine* 27 (1926): 189–203.

32. Worth, *Struggle for the Georgia Coast*, 102.

33. From Spanish reports of 1684, cited in ibid., 39–41.

34. Ibid., 194. A league represented about three statute miles.

35. Jefferies and Moore, "Mission San Joseph de Sapala," 352.

36. Spanish sources cited in John Tate Lanning, *The Spanish Missions of Georgia* (Chapel Hill: University of North Carolina Press, 1935), 61–62. Jefferies and Moore, "Mission San Joseph de Sapala," 348, notes that a survivor of a shipwreck off Sapelo in 1595 reported the island as un-inhabited, but Spanish manuscripts confirm Guale presence on the island in that period, likely the town of Espogue.

37. Jefferies and Moore, "Mission San Joseph de Sapala," 374.

38. "Journal. Capt. Dunlop's Voyage to the Southward, 1687," *South Carolina Historical and Genealogical Magazine* 30 (1929): 127–33.

39. Herbert E. Bolton and Mary Ross, *The Debatable Land* (Berkeley: University of California Press, 1925).

40. Kenneth Coleman, *Colonial Georgia: A History* (Athens: University of Georgia Press, 1976), 84–88.

41. Isaac Levy, advertisement, Sept. 13, 1759, document KRC042, Hargrett Rare Book and Manuscript Library, University of Georgia, Athens.

42. Petition of Isaac Levy to the King's Excellent Majority in Council, December 15, 1759, Document KRC041, Hargrett Rare Book and Manuscript Library; Petition to the King of England from Isaac Levy respecting the Islands of Sapelo, Ossabaw, and St. Catherines, 1760, document KRC043, Hargrett Rare Book and Manuscript Library.

43. Frances Howell Beckemeyer, comp., *Abstracts of Georgia Colonial Conveyance Book C-1, 1750–1761* (Atlanta: R. J. Taylor Foundation, 1975), 345–50. See also Steven C. Hahn, *The Life and Times of Mary Musgrove* (Gainesville: University Press of Florida, 2012).

44. Virginia Steele Wood and Mary R. Bullard, eds. *Journal of a Visit to the Georgia Islands of St. Catherines, Green, Ossabaw, Sapelo, St. Simons, Jekyll, and Cumberland* (Macon, Ga.: Mercer University Press, 1996), 22.

45. Fletcher Crowe and Anita Spring, "Fort Caroline: Research Suggests a New Site for America's Oldest Fortified Settlement," unpublished ms., Florida Museum of Natural History, Gainesville.

46. Pat Bryant, comp., *English Crown Grants in St. Andrew Parish in Georgia, 1755–1775* (Atlanta: Surveyor General Department, Georgia Department of Archives and History, 1972), 25.

47. "A Plan of the Islands of Sappola, Containing 9520 Acres, by Henry Yonge and Will DeBrahm, Surveyors General," September 30, 1760, Georgia Surveyor General Department, GDAH, Morrow.

48. Morgan R. Crook Jr., "A Place Known as Chocolate," Report of Investigations, Antonio J. Waring, Jr. Archaeological Laboratory, University of West Georgia, Carrollton, 2007. The naming of Chocolate is discussed in chapter 4 of this book.

49. "A Plan of the Islands of Sappola."

50. "The Beginning of Cotton Cultivation in Georgia," *Georgia Historical Quarterly* 1 (1917): 40; Kenneth Coleman and Stephen Gurr, eds., *Dictionary of Georgia Biography* (Athens: University of Georgia Press, 1983), 673.

51. *Georgia Gazette* (Savannah), November 8, 1775.

52. Ibid., September 16, 1784.

53. Walter C. Hartridge, ed., *The Letters of Don Juan McQueen to His Family* (Savannah: Georgia Society of the Colonial Dames of America, 1943), xxv–xxviii.

Chapter III. French Interlude

1. The biography of DuBignon is Martha L. Keber, *Seas of Gold, Seas of Cotton: Christophe Poulain DuBignon of Jekyll Island* (Athens: University of Georgia Press, 2002). Keber's use of French manuscripts places the Sapelo Company in context, particularly the convoluted path taken in the formation of the company. See also Kenneth H. Thomas Jr., "The Sapelo Company: Five Frenchmen on the Georgia Coast, 1789–1794," *Proceedings and Papers of the Georgia Association of Historians* 10 (1989): 37–64. Thomas's paper demythologized much of what had previously been written about the French period on Sapelo, correcting errors in the earlier literature. I am indebted to both Keber and Thomas on whose accounts part of this chapter is based. The professional courtesies and collegiality extended to me by both have been invaluable for many years.

2. The matter of finances relating to the lost vessel was satisfactorily resolved with Dumoussay when McQueen returned to Georgia in 1791. See Walter C. Hartridge, ed., *The Letters of Don Juan McQueen to His Family* (Columbia, S.C.: Georgia Society of the Colonial Dames of America, 1943), xxvii.

3. Quoted in Keber, *Seas of Gold*, 149–50.

4. Ibid., 147–49, 151–52.

5. Thomas, "Sapelo Company," 46–47.

6. *Georgia Gazette* (Savannah), July 24, 1794; Thomas, "Sapelo Company," 42–43. There is no site on Sapelo Island now named "Hermitage."

7. Chappedelaine to DuBignon, May 1792, cited in Keber, *Seas of Gold*, 173.

8. Keber, *Seas of Gold*, 171. The two letters from Chappedelaine to DuBignon quoted above were provided the author courtesy of Martha Keber in 1994. The translation is by Keber.

9. *Georgia Gazette* (Savannah), May 9, 1793.

10. Even though its primary effort was at Sapelo, the company had agricultural activity on Jekyll in 1791–92.

11. Keber, *Seas of Gold*, 182.

12. Richard K. Murdoch, "Correspondence of French Consuls in Charleston, South Carolina, 1793–1797," *South Carolina Historical Magazine* 74 (1973): 6–7, cited in Thomas, "Sapelo Company," 45.

13. Superior Court Minutes, July 1793, Liberty County Records; Deed Book C (1794), 108–10, Liberty County Records; "Agreement between the Concerned in the Islands of Sapelo for the Liquidation of the Business," November 18, 1793, record group 21, box 116, NARA, Southeast Region, Morrow, Georgia, cited in Thomas, "Sapelo Company," 46–49; Keber, *Seas of Gold*, 180. See also June Hall McCash, *Jekyll Island's Early Years* (Athens: University of Georgia Press, 2005), 106–7. Sapelo Island was then apportioned to Liberty County.

14. *Georgia Gazette*, May 15, 1794, June 5, 1794, June 19, 1794, and July 24, 1794; deed of agreement between DuBignon, Chappedelaine, and Dumoussay, June 14, 1794, Deed Book R, 248–50, Chatham County Records; Deed Book CD, 300–301; Glynn County Records, recorded January 11, 1800; Thomas, "Sapelo Company," 48–49. Keber's observation on Boisfeillet is from *Seas of Gold*, 181–82

15. Dumoussay probably died of food poisoning. His grave marker was recovered in the 1970s and displayed at the University of Georgia Marine Institute. It is now at the Sapelo Island Visitors Center. The French burials are discussed later in this chapter.

16. *Georgia Gazette*, September 25, 1794. The murder of Chappedelaine likely occurred at the house he was sharing with Dumoussay near Spanish Fort, but it could have occurred at the High Point house then occupied by Boisfeillet.

17. Boisfeillet Family Genealogy, Picot B. Floyd Collection, GHS, Savannah.

18. Rachel Laura DeVan Perrine, "Bourbon Field: Preliminary Investigations of a Barrier Island Plantation Site," master's thesis, University of Tennessee at Chattanooga, 2008.

19. *Darien Gazette*, August 30, 1819; Buddy Sullivan, *Early Days on the Georgia Tidewater: The Story of McIntosh County and Sapelo*, 6th ed. (Darien, Ga.: McIntosh County Commission, 2001), 205–7.

20. Grandclos Mesle to Dumoussay, October 25, 1791, cited in Keber, *Seas of Gold*, 198. Grandclos Mesle and Dumoussay were unhappy with Boisfeillet, feeling he was evading responsibility for paying his share of the company's expenses.

21. Boisfeillet Family Genealogy, GHS.

22. Thomas, "Sapelo Company," 50–52.

23. Ibid., 50.

24. For desVergers, see the *Columbian Museum and Savannah Advertiser*, July 28, 1797, and June 7, 1806. For Chevalier, see *Early Deaths in Savannah, Georgia, 1763–1803* (Savannah: Georgia Historical Society, 1993). For Louis Harrington's ownership of Sapelo property, see *Columbian Museum and Savannah Advertiser*, January 11, 1799. The chains of title to North End tracts are discussed in chapter 4.

25. Kenneth H. Thomas Jr., "Montalet of Savannah and Sapelo: The Man and the Myth," paper presented at the Georgia Historical Society, Savannah, November 1994; Savannah Writers Project, *Savannah River Plantations*, edited by Mary Granger (Savannah: Georgia Historical Society, 1947), 429–32.

26. *Savannah Republican*, June 11, 1814.

27. Deed Book T (1798), 145, App. 14; 189, App. 15, Chatham County Records.

28. *Savannah Republican*, June 11, 1814.

29. *Savannah River Plantations*, 430, 431.

30. Deed Book Y (1803), 4, App. 16, Chatham County Records.

31. Thomas, "Montalet of Savannah and Sapelo."

32. Montalet's slave dispositions are from ibid. Thomas's estimate of Montalet's ownership of as many as a hundred slaves on Sapelo is probably excessive.

33. Wayne-Stites-Anderson Papers, Collection 846, GHS.

34. *Savannah Republican*, June 11, 1814.

35. Deed Book 21 (1815), 336, App. 17, Chatham County Records; Thomas, "Montalet of Savannah and Sapelo."

36. Lefils Family Affidavit, Collection 490, Folder 1, GHS; Thomas, "Sapelo Company," 40. In his will Dumoussay left bequests to Bernard LeFils and his family.

37. Lefils Family Affidavit. The local citizens deposed in 1912 were C. O. Fulton (by executor), Charles L. Bass, Sarah S. McKinley, and Alexander Duplin McIntosh.

Chapter IV. Agrarian Sapelo

1. The Ashantilly estate was originally awarded to Sir Peter Spalding by Robert the Bruce in recognition of the former's exploits at Berwick Castle in 1318. Though outdated, the only biography of Spalding remains E. Merton Coulter, *Thomas Spalding of Sapelo* (Baton Rouge: Louisiana State University Press, 1940). Pages 1–10 cover Spalding's early life. A new biography of Spalding needs to be written.

2. Allen D. Candler, *The Revolutionary Records of the State of Georgia*, 3 volumes (Atlanta, 1908), I, 146. For James Spalding's activities during and after the Revolution, see Wilbur Henry Siebert, *Loyalists in East Florida, 1774–1785* (Deland: Florida State Historical Society, 1929), 9–10.

3. Candler, *Revolutionary Records of Georgia*, III, 255.

4. *Georgia Gazette* (Savannah), November 13, 1794.

5. Charles Spalding Wylly, "The Story of Sapelo," unpublished typescript, 1914, Buddy Sullivan Papers, collection 2433, GHS, 18; *Biographical Dictionary of the American Congress* (Washington, D.C.: Government Printing Office, 1928), 1551.

6. Richard Leake Plantation Account Book, 1785–1801, collection 485, GHS.

7. *Georgia Gazette*, November 12, 1795.

8. Richard Leake to Thomas Spalding, November 28, 1797, Spalding Family Papers, series 9, box 2.

9. Coulter, *Thomas Spalding*, 31.

10. Family Bible, Spalding Family Papers, box 3.

11. Kenneth H. Thomas, Jr., "The Sapelo Company: Five Frenchmen on the Georgia Coast, 1789–1794," *Proceedings and Papers of the Georgia Association of Historians* 10 (1989): 64n123. See also "Some Memoranda in Relation to Thomas Spalding, late of Sapelo Island, by his son, Charles Spalding," June 1878, Spalding Family Papers, series 2, box 1. Coulter makes no mention in his Spalding biography of Leake and Swarbreck's involvement in the purchase of the South End.

12. Glynn County deeds, 1804, in Spalding Family Papers, series 1, box 1. C. S. Wylly states that Spalding received a loan of $100,000 from London bankers at 3.5 percent interest, payable in ten years.

13. McIntosh County Tax Digest, 1825, GDAH.

14. Emory M. Thomas, "The South and the Sea: Some Thoughts on the Southern Maritime Tradition," *Georgia Historical Quarterly* 67 (Summer 1983): 160.

15. Coulter, *Thomas Spalding*, 128–29.

16. *Darien Gazette*, May 25, 1824.

17. Deed Book 2E (1818), 311–19, Chatham County Records.

18. *Savannah Georgian*, August 8, 1822; Deed Book 2L (1831), 310–13, Chatham County Records. The Savannah firm of William Mein and Robert Mackay distributed commodities to the coastal planters, specializing in imported wines.

19. Spalding, "Culture of Rice," *American Agriculturist* 4 (1845): 53.

20. Spalding, "Gama and Bermuda Grass," *American Agriculturist* 3 (1844): 335; Spalding, "On Manufacturing of Salt on the Coast of Carolina and Georgia," *Southern Agriculturist* 3 (1830): 187. Spalding apparently never pursued his salt-making project beyond the experimental stage.

21. Spalding, "Rice," *Southern Agriculturist* 8 (1835): 171–72.

22. Coulter, *Thomas Spalding*, 54–55.

23. Spalding, "On the Cotton Gin and the Introduction of Cotton," *Southern Agriculturist* 4, new series (1844): 106–11; *Georgia Gazette*, November 28, 1799; "The Beginning of Cotton Cultivation in Georgia," *Georgia Historical Quarterly* 1 (March 1917): 39–45; Lewis Cecil Gray, *History of Agriculture in the Southern United States to 1860* (Washington, D.C.: Carnegie Institution, 1933), 730–31; Richard D. Porcher and Sarah Fick, *The Story of Sea Island Cotton* (Charleston, S.C.: Charleston Museum, 2005), 78, 99. In 1828, Spalding noted that Philip Delegal planted twenty-two acres of cotton on the south end of Skidaway Island before the Revolution, adding that it was the green-seed, short-staple variety. *Athenian* (Athens, Ga.), June 17, 1828, reprinted from the *Savannah Georgian*.

24. *Columbian Museum and Savannah Advertiser*, October 15, 1799. For Francis Levett, see Siebert, *Loyalists in East Florida*, 328. For Julianton plantation, see Buddy Sullivan, *Early Days on the Georgia Tidewater: The Story of McIntosh County and Sapelo*, 6th ed. (Darien, Ga.: McIntosh County Commission, 2001), 230–32, 263–71, 782–86, 823–24; Sullivan, *Early Days on the Georgia Tidewater*, new revised ed., forthcoming, 2017.

25. *Georgia Gazette*, April 21, 1796.

26. "Day Book for the Estate of J. & P. Butler in Georgia, 1844," Margaret Davis Cate Papers, collection 997, GHS.

27. Roswell King Jr. to Thomas Butler, September 29, 1833, Butler Family Papers, Historical Society of Pennsylvania, Philadelphia.

28. James C. Bonner, *A History of Georgia Agriculture, 1732–1860* (Athens: University of Georgia Press, 1964), 51–52; Thomas Spalding, "Culture of Sea Island Cotton," *American Agriculturist* 3 (1844): 246.

29. Spalding, "Brief Notes," *Southern Agriculturist* 1 (December 1828): 60; Roswell King Jr., "On the Management of the Butler Estate, and the Cultivation of the Sugar Cane," *Southern Agriculturist* 1 (December 1828): 523–24.

30. Gray, *History of Agriculture*, 730–33.

31. John D. Legare, "Account of an Agricultural Excursion Made into the South of Georgia in the Winter of 1832," *Southern Agriculturist* 6 (1833): 138–47.

32. Charles E. Pearson, "Captain Charles Stevens and the Antebellum Georgia Coasting Trade," *Georgia Historical Quarterly* 75 (Fall 1991): 485–506.

33. *Savannah Daily Georgian*, January 16, 1843; *Savannah Daily Morning News*, March 17, 1859.

34. Fanny Kemble, *Journal of a Residence on a Georgian Plantation in 1838–1839*, edited by John A. Scott (New York: Alfred A. Knopf, 1961), 182–83 (first published in 1863). See also Malcolm Bell Jr., *Major Butler's Legacy: Five Generations of a Slaveholding Family* (Athens: University of Georgia Press, 1987).

35. *Savannah Republican*, March 8, 1828, March 15, 1828.

36. *Savannah Georgian*, August 27, 1833, September 3, 1833; Robert Manson Myers, ed., *The Children of Pride* (New Haven: Yale University Press, 1972), 1471.

37. Francis R. Goulding, *Sapelo, or Child Life on the Tide-Water* (New York: Dodd, Mead, 1870). Goulding was the pastor of the Darien Presbyterian Church from 1856 to 1862.

38. *Savannah Georgian*, April 23, 1849.

39. Ibid.

40. *Savannah Georgian*, December 4, 1846.

41. Buddy Sullivan, *A Georgia Tidewater Companion* (Charleston, S.C.: CreateSpace, 2014), 16–19, 154–63.

42. *Columbian Museum and Savannah Daily Gazette*, April 25, 1817.

43. "Survey of Sapelo Inlet by Lt. James Glynn, U.S. Navy," 1842, 27th Cong., 2nd sess., Doc. No. 159, House of Representatives; *Savannah Georgian*, February 15, 1840.

44. Coulter, *Thomas Spalding*, 165–66.

45. Contract dated September 14, 1819 between the United States and Winslow Lewis, Site File, Georgia, no. 2, 1st site, RG 26 (U.S. Coast Guard Records), NARA; Sullivan, *Early Days on the Georgia Tidewater* (2001), 125–28.

46. Morgan R. Crook Jr. and Patricia O'Grady, "Spalding's Sugar Works Site," in *Sapelo Papers: Researches in the History and Pre-History of Sapelo Island, Georgia* (Carrollton: West Georgia College Studies in the Social Sciences, 1980), 7.

47. Allen D. Candler, comp., *Colonial Records of the State of Georgia*, vol. 3 (Atlanta, 1905), collection 2433, 427–28. Slavery was legalized in the Georgia colony in 1750.

48. Elizabeth Spalding Willingham, "Sapelo Island," unpublished article, 1973, in Buddy Sullivan Papers, GHS; U.S. Census, 1850, McIntosh County, Slave Schedules.

49. Deed Book A (1841), 302–3, RMCG.

50. Coulter, *Thomas Spalding*, 85.

51. Ibid., 82.

52. *Columbian Museum and Savannah Advertiser*, March 7, 1807.

53. Porcher and Fick, *The Story of Sea Island Cotton*, 136–37.

54. Spalding, letter to J. A. Turner, in J. A. Turner, *The Cotton Planter's Manual* (New York, 1857).

55. Spalding, "Cotton—Its Introduction and Progress of Its Culture in the United States," *Southern Agriculturist* 8 (1835): 45–46.

56. King, "On the Management of the Butler Estate," 523.

57. Legare, "Account of an Agricultural Excursion," 146.

58. King, "On the Management of the Butler Estate," 524.

59. Ibid.

60. William McFeely, *Sapelo's People: A Long Walk into Freedom* (New York: W. W. Norton, 1994), 43; Kemble, *Journal*, 67–68, 98.

61. H. S. DuVal, *Topographical Reconnaissance of Sapelo Island, Georgia*, 1857, RG 23 (U.S. Coast and Geodetic Survey Records), NARA, cited hereafter as 1857 DuVal survey; Ray Crook, Cornelia Bailey, Norma Harris, and Karen Smith, *Sapelo Voices* (Carrollton: State University of West Georgia, 2003), 18–20.

62. U.S. Census, 1860, McIntosh County, Slave Schedules.

63. Thomas, "The Sapelo Company," 37–64; Wylly, "Story of Sapelo," 30–38.

64. I am indebted to Kenneth H. Thomas for information on Chucalate.

65. Wylly, "Story of Sapelo," 37–38.

66. Morgan R. Crook Jr., "A Place Known as Chocolate," unpublished paper, University of West Georgia, Antonio J. Waring Archaeological Laboratory, 2007.

67. Hopkins, pardoned in 1822, returned to McIntosh County. *Darien Gazette*, June 1, 1825.

68. John L. Hopkins, *Messalina's Questions, or, A Vindication of Slavery*, Liverpool, England, 1821.

69. See chapter 3 for particulars on Montalet.

70. Wylly, "Story of Sapelo," 30–38. Wylly's reference to Bourbon is misleading. Although Montalet administered the property he did not own the tract. It was held by the children of his late father-in-law, Picot de Boisfeillet, from whom Swarbreck acquired it. See chapter 3.

71. Kenneth H. Thomas Jr., "Montalet of Savannah and Sapelo: The Man and the Myth," paper presented to the Georgia Historical Society, Savannah, November 1994.

72. U.S. Census, 1850, 1860, Bryan County, Georgia, Slave Schedules, Agricultural Schedules.

73. U.S. Census, 1850, 1860, McIntosh County, Slave Schedules, Agricultural Schedules.

74. 1857 DuVal survey; *Sapelo Sound, Georgia*, 1859, Coast Survey of the United States, RG 23, NARA. The antebellum causeway is located in the same place as the present road and tidegate on the north end of the Duck Pond.

75. Wylly, "Story of Sapelo," 47; Myers, ed., *Children of Pride*, 1683, 792. On March 17, 1862, Spalding died in camp at the age of thirty-nine.

76. Deed Book A (1873), 196–99, RMCG.

77. Ibid.

78. U.S. Census, 1860, McIntosh County, Slave Schedules.

79. Deed Book A (1842), 542–44, Baldwin County Records, rerecorded in Deed Book B (1878), 208–11, RMCG. A list of the eighty-six slaves awarded by Spalding to Catherine Kenan in this deed was certified by the Baldwin County clerk in June 1851, five months after Spalding's death.

80. 1857 DuVal survey.

81. Rachel Laura DeVan Perrine, "Bourbon Field: Preliminary Investigations of a Barrier Island Plantation Site," master's thesis, University of Tennessee at Chattanooga, 2008, 66–67.

82. Mortgage Book A (1871), 11–12, RMCG. The acreage probably included contiguous salt marsh, which was usual in aggregating land sizes in the nineteenth century.

83. *Savannah Republican*, January 21, 1826.

84. Sullivan, *Early Days on the Georgia Tidewater* (2001), 151.

85. *Columbian Museum and Savannah Advertiser*, December 9, 1808; *Darien Gazette*, February 29, 1819, March 22, 1819; *Poulson's American Daily Advertiser* (Philadelphia), May 8, 1818.

86. Ronald H. Ridgley, "Thomas Spalding," *Dictionary of Georgia Biography* (Athens: University of Georgia Press, 1983), 913.

87. Coulter, *Thomas Spalding*, 285. The land adjoining the Spalding plot was deeded by C. H. Spalding for use as a public burial ground, St. Andrew's Cemetery, in 1870.

88. McIntosh County Probate Records, Will Book 49, Will of Thomas Spalding. The two grandsons in the codicil were Thomas Spalding Wylly (1831–1922) and Alexander C. Wylly (1833–1911).

89. *Southern Recorder* (Milledgeville), December 17, 1850.

90. *Savannah Georgian*, January 17, 1851.

91. Coulter, *Thomas Spalding*, 304–6.

Chapter V. Tabby

1. Thomas Spalding, "On the Culture of the Sugar Cane," *Southern Agriculturist* 1 (1828): 553–56; Spalding, "On the Cultivation of Sugar Cane, Erecting of Proper Buildings and Manufacturing of Sugar," *Southern Agriculturist* 2 (1829): 55; Carlyle Sitterson, *Sugar Country: The Cane Sugar Industry in the South, 1753–1950* (Lexington: University Press of Kentucky, 1953), 31–37. John McQueen Jr. (1773–1822) was the son of John McQueen, who owned Sapelo Island from 1784 to 1789.

2. E. Merton Coulter, *Thomas Spalding of Sapelo* (Baton Rouge: Louisiana State University Press, 1940), 111.

3. Spalding, "On the Cultivation of Sugar Cane, Erecting of Proper Buildings," 55.

4. Spalding, "On the Culture of the Sugar Cane," 553.

5. Roswell King Jr., "On the Management of the Butler Estate, and the Cultivation of the Sugar Cane," *Southern Agriculturist* 1 (1828): 523–24.

6. Thomas Spalding, "Brief Notes," *Southern Agriculturist* 1 (1828): 60.

7. Thomas Spalding, *Observations on the Method of Planting and Cultivating the Sugar-Cane of Georgia and South Carolina* (Charleston: Agricultural Society of South Carolina, 1816), in E. M. Coulter, ed., *Georgia's Disputed Ruins* (Chapel Hill: University of North Carolina Press, 1937), 234.

8. Spalding, "On the Cultivation of Sugar Cane, Erecting of Proper Buildings," 56.

9. *Savannah Republican*, November 23, 1825.

10. Spalding, *Observations on the Method of Planting and Cultivating the Sugar-Cane*, 228–63.

11. Spalding to N. C. Whiting, July 29, 1844, cited in Marmaduke Floyd, "Certain Tabby Ruins on the Georgia Coast," in Coulter, ed., *Georgia's Disputed Ruins*, 72–76.

12. Thomas Spalding, "On the Mode of Constructing Tabby Buildings and the Propriety of Improving Our Plantations in a Permanent Manner," *Southern Agriculturist* 3 (1830): 617–20; Spalding, "On the Construction of Sugar Mills," *Southern Agriculturist* 5 (1832): 281–85.

13. Spalding, unidentified communication, 1816, Spalding Family Papers, Collection 750, series 1, box 1, GHS.

14. Thomas Spalding, "A Sketch of the Life of General James Oglethorpe," Georgia Historical Society, *Collections* 1 (1840): 248; Spalding, "On the Mode of Constructing Tabby Buildings," 617.

15. Floyd, "Certain Tabby Ruins," 3–189.

16. See, for example, W. Robert Moore, "The Golden Isles of Guale," *National Geographic* 55 (February 1934): 235–264.

17. Floyd, "Certain Tabby Ruins," 76. See a cogent analysis of the controversy in Joseph Floyd, "The Ghosts of Guale: Sugar Houses, Spanish Missions, and the Struggle for Georgia's Colonial Heritage," *Georgia Historical Quarterly* 97 (Winter 2013): 387–410.

18. David Hurst Thomas, *St. Catherines: An Island in Time* (Athens: University of Georgia Press, 2011), 9.

19. Moore, "The Golden Isles of Guale," 235.

20. Floyd, "Certain Tabby Ruins," 184–85; Margaret Davis Cate, *Our Todays and Yesterdays*, 2nd ed. (Brunswick, Ga., 1930), 33–35.

21. Thomas Spalding II, son of Randolph and Mary Bass Spalding.

22. Kate McKinley Treanor to I. F. Arnow, October 31, 1932, in *Georgia's Disputed Ruins*, 218–19.

23. Spalding, "On the Cultivation of Sugar Cane, Erecting of Proper Buildings," 55; Thomas Spalding, "Culture of the Sugar Cane—No. II," *American Agriculturist* 3 (1844): 206.

24. Spalding, *Observations on the Method of Planting and Cultivating the Sugar-Cane*, 236–37.

25. Ibid., 237.

26. Spalding, "On the Culture of the Sugar Cane," 556.

27. John D. Legare, "Account of an Agricultural Excursion Made into the South of Georgia in the Winter of 1832," *Southern Agriculturist* 6 (1833): 138–47; Thomas Spalding, "Letter to the Editor," *Southern Agriculturist* 2 (February 1829): 100–102.

28. Floyd, "Certain Tabby Ruins," 106–8.

29. Ibid.

30. Archibald C. McKinley, journal entry of May 28, 1870, in Robert L. Humphries, ed., *The Journal of Archibald C. McKinley* (Athens: University of Georgia Press, 1991), 40.

31. *Columbian Museum and Savannah Daily Gazette*, February 10, 1817.

32. Floyd, "Certain Tabby Ruins," 120.

33. Spalding, "On the Cultivation of Sugar Cane, Erecting of Proper Buildings," 60.

34. Floyd, "Certain Tabby Ruins," 124–26.

35. *Savannah Georgian*, September 25, 1824. Carnochan is buried at Darien's Upper Mill Cemetery.

36. James A. Ford, "An Archaeological Report on the Elizafield Ruins," in Coulter, ed., *Georgia's Disputed Ruins*, 193–225.

37. Buddy Sullivan, *A Georgia Tidewater Companion* (Charleston, S.C.: CreateSpace, 2014), 165–71.

38. Coulter, *Thomas Spalding*, 43.

39. William G. Haynes Jr., "Thomas Spalding of Sapelo and Ashantilly," n.d., private collection, Ashantilly Center, Inc., Darien, Georgia.

40. Walter C. Hartridge, ed., *The Letters of Robert Mackay to His Wife, 1795–1816* (Athens: University of Georgia Press, 1949), 73.

41. Spalding to N. C. Whiting, July 29, 1844, in Floyd, "Certain Tabby Ruins," 72–76.

42. Spalding, "On the Mode of Constructing Tabby Buildings," 619; Daniel Mulford to Betsy Crane, January 22, 1810, Daniel Mulford Papers, Collection 579, GHS. Based on an unspecified reference to "family tradition," Floyd sets 1805 as the year the mansion was begun ("Certain Tabby Ruins," 77), but 1807 seems more reasonable.

43. Spalding to N. C. Whiting, in Floyd, "Certain Tabby Ruins," 76.

44. Daniel Mulford to Betsy Crane, January 22, 1810; Mills B. Lane, *Architecture of the Old South: Georgia* (Savannah, Ga.: Beehive Press, 1986), 67–71.

45. Charles Spalding Wylly, "The Story of Sapelo," unpublished typescript, 1914, Buddy Sullivan Papers, collection 2433, GHS; Coulter, *Thomas Spalding*, 54–55.

46. Judson Kratzer, "A Cultural Landscape Analysis of Ashantilly," draft report, Armstrong State University, Savannah, Ga., 1999.

47. Charles H. Spalding, "Some Memoranda in Relation to Thomas Spalding," (1878), Spalding Family Papers, series 2, box 1.

48. Spalding Family Papers, family Bible, box 3.

49. Ibid.

50. Charles H. Spalding, "Some Memoranda."

Chapter VI. Geechee Sapelo

1. William S. McFeely, *Sapelo's People: A Long Walk into Freedom* (New York: W. W. Norton, 1994), 86.

2. Ibid., 131–32.

3. "Report of A. P. Ketchum," microcopy 798, rolls 36, 38, RG 105 (Records of the Bureau of Refugees, Freedmen, and Abandoned Lands), NARA; McFeely, *Sapelo's People*, 82–92, 130–31.

4. "Report of Abandoned and Confiscated Lands for the Month Ending August 31, 1865," Records of South Carolina [including Georgia], July 1865–December 1866, microcopy 869, roll 33, 1–2, RG 105, NARA.

5. "Monthly Report of William F. Eaton, Agent, for the Month Ending September 30, 1865," Unregistered Letters, 1867–1868, E-1002, RG 105, NARA. Eaton's September 1865 report was filed with documents of 1867–68.

6. Russell Duncan, *Freedom's Shore: Tunis Campbell and the Georgia Freedmen* (Athens: University of Georgia Press, 1986), 33–34.

7. McFeely, *Sapelo's People*, 135–39. Dickson and McBride are not listed in the 1870 McIntosh County census.

8. Davis Tillson to O. O. Howard, September 22, 1866, Registers and Letters, microcopy 752, roll 37, p. 1065, RG 105, NARA.

9. T. G. Campbell to A. P. Ketchum, June 20, 30, 1865, "St. Catherines Island," Freedmen's Bureau Records, MS Collection 5915, GHS.

10. Whittington B. Johnson, "A Black Teacher and Her School in Reconstruction Darien," *Georgia Historical Quarterly* 75 (Spring 1991): 90–105.

11. Anthony Wilson report to American Missionary Association, January 1870, cited in McFeely, *Sapelo's People*, 103.

12. "Geechee" is the self-preferred term today for Georgia coastal and island people, their slave ancestors, and their culture (including language). It is the equivalent of "Gullah," a term that originated in South Carolina and continues to be used there.

13. U.S. Census, 1870, McIntosh County, Population and Agricultural Schedules; *Savannah Morning News*, September 2, 1870. A genealogical resource for families of the freedmen and their descendants is Mae Ruth Green, "Sapelo Island Families: Studies of Forty-four Families," unpublished, compiled 1981–84, Real Estate Division, GDNR, Atlanta.

14. There is the possibility of an additional settlement. In its Sapelo Island chapter, Georgia Writers' Project, *Drums and Shadows* (Athens: University of Georgia Press, 1940) mentions a praise house at "Silver Bluff" in the 1930s (p. 169) and displays a photograph by Muriel and Malcolm Bell (plate 43) depicting a simple wood-frame structure with a brass bell at the entrance. The location of Silver Bluff is undetermined; no mention of the site has been found in any of the primary or secondary Sapelo literature. Cornelia Bailey relates that there were three praise houses on Sapelo: at Hog Hammock, Shell Hammock, and Lumber Landing. Author's conversations with Cornelia Bailey, 2012, 2014.

15. Ray Crook, Cornelia Bailey, Norma Harris, and Karen Smith, eds., *Sapelo Voices: Historical Anthropology and the Oral Traditions of Gullah-Geechee Communities on Sapelo Island, Georgia* (Carrollton: State University of West Georgia, 2003), 25–26.

16. It could be argued that the tabby foundation ruins at High Point are from the Montalet house, enlarged around 1809 from an earlier structure.

17. Deed Book A (1873), 196–200, RMCG; Spalding Family Papers, Collection 750, series 4, box 1, series 5, box 1, GHS. The three hammocks are on the Duplin River, north of Little Sapelo.

18. I am indebted to Malcolm Bell III for information on Priscilla Sawyer Barrow, e-mail communication, June 26, 2014. Mr. Bell is the son of the late Muriel (Barrow) and Malcolm Bell Jr. of Savannah and thus a descendant of David C. and Priscilla Barrow. The Bells photographed the African American people of Sapelo Island for *Drums and Shadows* in the 1930s. For Arthur A. Loomis, see *Daily Transcript* (Holyoke, Mass.), December 26, 1885.

19. Spalding Family Papers, series 4, box 1; Kenneth H. Thomas, principal investigator, National Register of Historic Places application for Hog Hammock and Behavior Cemetery, 1996, page 16, GDNR, Historic Preservation Division, Atlanta.

20. U.S. Census, 1870, McIntosh County.

21. McKinley had an adventurous trip bringing the steamer from Morehead City, North Carolina, to Sapelo. See Robert L. Humphries, ed., *The Journal of Archibald C. McKinley* (Athens: University of Georgia Press, 1991), 173–76; Buddy Sullivan, *Early Days on the Georgia Tidewater: The Story of McIntosh County and Sapelo*, 6th ed. (Darien, Ga.: McIntosh County Commission, 2001), 390–92, 401–3; Buddy Sullivan, *Early Days on the Georgia Tidewater*, new revised ed., forthcoming, 2017.

22. Buddy Sullivan, *High Water on the Bar* (Darien, Ga.: Downtown Development Authority, 2009), 7–37, discusses the Darien timber port, 1866–1916.

23. *Darien Timber Gazette*, September 6, 1884; *Macon Telegraph & Messenger*, January 28, 1885.

24. *Annual Report of the Lighthouse Board*, 1868, no. 294, RG 26 (U.S. Coast Guard Records), NARA; U.S. Coast Survey, *Doboy Sound and Vicinity, Georgia*, 1868, RG 23 (U.S. Coast and Geodetic Survey Records), NARA.

25. Sullivan, *Early Days on the Georgia Tidewater* (2001), 416–26. The Wolf Island beacon was badly damaged in the 1898 hurricane, and it was deactivated the following year by the Lighthouse Service.

26. Deed Book A (1875), 498–99, RMCG.

27. Deed Book C (recorded 1886), 485–86, RMCG.

28. Plat of Sapelo lighthouse island, surveyed October 10, 1902, Site File, Georgia, No. 2, 1st Site, RG 26, NARA.

29. T. R. R. Cobb in *Atlanta Constitution*, July 1894; see also *Darien Timber Gazette*, February 15, 1890.

30. Buddy Sullivan Papers, Collection 2433, GHS. See also Sullivan, *Early Days on the Georgia Tidewater* (2001), 405–7; Sullivan, *Early Days on the Georgia Tidewater* (new revised ed., forthcoming).

31. Thomas, National Register application, 11.

32. Mortgage Book A (1871), 11–12, Deed Book A (1874), 518–19, RMCG.

33. Resurvey of Raccoon Bluff tract by Paul Wilder, Real Estate Division, GDNR, 2000.

34. Crook et al., *Sapelo Voices*, 24; McFeely, *Sapelo's People*, 141–42.

35. U.S. Census, 1880, McIntosh County, Agricultural Schedules.

36. McFeely, *Sapelo's People*, 143.

37. Sullivan, *Early Days on the Georgia Tidewater* (2001), 474–88.

38. U.S. Census, 1910, McIntosh County, Population Schedules; Crook et al., *Sapelo Voices*, 26.

39. U.S. Census, 1900, McIntosh County; Sullivan, *Early Days* (2001), 488–98, 511–14, details the timber industry in Sapelo Sound and the 1898 hurricane; also Sullivan, introduction to *High Water on the Bar*.

40. *Annual Report of the Surgeon-in-Charge*, South Atlantic Quarantine, 1896, in Annual Reports, RG 90, United States Marine Hospital Service Records, NARA.

41. Crook et al., *Sapelo Voices*, 26.

42. Nathaniel H. Bishop, *Voyage of the Paper Canoe* (Boston: Lee and Shepard, 1878), 296–99.

43. Author's conversation with Cornelia Walker Bailey, July 15, 2014; see archaeological field reports, Historic Preservation Division, GDNR, Atlanta. The slave settlements are discussed in chapter 4.

44. Capt. Rotheus Drinkwater was the son-in-law of James Shearwood, navy timber contractor of Sapelo Island (see chapter 4).

45. Deed Book B (1878), 221–23, RMCG; Crook et al., *Sapelo Voices*, 34–36; Thomas, National Register application, 16.

46. Crook et al., *Sapelo Voices*, 24–25; McFeely, *Sapelo's People*, 83–84; Thomas, National Register application, 24.

47. Survey Plat, Sapelo Island, "The South End," by Alexander C. Wylly, June 1891, Surveyor General's Department, GDAH.

48. Thomas, National Register application, 25–26.

49. According to the 1910 census two Geechee women, Rose Hillery, a cook, and Mary Olane, a laundress, were also listed in the household of Jimmy and Daniel Cromley.

50. *Annual Reports* of the Lighthouse Board and keepers lists, Site File, Georgia, No. 12, 2nd site, 1905–33, RG 26, NARA; "Sapelo Light-Station, Georgia," U.S. Lighthouse Service, Site File, Michigan, RG 26, NARA. The drawings of the second Sapelo lighthouse are not among the Sapelo records in RG 26. The sketches were only located in 1997 in the RG 26 file for South Fox Island, Michigan, to which Sapelo's tower was moved in 1934.

51. *Darien Gazette*, October 8, 1898.

52. A. C. McKinley to William M. Cobb, November 4, 1898. The full letter is in Humphries, ed., *The Journal of Archibald C. McKinley*, 232–33. Cobb, of Athens, was a nephew of A. C. McKinley.

53. *Darien Timber Gazette*, March 29, 1890; *Atlanta Constitution*, August 24, 1897.

54. Deed Book G (1900), 484–85, 519–20, RMCG.

55. Deed Book K (1910), 172–73, RMCG.

56. Sullivan, *Early Days on the Georgia Tidewater* (2001), 818–19.

57. Site Files, 1891–1914, RG 28 (U.S. Postal Service Records), NARA.

58. Charles S. Wylly, "The Story of Sapelo," unpublished typescript, 1914, Buddy Sullivan Papers, collection 2433, GHS.

59. McFeely, *Sapelo's People* (2001), 143.

Chapter VII. Sapelo Regenesis

1. Burnette Vanstory, *Howard Earle Coffin* (Sea Island, Ga.: Sea Island Co., 1969), 7; Maxwell Taylor Courson, "Howard Earle Coffin, King of the Georgia Coast," *Georgia Historical Quarterly* 83 (1999): 321–24.

2. Harold Martin, *This Happy Isle: The Story of Sea Island and the Cloister* (Sea Island, Ga.: Sea Island Co., 1977), 7.

3. "Sapelo Sold to Westerner," *Savannah Morning News*, June 13, 1912; *Darien Gazette*, June 15, 1912.

4. The lower section of Barn Creek fronting Long Tabby and the former McKinley house later became known as Post Office Creek.

5. Deed Book K (1912), 172–75, 205–6, 234–35, 310–14, Deed Book Q (1920), 533, Deed Book 6 (1934), 16, RMCG. Specifics and property demarcations of the multiple transactions are outlined in Buddy Sullivan, *Early Days on the Georgia Tidewater: The Story of McIntosh County and Sapelo*, 6th ed. (Darien, Ga.: McIntosh County Commission, 2001), 601–6.

6. Ray Crook, Cornelia Bailey, Norma Harris, and Karen Smith, *Sapelo Voices* (Carrollton: State University of West Georgia, 2003), 25–26.

7. Vanstory, *Howard Earle Coffin*, 19.

8. *Soil Survey of McIntosh County, Georgia*, Series 1929, U.S. Department of Agriculture, Field Operations, Bureau of Chemistry and Soils, 1932. This was the first scientific analysis of Sapelo Island's soils.

9. Martin, *This Happy Isle*, 14, 17.

10. *Soil Survey of McIntosh County*; Sullivan, *Early Days* (2001), 621–27, 794; Buddy Sullivan, *Early Days on the Georgia Tidewater*, new revised ed., forthcoming, 2017.

11. Coffin Papers, Sea Island Company archives, Sea Island, Georgia.

12. Ibid.

13. Author interview with Patty Wylly Davis, July 25, 1992.

14. Jones quoted in Martin, *This Happy Isle*, 22; Paul S. Galtsoff and R. H. Luce, *Oyster Investigations in Georgia* (Washington, D.C.: U.S. Department of Commerce, Bureau of Fisheries, 1930).

15. Niles H. Schuh to Corps of Engineers, Savannah District, January 17, 1928, Coffin Papers, Sea Island Company archives.

16. Martin, *This Happy Isle*, 16.

17. Ibid., 21.

18. *Savannah News-Press*, May 28, 1930.

19. Martin, *This Happy Isle*, 16.

20. W. Robert Moore, "The Golden Isles of Guale," *National Geographic* 65 (February 1934): 242; Vanstory, *Howard Earle Coffin*, 20. Moore's piece featured Coffin, Sapelo, and Sea Island; *The Cloister Bells*, a special publication of the Sea Island Company, 1930, Sea Island Company archives, features a photogravure spread on the Sapelo house.

21. *Brunswick (Ga.) News*, December 26, 1928.

22. *Atlanta Constitution*, December 31, 1928. A section of photographs accompanying the article was captioned "President and Mrs. Coolidge Enjoy Georgia Vacation" and depicted scenes of the rodeo and the president viewing the proceedings wearing his "eleven-gallon" hat.

23. Frank O. Salisbury, *Portrait and Pageant: Kings, Presidents, and People* (London: J. Murray, 1944), 91–96.

24. After Sapelo's sale to R. J. Reynolds Jr., the Coffins' paintings were moved to the Cloister, later being donated to the state of Georgia by A. W. Jones Sr. after the state's acquisition of the island.

25. *Brunswick (Ga.) News*, February 15, 1929.

26. Coffin guest register, Sapeloe Island, 1917–34, Sea Island Company archives.

27. *Soil Survey of McIntosh County.*

28. Revocable license dated May 4, 1933, issued to R. H. Cromley from the U.S. Lighthouse Service, Site File, Georgia, No. 12, 2nd site, RG 26, NARA; *Darien Gazette*, May 26, 1933.

29. Diane Maddex, *Sea Island: Seventy-Five Years of Gracious Hospitality* (Sea Island, Ga.: Sea Island Company, 2003), 21–48.

30. Howard E. Coffin, "Georgia's Future and Some of Her Undeveloped Resources: An Address before the Annual Meeting of the Georgia Bar Association, the Cloister Hotel, Sea Island Beach, Ga.," 1930, Sea Island Company archives.

31. Martin, *This Happy Isle*, 64–65.

32. "Sapeloe Island, The Queen of the Golden Isles," promotional booklet, 1933, Sea Island Company archives.

33. Martin, *This Happy Isle*, 67.

34. Patrick Reynolds and Tom Shachtman, *The Gilded Leaf: Triumph, Tragedy and Tobacco, Three Generations of the R. J. Reynolds Family and Fortune* (Boston: Little, Brown, 1989), 188–89.

35. Deed Book 6 (1934), 43–47, Deed Book 18 (1949), 135–39, RMCG. The latter document pertains to the mainland Meridian Landing tract, the point of boat access to and from Sapelo Island.

36. Martin, *This Happy Isle*, 70–71.

37. Ibid., 71.

38. Crook et al., *Sapelo Voices*, 28–29.

39. *Soil Survey of McIntosh County.*

40. U.S. Census, 1930, McIntosh County, Population Schedules; Allen Green, conversations with the author, 1993–94; Crook et al., *Sapelo Voices*, 32–33.

41. U.S. Census, 1920, 1930, McIntosh County.

42. *Soil Survey of McIntosh County.* The survey's information about rice corroborates that Raccoon Bluff was conducive to planting that staple, first practiced by the French in 1791–92.

43. Crook et al., *Sapelo Voices*, 85–86; Allen Green, conversations with the author, 1993.

44. Georgia Writers' Project, *Drums and Shadows: Survival Studies among the Georgia Coastal Negroes* (Athens: University of Georgia Press, 1940). The cover and interior photographs of

Eddie Hall guiding his oxcart down a sandy Sapelo road has long been incorrectly captioned as depicting Julius Bailey (1911–50). Author's conversation with Cornelia Walker Bailey, July 15, 2014; e-mail communication from Malcolm Bell III, June 22, 2014 ("Cornelia Bailey and Julius Bailey, Jr. say this is Eddie Hall.")

45. Ibid., 158–59.

46. U.S. Census, 1930.

47. Ibid. See also Crook et al. *Sapelo Voices*, 35.

48. Crook et al., *Sapelo Voices*, 124–79.

49. Cornelia Bailey, conversations with the author, 2012.

50. *Soil Survey of McIntosh County*; Crook et al., *Sapelo Voices*, 31.

Chapter VIII. Sapelo in the 1950s

1. *Coastlines Georgia*, Coastal Resources Division, GDNR, 1981.

2. "Study of a National Seashore Recreational Area: Sapelo Island, Georgia," National Park Service, Washington, D.C., 1934. The estimated purchase cost included the acquisition of Creighton Island.

3. Paul H. Silverstone, comp., *The Navy of World War II, 1922–1947* (New York: Routledge, 2008), 25–26.

4. Patrick Reynolds and Tom Shachtman, *The Gilded Leaf* (Boston: Little, Brown, 1989), 235.

5. Shutze's plans for the modernization are on deposit at Georgia Tech. Another Georgia Tech architectural graduate, Augustus E. Constantine, designed the South End farm complex built by Reynolds during 1935–37.

6. R. N. White Jr., Survey of Sapelo Island, 1940, Surveyor General's Office, GDAH.

7. Darien Telephone Company archives, Darien, Georgia.

8. *Atlanta Journal-Constitution Sunday Magazine*, July 17, 1949.

9. Reynolds and Shachtman, *Gilded Leaf*, 241–42.

10. Typescript dated November 19, 1955, copy in Buddy Sullivan Papers, Collection 2433, GHS.

11. Author's conversation with Charles Durant (b. 1931), July 17, 2014.

12. Reynolds and Shachtman, *Gilded Leaf*, 265, 266.

13. Ibid., 266.

14. Ibid., 274.

15. *Darien News*, May 10, May 17, 1962.

16. Reynolds and Shachtman, *Gilded Leaf*, 284

17. Ibid., 286.

18. Ibid., 292. Reynolds and Schachtment believed Reynolds's death to have been hastened by the intake of excessive pure oxygen.

19. Heidi Schnakenberg, *Kid Carolina: R. J. Reynolds Jr., a Tobacco Fortune, and the Mysterious Death of a Southern Icon* (New York: Center Street, 2010), 253–55; Reynolds and Shachtman, *Gilded Leaf,* 296.

Chapter IX. Scientific Sapelo

1. Betty Jean Craige, *Eugene Odum: Ecosystem Ecologist and Environmentalist* (Athens: University of Georgia Press, 2001), 54–58.

2. Ibid., 56.

3. Mildred Teal and John Teal, *Portrait of an Island* (New York: Atheneum, 1964); Mildred Teal and John Teal, *Life and Death of a Salt Marsh* (New York: Atlantic, 1969).

4. Eugene P. Odum, "Living Marsh," introduction to Robert Hanie, *Guale: The Golden Coast of Georgia* (San Francisco: Friends of the Earth, 1974), 19–28.

5. For example, see J. H. Hoyt and V. J. Henry, "Influence of Island Migration on Barrier Island Sedimentation," *Geological Society of America Bulletin* 78 (1967): 77–86. Hoyt died in a glider accident in 1970.

6. See L. R. Pomeroy, "Algal Productivity in Salt Marshes of Georgia," *Limnology and Oceanography* 4 (1959): 386–97.

7. E. P. Odum, "A Proposal for a Marshbank and the Strategy of Ecosystem Development for the Estuarine Zone of Georgia," in *The Future of the Marshlands and Sea Islands of Georgia*, ed. David S. Maney, Frederick C. Marland, and Clifford B. West (Brunswick, Ga.: Coastal Area Planning and Development Commission, 1968), 74–85.

8. Emory M. Thomas, "The South and the Sea: Some Thoughts on the Southern Maritime Tradition," *Georgia Historical Quarterly* 67 (Summer 1983): 162.

9. *Proceedings of the Salt Marsh Conference Held at the Marine Institute of the University of Georgia, March 25–28, 1958* (Athens: University of Georgia Marine Institute, 1959).

10. R. J. Reimold, "The Movement of Phosphorous through the Salt Marsh Cordgrass," *Limnology and Oceanography* 17 (1972): 606–11.

11. David S. Maney, Frederick C. Marland, and Clifford B. West, eds., *The Future of the Marshlands and Sea Islands of Georgia* (Brunswick, Ga.: Coastal Area Planning and Development Commission, 1968).

12. The most comprehensive compilation of research at the UGAMI is *Collected Reprints of the University of Georgia Marine Institute*, 28 vols., 1962–2004, containing papers published in academic journals by scientists conducting research at Sapelo Island. The material in this

chapter relating specifics of UGAMI research is synthesized from *Sapelo Island National Estuarine Research Reserve Management Plan 1999–2004* (Washington, D.C.: National Oceanic and Atmospheric Administration, 1999), 44–46. See also Barbara Kinsey, *Sapelo Island Handbook* (Sapelo Island, Ga.: Sapelo Island Research Foundation, 1982), 40–45.

13. *Sapelo Island National Estuarine Research Reserve Management Plan 2008–2013* (Washington, D.C.: National Oceanic and Atmospheric Administration, 2008), 115–28.

14. R. Welch, M. Remillard, A. Chalmers, and J. J. Alberts, "Integration of GPS, Remote Sensing and GIS Techniques for Coastal Resource Management," *Photogrammetric Engineering and Remote Sensing* 58 (1992): 1571–78.

15. Now called the Sapelo Foundation.

16. *Sapelo Island National Estuarine Research Reserve Management Plan 1990* (Washington, D.C.: National Oceanic and Atmospheric Administration, 1990), 21.

17. Board of Regents of the University System of Georgia and the Georgia Department of Natural Resources, "A Proposal to Establish a National Estuarine Sanctuary in the State of Georgia," State Office of Planning and Budget, Atlanta, January 10, 1975.

18. The full text of the lease agreement is contained in *Sapelo Island National Estuarine Research Reserve Management Plan 1999–2004*, appendix C.

19. For an overview of the national program, including the Sapelo Island National Estuarine Research Reserve, see National Estuarine Research Reserve System, www.nerrs.noaa.gov. For specifics on the SINERR, Sapelo Island National Estuarine Research Reserve, see www.sapelonerr.org.

20. Game Management Section records, Wildlife Resources Division, GDNR, Brunswick, Georgia.

21. *Sapelo Island National Estuarine Research Reserve Management Plan 1999–2004*, appendix F.

22. Darien attorney Paul Varner represented Reynolds's local legal affairs in the 1940s and 1950s.

23. Kenneth H. Thomas, National Register of Historic Places Registration Document, GDNR, Atlanta, 1996; Ray Crook, Cornelia Bailey, Norma Harris, and Karen Smith, *Sapelo Voices* (Carrollton: University of West Georgia, 2003), 37–39.

24. Patrick Reynolds and Tom Shachtman, *The Gilded Leaf* (Boston: Little, Brown, 1989), 193.

25. Author's conversations with Allen Green, 1993, 1994; William S. McFeely, *Sapelo's People: A Long Walk into Freedom* (New York: W. W. Norton, 1994), 142.

26. McFeely, *Sapelo's People*, 151.

27. Reynolds and Shachtman, *Gilded Leaf*, 313.

28. *New York Times*, May 4, 2008.

29. 2010 Georgia Code, § 12–3–441 Title 12, Conservation and Natural Resources, Part 7, Sapelo Island Heritage Authority.

30. *Charleston Post and Courier*, November 27, 2013.

Afterword

Epigraph from *The Prince of Tides*, by Pat Conroy. Copyright 1986 by Pat Conroy. Reprinted by permission of Houghton Mifflin Harcourt Publishing Company. All rights reserved.

1. William S. McFeely, *Sapelo's People* (New York: W. W. Norton, 1994), 170.

Index